Formalized Music

Formalized Music

THOUGHT AND MATHEMATICS IN COMPOSITION

Iannis Xenakis

Indiana University Press

BLOOMINGTON   LONDON

Library of Congress catalog card number: 76–135017
ISBN: 0–253–32378–9

Manufactured in the United States of America

4 5 79 78 77

Contents

Preface to the Second Edition

The formalization that I attempted in trying to reconstruct part of the musical edifice ex nihilo has not used, for want of time or of capacity, the most advanced aspects of philosophical and scientific thought. But the escalade is started and others will certainly enlarge and extend the new thesis. This book is addressed to a hybrid public, but interdisciplinary hybridization frequently produces superb specimens.

I could sum up twenty years of personal efforts by the progressive filling in of the following Table of Coherences. My musical, architectural, and visual works are the chips of this mosaic. It is like a net whose variable lattices capture fugitive virtualities and entwine them in a multitude of ways. This table, in fact, sums up the true coherences of the successive chronological chapters of this book. The chapters stemmed from monographs, which tried as much as possible to avoid overlapping.

But the profound lesson of such a table of coherences is that any theory or solution given on one level can be assigned to the solution of problems on another level. Thus the solutions in macrocomposition on the Families level (programmed stochastic mechanisms) can engender simpler and more powerful new perspectives in the shaping of microsounds than the usual trigonometric (periodic) functions can. Therefore, in considering clouds of points and their distribution over a pressure-time plane, we can bypass the heavy harmonic analyses and syntheses and create sounds that have never before existed. Only then will sound synthesis by computers and digital-to-analogue converters find its true position, free of the rooted but ineffectual tradition of electronic, concrete, and instrumental music that makes use of Fourier synthesis despite the failure of this theory. Hence, in this book, questions having to do mainly with orchestral sounds (which are more diversified and more manageable) find a rich and immediate application as soon as they are transferred to the Microsound level in the pressure-time space. All music is thus automatically homogenized and unified.

"Everything is everywhere" is the word of this book and its Table of Coherences; Herakleitos would say that the ways up and down are one.

The French edition, *Musiques Formelles*, was produced thanks to Albert Richard, director of *La Revue Musicale*. The English edition, a corrected and completed version, results from the initiative of Mr. Christopher Butchers, who translated the first six chapters. My thanks also go to Mr. G. W. Hopkins, and Mr. and Mrs. John Challifour, who translated Chapters VII and VIII, respectively; to Mr. Michael Aronson and Mr. Bernard Perry of Indiana University Press, who decided to publish it; and finally to Mrs. Natalie Wrubel, who edited this difficult book with infinite patience, correcting and rephrasing many obscure passages.

I. X.

1970

Table (mosaic) of Coherences

Philosophy (in the etymological sense)
Thrust towards truth, revelation. Quest in everything, interrogation, harsh criticism, active knowledge through creativity.

Chapters (in the sense of the methods followed)

Partially inferential and experimental	Entirely inferential and experimental	Other methods to come
ARTS (VISUAL, SONIC, MIXED . . .)	SCIENCES (OF MAN, NATURAL)	?
	PHYSICS, MATHEMATICS, LOGIC	

This is why the arts are freer, and can therefore guide the sciences, which are entirely inferential and experimental.

Categories of Questions (fragmentation of the directions leading to creative knowledge, to philosophy)

REALITY (EXISTENTIALITY); CAUSALITY; INFERENCE: CONNEXITY; COMPACTNESS; TEMPORAL AND SPATIAL UBIQUITY AS A CONSEQUENCE OF NEW MENTAL STRUCTURES;   INDETERMINISM . . .   ← bi-pole → . . . DETERMINISM; . .

Families of Solutions or Procedures (of the above categories)

?	FREE STOCHASTIC materialized by a computer program	MARKOVIAN	GAMES	GROUPS

Pieces (examples of particular realization)

?	ACHORRIPSIS ST/10–1, 080262 ST/48–1, 240162 ATRÉES MORSIMA-AMORSIMA	ANALOGIQUE A ANALOGIQUE B SYRMOS	DUEL STRATÉGIE	AKRATA NOMOS ALPHA NOMOS GAMMA

Classes of Sonic Elements (sounds that are heard and recognized as a whole, and classified with respect to their sources)
ORCHESTRAL, ELECTRONIC (produced by analogue devices), CONCRETE (microphone collected), DIGITAL (realized with computers and digital-to-analogue converters), . . .

Microsounds
Forms and structures in the pressure-time space, recognition of the classes to which microsounds belong or which microstructures produce.
Microsound types result from questions and solutions that were adopted at the CATEGORIES, FAMILIES, and PIECES levels.

Preface to *Musiques Formelles*

This book is a collection of explorations in musical composition pursued in several directions. The effort to reduce certain sound sensations, to understand their logical causes, to dominate them, and then to use them in wanted constructions; the effort to materialize movements of thought through sounds, then to test them in compositions; the effort to understand better the pieces of the past, by searching for an underlying unit which would be identical with that of the scientific thought of our time; the effort to make "art" while "geometrizing," that is, by giving it a reasoned support less perishable than the impulse of the moment, and hence more serious, more worthy of the fierce fight which the human intelligence wages in all the other domains —all these efforts have led to a sort of abstraction and formalization of the musical compositional act. This abstraction and formalization has found, as have so many other sciences, an unexpected and, I think, fertile support in certain areas of mathematics. It is not so much the inevitable use of mathematics that characterizes the attitude of these experiments, as the overriding need to consider sound and music as a vast potential reservoir in which a knowledge of the laws of thought and the structured creations of thought may find a completely new medium of materialization, i.e., of communication.

For this purpose the qualification "beautiful" or "ugly" makes no sense for sound, nor for the music that derives from it; the quantity of intelligence carried by the sounds must be the true criterion of the validity of a particular music.

This does not prevent the utilization of sounds defined as pleasant or beautiful according to the fashion of the moment, nor even their study in their own right, which may enrich symbolization and algebration. *Efficacy* is in itself a sign of intelligence. We are so convinced of the historical necessity of this step, that we should like to see the visual arts take an analogous path—unless, that is, "artists" of a new type have not already done it in laboratories, sheltered from noisy publicity.

These studies have always been matched by actual works which mark out the various stages. My compositions constitute the experimental dossier of this undertaking. In the beginning my compositions and research were recognized and published, thanks to the friendship and moral and material support of Prof. Hermann Scherchen. Certain chapters in the present work reflect the results of the teaching of certain masters, such as H. Scherchen and Olivier Messiaen in music, and Prof. G. Th. Guilbaud in mathematics, who, through the virtuosity and liberality of his thought, has given me a clearer view of the algebras which constitute the fabric of the chapter devoted to Symbolic Music.

I. X.

1962

Formalized Music

Chapter I

Free Stochastic Music

Art, and above all, music has a fundamental function, which is to catalyze the sublimation that it can bring about through all means of expression. It must aim through fixations which are landmarks to draw towards a total exaltation in which the individual mingles, losing his consciousness in a truth immediate, rare, enormous, and perfect. If a work of art succeeds in this undertaking even for a single moment, it attains its goal. This tremendous truth is not made of objects, emotions, or sensations; it is beyond these, as Beethoven's Seventh Symphony is beyond music. This is why art can lead to realms that religion still occupies for some people.

But this transmutation of every-day artistic material which transforms trivial products into meta-art is a secret. The "possessed" reach it without knowing its "mechanisms." The others struggle in the ideological and technical mainstream of their epoch which constitutes the perishable "climate" and the stylistic fashion. Keeping our eyes fixed on this supreme meta-artistic goal, we shall attempt to define in a more modest manner the paths which can lead to it from our point of departure, which is the magma of contradictions in present music.

There exists a historical parallel between European music and the successive attempts to explain the world by reason. The music of antiquity, causal and deterministic, was already strongly influenced by the schools of Pythagoras and Plato. Plato insisted on the principle of causality, "for it is impossible for anything, to come into being without cause" (*Timaeus*). Strict causality lasted until the nineteenth century when it underwent a

The English translation of Chaps. I–VI is by Christopher A. Butchers.

1

Fig. I–1. Score of *Metastasis*, 1953/54, Bars 309–17

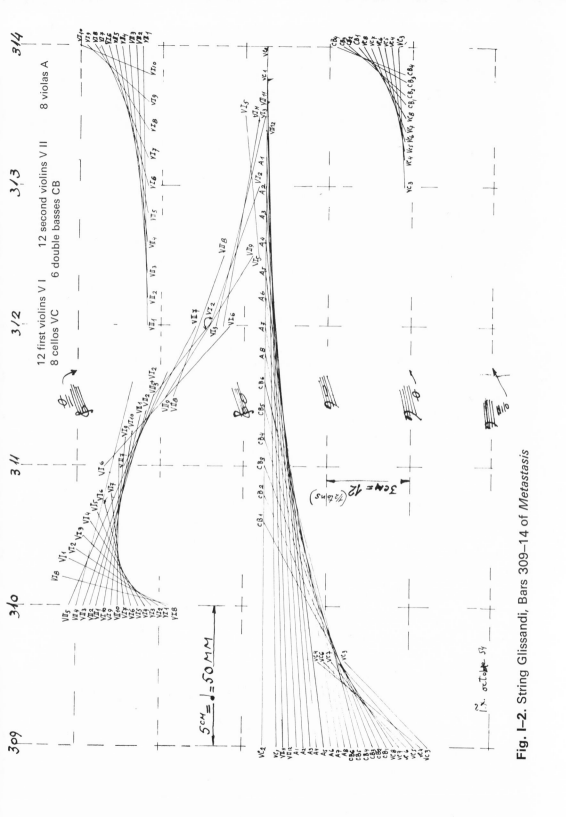

Fig. I–2. String Glissandi, Bars 309–14 of *Metastasis*

brutal and fertile transformation as a result of statistical theories in physics. Since antiquity the concepts of chance (*tyche*), disorder (*ataxia*), and disorganization were considered as the opposite and negation of reason (*logos*), order (*taxis*), and organization (*systasis*). It is only recently that knowledge has been able to penetrate chance and has discovered how to separate its degrees—in other words to rationalize it progressively, without, however, succeeding in a definitive and total explanation of the problem of "pure chance."

After a time lag of several decades, atonal music broke up the tonal function and opened up a new path parallel to that of the physical sciences, but at the same time constricted by the virtually absolute determinism of serial music.

It is therefore not surprising that the presence or absence of the principle of causality, first in philosophy and then in the sciences, might influence musical composition. It caused it to follow paths that appeared to be divergent, but which, in fact, coalesced in probability theory and finally in polyvalent logic, which are kinds of generalization and enrichments of the principle of causality. The explanation of the world, and consequently of the sonic phenomena which surround us or which may be created, necessitated and profited from the enlargement of the principle of causality, the basis of which enlargement is formed by the law of large numbers. This law implies an asymptotic evolution towards a stable state, towards a kind of goal, of *stochos*, whence comes the adjective "stochastic."

But everything in pure determinism or in less pure indeterminism is subjected to the fundamental operational laws of logic, which were disentangled by mathematical thought under the title of general algebra. These laws operate on isolated states or on sets of elements with the aid of operations, the most primitive of which are the union, notated $\cup$, the intersection, notated $\cap$, and the negation. Equivalence, implication, and quantifications are elementary relations from which all current science can be constructed.

Music, then, may be defined as an organization of these elementary operations and relations between sonic entities or between functions of sonic entities. We understand the first-rate position which is occupied by set theory, not only for the construction of new works, but also for analysis and better comprehension of the works of the past. In the same way a stochastic construction or an investigation of history with the help of stochastics cannot be carried through without the help of logic—the queen of the sciences, and I would even venture to suggest, of the arts—or its mathematical form algebra. For everything that is said here on the subject is also valid for all forms of art (painting, sculpture, architecture, films, etc.).

From this very general, fundamental point of view, from which we wish to examine and *make* music, primary time appears as a wax or clay on which operations and relations can be inscribed and engraved, first for the purposes of work, and then for communication with a third person. On this level, the asymmetric, noncommutative character of time is use (B after $A \neq A$ after B, i.e., lexicographic order). Commutative, metric time (symmetrical) is subjected to the same logical laws and can therefore also aid organizational speculations. What is remarkable is that these fundamental notions, which are necessary for construction, are found in man from his tenderest age, and it is fascinating to follow their evolution as Jean Piaget[1] has done.

After this short preamble on generalities we shall enter into the details of an approach to musical composition which I have developed over several years. I call it "stochastic," in honor of probability theory, which has served as a logical framework and as a method of resolving the conflicts and knots encountered.

The first task is to construct an abstraction from all inherited conventions and to exercise a fundamental critique of acts of thought and their materialization. What, in fact, does a musical composition offer strictly on the construction level? It offers a collection of sequences which it wishes to be causal. When, for simplification, the major scale implied its hierarchy of tonal functions—tonics, dominants, and subdominants—around which the other notes gravitated, it constructed, in a highly deterministic manner, linear processes, or melodies on the one hand, and simultaneous events, or chords, on the other. Then the serialists of the Vienna school, not having known how to master logically the indeterminism of atonality, returned to an organization which was extremely causal in the strictest sense, more abstract than that of tonality; however, this abstraction was their great contribution. Messiaen generalized this process and took a great step in systematizing the abstraction of all the variables of instrumental music. What is paradoxical is that he did this in the modal field. He created a multimodal music which immediately found imitators in serial music. At the outset Messiaen's abstract systematization found its most justifiable embodiment in a multiserial music. It is from here that the postwar neo-serialists have drawn their inspiration. They could now, following the Vienna school and Messiaen, with some occasional borrowing from Stravinsky and Debussy, walk on with ears shut and proclaim a truth greater than the others. Other movements were growing stronger; chief among them was the systematic exploration of sonic entities, new instruments, and "noises." Varèse was the

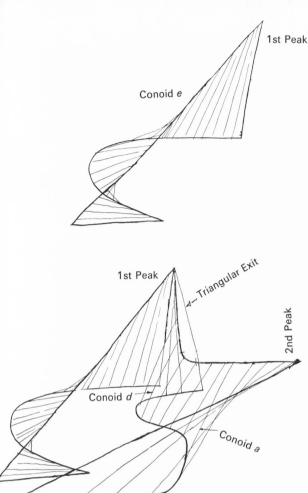

1st Peak

Conoid e

A. Ground profile of the *left half* of the "stomach." The intention was to build a shell, composed of as few ruled surfaces as possible, over the ground plan. A conoid (*e*) is constructed through the ground profile curve ; this wall is bounded by two straight lines : the straight directrix (rising from the left extremity of the ground profile), and the outermost generatrix (passing through the right extremity of the ground profile). This produces the first "peak" of the pavilion.

1st Peak

← Triangular Exit

2nd Peak

Conoid d

Conoid a

B. A ruled surface consisting of *two* conoids, *a* and *d*, is laid through the curve bounding the *right half* of the "stomach." The straight directrix of *d* passes through the first peak, and the outermost generatrix at this side forms a triangular exit with the generatrix of *e*. The straight directrix of *a* passes through a second peak and is joined by an arc to the directrix of *d*.

This basic form is the one used in the first design and was retained, with some modifications, in the final structure. The main problem of the design was to establish an aesthetic balance between the two peaks.

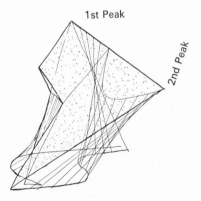

1st Peak

2nd Peak

C. Attempt to close the space between the two ruled surfaces of the first design by flat surfaces (which might serve as projection walls).

Fig. I–3. Stages in the Development of the First Design of the Philips Pavilion

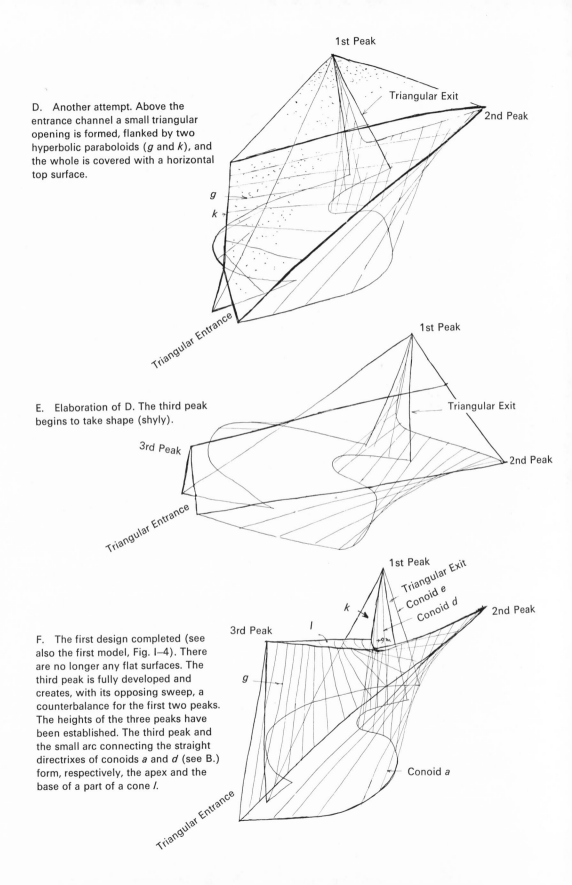

D. Another attempt. Above the entrance channel a small triangular opening is formed, flanked by two hyperbolic paraboloids (*g* and *k*), and the whole is covered with a horizontal top surface.

1st Peak

Triangular Exit

2nd Peak

g

k

Triangular Entrance

E. Elaboration of D. The third peak begins to take shape (shyly).

1st Peak

Triangular Exit

3rd Peak

2nd Peak

Triangular Entrance

F. The first design completed (see also the first model, Fig. I–4). There are no longer any flat surfaces. The third peak is fully developed and creates, with its opposing sweep, a counterbalance for the first two peaks. The heights of the three peaks have been established. The third peak and the small arc connecting the straight directrixes of conoids *a* and *d* (see B.) form, respectively, the apex and the base of a part of a cone *l*.

1st Peak

Triangular Exit

Conoid *e*

Conoid *d*

k

2nd Peak

3rd Peak

l

g

Conoid *a*

Triangular Entrance

pioneer in this field, and electromagnetic music has been the beneficiary (electronic music being a branch of instrumental music). However, in electromagnetic music, problems of construction and of morphology were not faced conscientiously. Multiserial music, a fusion of the multimodality of Messiaen and the Viennese school, remained, nevertheless, at the heart of the fundamental problem of music.

But by 1954 it was already in the process of deflation, for the completely deterministic complexity of the operations of composition and of the works themselves produced an auditory and ideological nonsense. I described the inevitable conclusion in "The Crisis of Serial Music":

> Linear polyphony destroys itself by its very complexity; what one hears is in reality nothing but a mass of notes in various registers. The enormous complexity prevents the audience from following the inter-twining of the lines and has as its macroscopic effect an irrational and fortuitous dispersion of sounds over the whole extent of the sonic spectrum. There is consequently a contradiction between the poly-phonic linear system and the heard result, which is surface or mass. This contradiction inherent in polyphony will disappear when the independence of sounds is total. In fact, when linear combinations and their polyphonic superpositions no longer operate, what will count will be the statistical mean of isolated states and of transforma-tions of sonic components at a given moment. The macroscopic effect can then be controlled by the mean of the movements of elements which we select. The result is the introduction of the notion of proba-bility, which implies, in this particular case, combinatory calculus. Here, in a few words, is the possible escape route from the "linear category" in musical thought.[2]

This article served as a bridge to my introduction of mathematics in music. For if, thanks to complexity, the strict, deterministic causality which the neo-serialists postulated was lost, then it was necessary to replace it by a more general causality, by a probabilistic logic which would contain strict serial causality as a particular case. This is the function of stochastic science. "Stochastics" studies and formulates the law of large numbers, which has already been mentioned, the laws of rare events, the different aleatory procedures, etc. As a result of the impasse in serial music, as well as other causes, I originated in 1954 a music constructed from the principle of indeterminism; two years later I named it "Stochastic Music." The laws of the calculus of probabilities entered composition through musical necessity.

But other paths also led to the same stochastic crossroads—first of all, natural events such as the collision of hail or rain with hard surfaces, or the song of cicadas in a summer field. These sonic events are made out of thousands of isolated sounds; this multitude of sounds, seen as a totality, is a new sonic event. This mass event is articulated and forms a plastic mold of time, which itself follows aleatory and stochastic laws. If one then wishes to form a large mass of point-notes, such as string pizzicati, one must know these mathematical laws, which, in any case, are no more than a tight and concise expression of chain of logical reasoning. Everyone has observed the sonic phenomena of a political crowd of dozens or hundreds of thousands of people. The human river shouts a slogan in a uniform rhythm. Then another slogan springs from the head of the demonstration; it spreads towards the tail, replacing the first. A wave of transition thus passes from the head to the tail. The clamor fills the city, and the inhibiting force of voice and rhythm reaches a climax. It is an event of great power and beauty in its ferocity. Then the impact between the demonstrators and the enemy occurs. The perfect rhythm of the last slogan breaks up in a huge cluster of chaotic shouts, which also spreads to the tail. Imagine, in addition, the reports of dozens of machine guns and the whistle of bullets adding their punctuations to this total disorder. The crowd is then rapidly dispersed, and after sonic and visual hell follows a detonating calm, full of despair, dust, and death. The statistical laws of these events, separated from their political or moral context, are the same as those of the cicadas or the rain. They are the laws of the passage from complete order to total disorder in a continuous or explosive manner. They are stochastic laws.

Here we touch on one of the great problems that have haunted human intelligence since antiquity: continuous or discontinuous transformation. The sophisms of movement (e.g., Achilles and the tortoise) or of definition (e.g., baldness), especially the latter, are solved by statistical definition; that is to say, by stochastics. One may produce continuity with either continuous or discontinuous elements. A multitude of short glissandi on strings can give the impression of continuity, and so can a multitude of pizzicati. Passages from a discontinuous state to a continuous state are controllable with the aid of probability theory. For some time now I have been conducting these fascinating experiments in instrumental works; but the mathematical character of this music has frightened musicians and has made the approach especially difficult.

Here is another direction that converges on indeterminism. The study of the variation of rhythm poses the problem of knowing what the limit of total asymmetry is, and of the consequent complete disruption of causality among durations. The sounds of a Geiger counter in the proximity of a radioactive source give an impressive idea of this. Stochastics provides the necessary laws.

Before ending this short inspection tour of events rich in the new logic, which were closed to the understanding until recently, I would like to include a short parenthesis. If glissandi are long and sufficiently interlaced, we obtain sonic spaces of continuous evolution. It is possible to produce ruled surfaces by drawing the glissandi as straight lines. I performed this experiment with *Metastasis* (this work had its premiere in 1955 at Donaueschingen). Several years later, when the architect Le Corbusier, whose collaborator I was, asked me to suggest a design for the architecture of the Philips Pavilion in Brussels, my inspiration was pin-pointed by the experiment with *Metastasis*. Thus I believe that on this occasion music and architecture found an intimate connection.[3] Figs. I–1–5 indicate the causal chain of ideas which led me to formulate the architecture of the Philips Pavilion from the score of *Metastasis*.

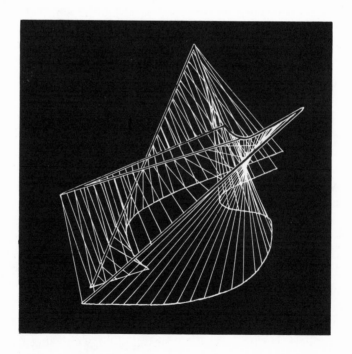

Fig. I–4. First Model of Philips Pavilion

Fig. I–5. Philips Pavilion, Brussels World's Fair, 1958

STOCHASTIC LAWS AND INCARNATIONS

I shall give quickly some of the stochastic laws which I introduced into composition several years ago. We shall examine one by one the independent components of an instrumental sound.

DURATIONS

Time (metrical) is considered as a straight line on which the points corresponding to the variations of the other components are marked. The interval between two points is identical with the duration. Among all the possible sequences of points, which shall we choose? Put thus, the question makes no sense.

If a mean number of points is designated on a given length the question becomes: Given this mean, what is the number of segments equal to a length fixed in advance?

The following formula, which derives from the principles of continuous probability, gives the probabilities for all possible lengths when one knows the mean number of points placed at random on a straight line.

$$P_x = \delta e^{-\delta x} \, dx, \qquad \text{(See Appendix I.)}$$

in which δ is the linear density of points, and x the length of any segment.

If we now choose some points and compare them to a theoretical distribution obeying the above law or any other distribution, we can deduce the amount of chance included in our choice, or the more or less rigorous adaptation of our choice to the law of distribution, which can even be absolutely functional. The comparison can be made with the aid of tests, of which the most widely used is the χ^2 criterion of Pearson. In our case, where all the components of sound can be measured to a first approximation, we shall use in addition the correlation coefficient. It is known that if two populations are in a linear functional relationship, the correlation coefficient is one. If the two populations are independent, the coefficient is zero. All intermediate degrees of relationship are possible.

Clouds of Sounds

Assume a given duration and a set of sound-points defined in the intensity-pitch space realized during this duration. Given the mean superficial density of this tone cluster, what is the probability of a particular density occurring in a given region of the intensity-pitch space? Poisson's Law answers this question:

$$P_\mu = \frac{\mu_0^\mu}{\mu!} e^{-\mu_0},$$

where μ_0 is the mean density and μ is any particular density. As with durations, comparisons with other distributions of sound-points can fashion the law which we wish our cluster to obey.

INTERVALS OF INTENSITY, PITCH, ETC.

For these variables the simplest law is

$$\theta(\gamma)\,d\gamma = \frac{2}{a}\left(1 - \frac{\gamma}{a}\right) d\gamma, \qquad \text{(See Appendix I.)}$$

which gives the probability that a segment (interval of intensity, pitch, etc.) within a segment of length a, will have a length included within γ and $\gamma + d\gamma$, for $0 \leq \gamma \leq a$.

SPEEDS

We have been speaking of sound-points, or granular sounds, which are in reality a particular case of sounds of continuous variation. Among these let us consider glissandi. Of all the possible forms that a glissando sound can take, we shall choose the simplest—the uniformly continuous glissando. This glissando can be assimilated sensorially and physically into the mathematical concept of speed. In a one-dimensional vectorial representation, the scalar size of the vector can be given by the hypotenuse of the right triangle in which the duration and the melodic interval covered form the other two sides. Certain mathematical operations on the continuously variable sounds thus defined are then permitted. The traditional sounds of wind instruments are, for example, particular cases where the speed is zero. A glissando towards higher frequencies can be defined as positive, towards lower frequencies as negative.

We shall demonstrate the simplest logical hypotheses which lead us to a mathematical formula for the distribution of speeds. The arguments which follow are in reality one of those "logical poems" which the human intelligence creates in order to trap the superficial incoherencies of physical phenomena, and which can serve, on the rebound, as a point of departure for building abstract entities, and then incarnations of these entities in sound or light. It is for these reasons that I offer them as examples:

Homogeneity hypotheses [11]*

1. The density of speed-animated sounds is constant; i.e., two regions of equal extent on the pitch range contain the same average number of mobile sounds (glissandi).

* The numbers in brackets correspond to the numbers in the Bibliography at the end of the book.

2. The absolute value of speeds (ascending or descending glissandi) is spread uniformly; i.e., the mean quadratic speed of mobile sounds is the same in different registers.

3. There is isotropy; that is, there is no privileged direction for the movements of mobile sounds in any register. There is an equal number of sounds ascending and descending.

From these three hypotheses of symmetry, we can define the function $f(v)$ of the probability of the absolute speed v. ($f(v)$ is the relative frequency of occurrence of v.)

Let n be the number of glissandi per unit of the pitch range (density of mobile sounds), and r any portion taken from the range. Then the number of speed-animated sounds between v and $v + dv$ and positive, is, from hypotheses 1 and 3:

$$n r \tfrac{1}{2} f(v)\, dv \quad \text{(the probability that the sign is } + \text{ is } \tfrac{1}{2}).$$

From hypothesis 2 the number of animated sounds with speed of absolute value v is a function which depends on v^2 only. Let this function be $g(v^2)$. We then have the equation

$$n r \tfrac{1}{2} f(v)\, dv = n r\, g(v^2)\, dv.$$

Moreover if $|x| = v$, the probability function $g(v^2)$ will be equal to the law of probability H of x, whence $g(v^2) = H(x)$, or $\log g(v^2) = h(x)$.

In order that $h(x)$ may depend only on $x^2 = v^2$, it is necessary and sufficient that the differentials $d \log g(v^2) = h'(x)\, dx$ and $v\, dv = x\, dx$ have a constant ratio:

$$\frac{d \log g(v^2)}{v\, dv} = \frac{h'(x)\, dx}{x\, dx} = \text{constant} = -2j,$$

whence $h'(x) = -2jx$, $h(x) = -jx^2 + c$, and $H(x) = ke^{-jx^2}$.

But $H(x)$ is a function of elementary probabilities; therefore its integral from $-\infty$ to $+\infty$ must be equal to 1. j is positive and $k = \sqrt{j}/\sqrt{\pi}$. If $j = 1/a^2$, it follows that

$$\tfrac{1}{2} f(v) = g(v^2) = H(x) = \frac{1}{a\sqrt{\pi}}\, e^{-v^2/a^2}$$

and

$$f(v) = \frac{2}{a\sqrt{\pi}}\, e^{-v^2/a^2}$$

for $v = |x|$, which is a Gaussian distribution.

This chain of reasoning borrowed from Paul Lévy was established after Maxwell, who, with Boltzmann, was responsible for the kinetic theory of gases. The function $f(v)$ gives the probability of the speed v; the constant a defines the "temperature" of this sonic atmosphere. The arithmetic mean of v is equal to $a/\sqrt{\pi}$, and the standard deviation is $a/\sqrt{2}$.

We offer as an example several bars from the work *Pithoprakta* for string orchestra (Fig. I–6), written in 1955–56, and performed by Prof. Hermann Scherchen in Munich in March 1957.[4] The graph (Fig. I–7) represents a set of speeds of temperature proportional to $a = 35$. The abscissa represents time in units of 5 cm = 26 MM (Mälzel Metronome). This unit is subdivided into three, four, and five equal parts, which allow very slight differences of duration. The pitches are drawn as the ordinates, with the unit 1 semitone = 0.25 cm. 1 cm on the vertical scale corresponds to a major third. There are 46 stringed instruments, each represented by a jagged line. Each of the lines represents a speed taken from the table of probabilities calculated with the formula

$$f(v) = \frac{2}{a\sqrt{\pi}} e^{-v^2/a^2}.$$

A total of 1148 speeds, distributed in 58 distinct values according to Gauss's law, have been calculated and traced for this passage (measures 52–60, with a duration of 18.5 sec.). The distribution being Gaussian, the macroscopic configuration is a plastic modulation of the sonic material. The same passage was transcribed into traditional notation. To sum up we have a sonic compound in which:

1. The durations do not vary.
2. The mass of pitches is freely modulated.
3. The density of sounds at each moment is constant.
4. The dynamic is ff without variation.
5. The timbre is constant.
6. The speeds determine a "temperature" which is subject to local fluctuations. Their distribution is Gaussian.

As we have already had occasion to remark, we can establish more or less strict relationships between the component parts of sounds.[5] The most useful coefficient which measures the degree of correlation between two variables x and y is

$$r = \frac{\sum (x - \bar{x})(y - \bar{y})}{\sqrt{\sum (x - \bar{x})^2}\sqrt{\sum (y - \bar{y})^2}},$$

where $\bar{x}$ and $\bar{y}$ are the arithmetic means of the two variables.

Here then, is the technical aspect of the starting point for a utilization of the theory and calculus of probabilities in musical composition. With the above, we already know that:

1. We can control continuous transformations of large sets of granular and/or continuous sounds. In fact, densities, durations, registers, speeds, etc., can all be subjected to the law of large numbers with the necessary approximations. We can therefore with the aid of means and deviations shape these sets and make them evolve in different directions. The best known is that which goes from order to disorder, or vice versa, and which introduces the concept of entropy. We can conceive of other continuous transformations: for example, a set of plucked sounds transforming continuously into a set of arco sounds, or in electromagnetic music, the passage from one sonic substance to another, assuring thus an organic connection between the two substances. To illustrate this idea, I recall the Greek sophism about baldness: "How many hairs must one remove from a hairy skull in order to make it bald?" It is a problem resolved by the theory of probability with the standard deviation, and known by the term *statistical definition.*

2. A transformation may be explosive when deviations from the mean suddenly become exceptional.

3. We can likewise confront highly improbable events with average events.

4. Very rarified sonic atmospheres may be fashioned and controlled with the aid of formulae such as Poisson's. Thus, even music for a solo instrument can be composed with stochastic methods.

These laws, which we have met before in a multitude of fields, are veritable diamonds of contemporary thought. They govern the laws of the advent of being and becoming. However, it must be well understood that they are not an end in themselves, but marvelous tools of construction and logical lifelines. Here a backfire is to be found. This time it is these stochastic tools that pose a fundamental question: "What is the minimum of logical constraints necessary for the construction of a musical process?" But before answering this we shall sketch briefly the basic phases in the construction of a musical work.

Fig. I–6. Bars 52–57 of *Pithoprakta*

B. & H. 19583

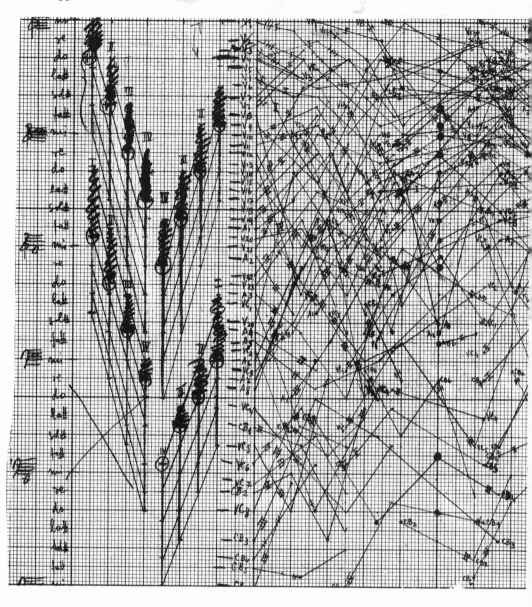

Fig. I–7. Graph of Bars 52–57 of *Pithoprakta*

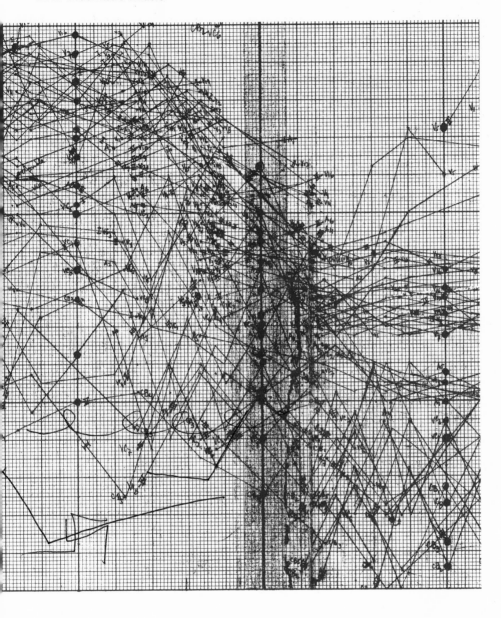

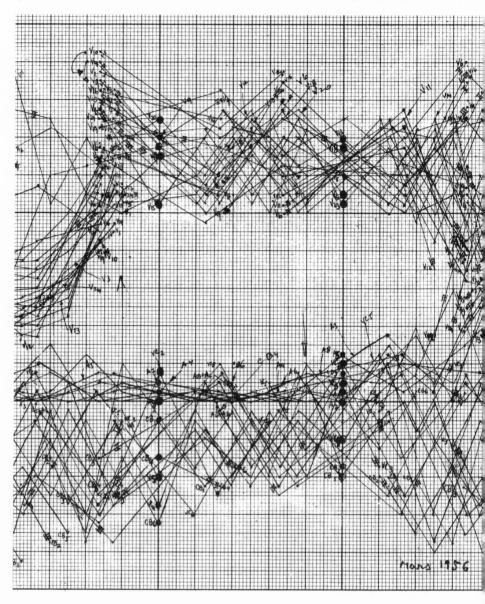

Fig. I–7 *(continued)*

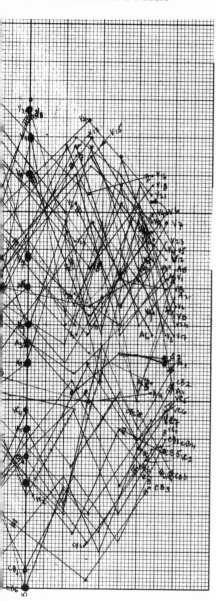

FUNDAMENTAL PHASES OF A MUSICAL WORK

1. *Initial conceptions* (intuitions, provisional or definitive data);

2. *Definition of the sonic entities* and of their symbolism communicable with the limits of possible means (sounds of musical instruments, electronic sounds, noises, sets of ordered sonic elements, granular or continuous formations, etc.);

3. *Definition of the transformations* which these sonic entities must undergo in the course of the composition (macrocomposition: general choice of logical framework, i.e., of the elementary algebraic operations and the setting up of relations between entities, sets, and their symbols as defined in 2.); and the arrangement of these operations in lexicographic time with the aid of succession and simultaneity);

4. *Microcomposition* (choice and detailed fixing of the functional or stochastic relations of the elements of 2.), i.e., algebra outside-time, and algebra in-time;

5. *Sequential programming* of 3. and 4. (the schema and *pattern* of the work in its entirety);

6. *Implementation of calculations*, verifications, feedbacks, and definitive modifications of the sequential program;

7. *Final symbolic result* of the programming (setting out the music on paper in traditional notation, numerical expressions, graphs, or other means of solfeggio);

8. *Sonic realization* of the program (direct orchestral performance, manipulations of the type of electromagnetic music, computerized construction of the sonic entities and their transformations).

The order of this list is not really rigid. Permutations are possible in the course of the working out of a composition. Most of the time these phases are unconscious and defective. However, this list does establish ideas and allows speculation about the future. In fact, computers can take in hand phases 6. and 7., and even 8. But as a first approach, it seems that only phases 6. and 7. are immediately accessible. That is to say, that the final symbolic result, at least in France, may be realized only by an orchestra or by manipulations of electroacoustic music on tape recorders, emitted by the existing electroacoustic channels; and not, as would be desirable in the very near future, by an elaborate mechanization which would omit orchestral or tape interpreters, and which would assume the computerized fabrication of the sonic entities and of their transformations.

Here now is an answer to the question put above, an answer that is true for instrumental music, but which can be applied as well to all kinds of sound production. For this we shall again take up the phases described:

2. Definition of sonic entities. The sonic entities of the classical orchestra can be represented in a first approximation by vectors of four usually independent variables, $E_r(c, h, g, u)$:

c_a = timbre or instrumental family
h_i = pitch of the sound
g_j = intensity of the sound, or dynamic form
u_k = duration of the sound.

The vector E_r defines a point M in the *multidimensional space* provided by a *base* (c, h, g, u). This point M will have as *coordinates* the numbers c_a, h_i, g_j, u_k. For example: c_3 played arco and forte on a violin, one eighth note in length, at one eighth note = 240 MM, can be represented as $c_{\text{viol. arco}}$, h_{39} (= c_3), g_4 (= forte), u_5 (= $\frac{1}{4}$ sec.). Suppose that these points M are plotted on an axis which we shall call E_r, and that through its origin we draw another axis t, at right angles to axis E_r. We shall represent on this axis, called the *axis of lexicographic time*, the lexicographic-temporal succession of the points M. Thus we have defined and conveniently represented a two-dimensional space (E_r, t). This will allow us to pass to phase 3., definition of transformation, and 4., microcomposition, which must contain the answer to the problem posed concerning the minimum of constraints.

To this end, suppose that the points M defined above can appear with no necessary condition other than that of obeying an aleatory law without memory. This hypothesis is equivalent to saying that we admit a stochastic distribution of the events E_r in the space (E_r, t). Admitting a sufficiently weak superficial distribution n, we enter a region where the law of Poisson is applicable:

$$P_k = \frac{n^k}{K!} e^{-n}.$$

Incidentally we can consider this problem as a synthesis of several conveniently chosen linear stochastic processes (law of radiation from radioactive bodies). (The second method is perhaps more favorable for a mechanization of the transformations.)

A sufficiently long fragment of this distribution constitutes the musical work. The basic law defined above generates a whole family of compositions as a function of the superficial density. So we have a formal archetype of composition in which the basic aim is to attain the greatest possible *asymmetry* (in the etymological sense) and the *minimum of constraints, causalities, and rules*. We think that from this archetype, which is perhaps the most general one, we can redescend the ladder of forms by introducing progressively more numerous constraints, i.e., choices, restrictions, and negations. In the analysis in several linear processes we can also introduce other processes: those of Wiener-Lévy, P. Lévy's infinitely divisibles, Markov chains, etc., or mixtures of several. It is this which makes this second method the more fertile.

The exploration of the limits a and b of this archetype $a \leq n \leq b$ is equally interesting, but on another level—that of the mutual comparison of samples. This implies, in effect, a gradation of the increments of n in order that the differences between the families n_i may be recognizable. Analogous remarks are valid in the case of other linear processes.

If we opt for a Poisson process, there are two necessary hypotheses which answer the question of the minimum of constraints: 1. there exists in a given space musical instruments and men; and 2. there exist means of contact between these men and these instruments which permit the emission of rare sonic events.

This is the only hypothesis (cf. the *ekklisis* of Epicurus). From these two constraints and with the aid of stochastics, I built an entire composition without admitting any other restrictions. *Achorripsis* for 21 instruments was composed in 1956–57, and had its first performance in Buenos Aires in 1958 under Prof. Hermann Scherchen. (See Fig. I–8.)

At that time I wrote:*

τὸ γὰρ αὐτὸ νοεῖν ἐστίν τε καὶ εἶναι

τὸ γὰρ αὐτὸ εἶναι ἐστίν τε καὶ οὐκ εἶναι†

ONTOLOGY

In a universe of nothingness. A brief train of waves, so brief that its end and beginning coincide (negative time) disengaging itself endlessly.

Nothingness resorbs, creates.

It engenders being.

Time, Causality.

These rare sonic events can be something more than isolated sounds. They can be melodic figures, cell structures, or agglomerations whose

---

* The following excerpt (through p. 37) is from "In Search of a Stochastic Music," *Gravesaner Blätter*, no. 11/12.

† "For it is the same to think as to be" (*Poem* by Parmenides); and my paraphrase, "For it is the same to be as not to be."

characteristics are also ruled by the laws of chance, for example, clouds of sound-points or speed-temperatures.[6] In each case they form a sample of a succession of rare sonic events.

This sample may be represented by either a simple table of probabilities or a double-entry table, a matrix, in which the cells are filled by the frequencies of events. The rows represent the particular qualifications of the events, and the columns the dates (see Matrix M, Fig. I–9). The frequencies in this matrix are distributed according to Poisson's formula, which is the law for the appearances of rare random events.

We should further define the sense of such a distribution and the manner in which we realize it. There is an advantage in defining chance as an aesthetic law, as a normal philosophy. Chance is the limit of the notion of evolving symmetry. Symmetry tends to asymmetry, which in this sense is equivalent to the negation of traditionally inherited behavioral frameworks. This negation not only operates on details, but most importantly on the composition of structures, hence tendencies in painting, sculpture, architecture, and other realms of thought. For example, in architecture, plans worked out with the aid of regulating diagrams are rendered more complex and dynamic by exceptional events. Everything happens as if there were one-to-one oscillations between symmetry, order, rationality, and asymmetry, disorder, irrationality in the reactions between the epochs of civilizations.

At the beginning of a transformation towards asymmetry, exceptional events are introduced into symmetry and act as aesthetic stimuli. When these exceptional events multiply and become the general case, a jump to a higher level occurs. The level is one of disorder, which, at least in the arts and in the expressions of artists, proclaims itself as engendered by the complex, vast, and rich vision of the brutal encounters of modern life. Forms such as abstract and decorative art and action painting bear witness to this fact. Consequently chance, by whose side we walk in all our daily occupations, is nothing but an extreme case of this controlled disorder (that which signifies the richness or poverty of the connections between events and which engenders the dependence or independence of transformations); and by virtue of the negation, it conversely enjoys all the benevolent characteristics of an artistic regulator. It is a regulator also of sonic events, their appearance, and their life. But it is here that the iron logic of the laws of chance intervenes; this chance cannot be created without total submission to its own laws. On this condition, chance checked by its own force becomes a hydro-electric torrent.

Fig. I–8. Bars 104–111 of *Achorripsis*

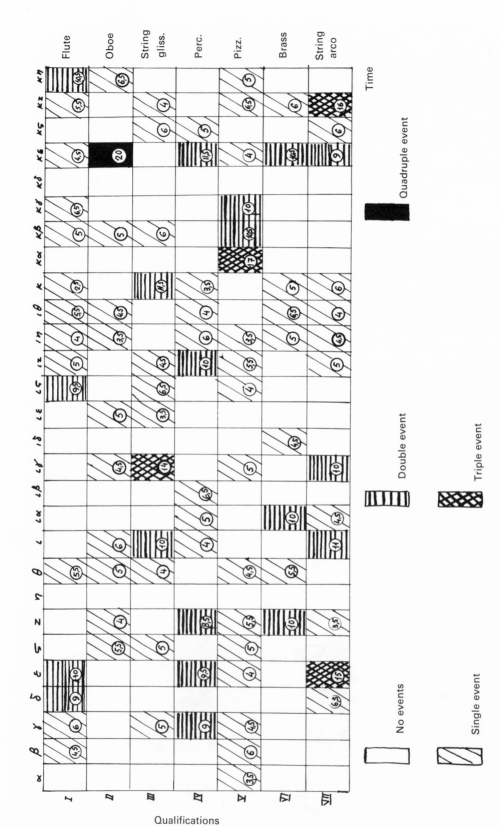

Fig. I–9. Vector Matrix *M*, Matrix of *Achorripsis*

However, we are not speaking here of cases where one merely plays heads and tails in order to choose a particular alternative in some trivial circumstance. The problem is much more serious than that. It is a matter here of a philosophic and aesthetic concept ruled by the laws of probability and by the mathematical functions that formulate that theory, of a coherent concept in a new region of coherence.

The analysis that follows is taken from *Achorripsis*.

For convenience in calculation we shall choose a priori a mean density of events

$$\lambda = 0.6 \text{ events/unit.}$$

Applying Poisson's formula,

$$P_k = \frac{\lambda^k}{K!} e^{-\lambda}$$

we obtain the table of probabilities:

$$
\begin{aligned}
P_0 &= 0.5488 \\
P_1 &= 0.3293 \\
P_2 &= 0.0988 \\
P_3 &= 0.0198 \\
P_4 &= 0.0030 \\
P_5 &= 0.0004.
\end{aligned}
\tag{1}
$$

P_i is the probability that the event will occur i times in the unit of volume, time, etc. In choosing a priori 196 units or cells, the distribution of the frequencies among the cells is obtained by multiplying the values of P_i by 196.

	Number of cells
i	$196\ P_i$
0	107
1	65
2	19
3	4
4	1

(2)

The 196 cells may be arranged in one or several groups of cells, qualified as to timbre and time, so that the number of groups of timbres times the number of groups of durations = 196 cells. Let there be 7 distinct timbres; then $196/7 = 28$ units of time. Thus the 196 cells are distributed over a two-dimensional space as shown in (3).

Timbre ▲

Flute						
Oboe						
String gliss.						
Percussion						
Pizzicato						
Brass						
String arco						

(3)

0 1 2 3 28   Time

If the musical sample is to last 7 minutes (a subjective choice) the unit of time U_t will equal 15 sec., and each U_t will contain 6.5 measures at MM = 26.

How shall we distribute the frequencies of zero, single, double, triple, and quadruple events per cell in the two-dimensional space of Matrix (3)? Consider the 28 columns as cells and distribute the zero, single, double, triple, and quadruple events from table (2) in these 28 new cells. Take as an example the single event; from table (2) it must occur 65 times. Everything happens as if one were to distribute events in the cells with a mean density $\lambda = 65/28 = 2.32$ single events per cell (here cell = column).

In applying anew Poisson's formula with the mean density $\lambda = 2.32$ ($2.32 \ll 30$) we obtain table (4).

Poisson Distribution

Frequency K	No. of Columns	Product col $\times K$	
0	3	0	
1	6	6	
2	8	16	
3	5	15	(4)
4	3	12	
5	2	10	
6	1	6	
7	0	0	
Totals	28	65	

Arbitrary Distribution

Frequency K	No. of Columns	Product col $\times K$	
0	10	0	
1	3	3	
2	0	0	
3	9	27	(5)
4	0	0	
5	1	5	
6	5	30	
7	0	0	
Totals	28	65	

One could choose any other distribution on condition that the sum of single events equals 65. Table (5) shows such a distribution.

But in this axiomatic research, where chance must bathe all of sonic space, we must reject every distribution which departs from Poisson's law. And the Poisson distribution must be effective not only for the columns but also for the rows of the matrix. The same reasoning holds true for the diagonals, etc.

Contenting ourselves just with rows and columns, we obtain a homogeneous distribution which follows Poisson. It was in this way that the distributions in rows and columns of Matrix (M) (Fig. I–9) were calculated.

So a *unique* law of chance, the law of Poisson (for rare events) through the medium of the arbitrary mean λ is capable of conditioning, on the one hand, a whole sample matrix, and on the other, the partial distributions following the rows and columns. The a priori, arbitrary choice admitted at the beginning therefore concerns the variables of the "vector-matrix."

Variables or entries of the "vector-matrix"

1. Poisson's Law
2. The mean λ
3. The number of cells, rows, and columns

The distributions entered in this matrix are not always rigorously defined. They really depend, for a given λ, on the number of rows or columns. The greater the number of rows or columns, the more rigorous is the definition. This is the law of large numbers. But this indeterminism allows free will if the artistic inspiration wishes it. It is a second door that is open to the subjectivism of the composer, the first being the "state of entry" of the "Vector-Matrix" defined above.

Now we must specify the unit-events, whose frequencies were adjusted in the standard matrix (M). We shall take as a single event a cloud of sounds with linear density δ sounds/sec. Ten sounds/sec is about the limit that a normal orchestra can play. We shall choose $\delta = 5$ sounds/measure at MM 26, so that $\delta = 2.2$ sounds/sec ($\approx 10/4$).

We shall now set out the following correspondence:

Event	Cloud of density δ =		Mean number of sounds/cell (15 sec)
	Sounds/ measure 26MM	Sounds/ sec	
zero	0	0	0
single	5	2.2	32.5
double	10	4.4	65
triple	15	6.6	97.5
quadruple	20	8.8	130

The hatchings in matrix (M) show a Poisson distribution of frequencies, homogeneous and verified in terms of rows and columns. We notice that the rows are interchangeable (= interchangeable timbres). So are the columns. This leads us to admit that the determinism of this matrix is weak in part, and that it serves chiefly as a basis for thought—for thought which manipulates frequencies of events of all kinds. The true work of molding sound consists of distributing the clouds in the two-dimensional space of the matrix, and of anticipating a priori all the sonic encounters before the calculation of details, eliminating prejudicial positions. It is a work of patient research which exploits all the creative faculties instantaneously. This matrix is like a game of chess for a single player who must follow certain rules of the game for a prize for which he himself is the judge. This game matrix has no unique strategy. It is not even possible to disentangle any balanced goals. It is very general and incalculable by pure reason.

Up to this point we have placed the cloud densities in the matrix. Now with the aid of calculation we must proceed to the coordination of the aleatory sonic elements.

HYPOTHESES OF CALCULATION

Let us analyze as an example cell III, ιz of the matrix: third row, sounds of continuous variation (string glissandi), seventeenth unit of time (measures 103–11). The density of the sounds is 4.5 sounds/measure at MM 26 ($\delta = 4.5$); so that 4.5 sounds/measure times 6.5 measures = 29 sounds for this cell. How shall we place the 29 glissando sounds in this cell?

Hypothesis 1. The acoustic characteristic of the glissando sound is assimilated to the speed $v = df/dt$ of a uniformly continuous movement. (See Fig. I–10.)

Hypothesis 2. The quadratic mean α of all the possible values of v is proportional to the sonic density δ. In this case $\alpha = 3.38$ (temperature).

Hypothesis 3. The values of these speeds are distributed according to the most complete asymmetry (chance). This distribution follows the law of

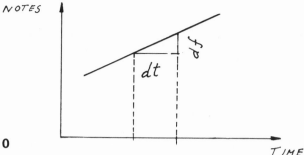

Fig. I–10

Gauss. The probability $f(v)$ for the existence of the speed v is given by the function

$$f(v) = \frac{2}{a\sqrt{\pi}}\, e^{-v^2/a^2}\, ;$$

and the probability $P(\lambda)$ that v will lie between v_1 and v_2, by the function

$$P(\lambda) = \theta(\lambda_2) - \theta(\lambda_1),$$

in which $\lambda_1 = v_1/a$ and

$$\theta(\lambda) = \frac{2}{\sqrt{\pi}} \int_0^\lambda e^{-\lambda^2}\, d\lambda \quad \text{(normal distribution)}.$$

Hypothesis 4. A glissando sound is essentially characterized by *a.* the moment of its departure; *b.* its speed $v_m = df/dt$, $(v_1 < v_m < v_2)$; and *c.* its register.

Hypothesis 5. Assimilate time to a line and make each moment of departure a point on that line. It is as if one were to distribute a number of points on a line with a linear density $\delta = 4.5$ points at MM $= 26$. This, then, is a problem of continuous probabilities. These points define segments and the probability that the *i*-th segment will have a length x_i between x and $x + dx$ is

$$P_x = \delta e^{-\delta x}\, dx.$$

Hypothesis 6. The moment of departure corresponds to a sound. We shall attempt to define its pitch. The strings have a range of about 80 semitones, which may be represented by a line of length $a = 80$ semitones. Since between two successive or simultaneous glissandi there exists an interval between the pitches at the moments of departure, we can define not only the note of attack for the first glissando, but also the melodic interval which separates the two origins.

Put thus, the problem consists of finding the probability that a segment *s* within a line segment of length *a* will have a length between *j* and *j* + *dj* (0 ≤ *j* ≤ *a*). This probability is given by the formula

$$\theta(j) \; dj = \frac{2}{a} \left(1 - \frac{j}{a}\right) dj. \qquad \text{(See Appendix I.)}$$

Hypothesis 7. The three essential characteristics of the glissando sound defined in Hypothesis 4 are independent.

From these hypotheses we can draw up the three tables of probability: a table of durations, a table of speeds, and a table of intervals.

All these tables furnish us with the elements which materialize in cell III, *ιz*. The reader is encouraged to examine the score to see how the results of the calculations have been used. Here also, may we emphasize, a great liberty of choice is given the composer. The restrictions are more of a general canalizing kind, rather than peremptory. The theory and the calculation define the tendencies of the sonic entity, but they do not constitute a slavery. Mathematical formulae are thus tamed and subjugated by musical thought. We have given this example of glissando sounds because it contains all the problems of stochastic music, controlled, up to a certain point, by calculation.

Table of Durations

δ = 4.5 sounds/measure at MM 26

Unit *x* = 0.10 of the measure at 26 MM

4.5 · 6.5 = 29 sounds/cell, i.e., 28 durations

x	δx	$e^{-\delta x}$	$\delta e^{-\delta x}$	$\delta e^{-\delta x} \, dx$	$28P_x$
0.00	0.00	1.000	4.500	0.362	10
0.10	0.45	0.638	2.870	0.231	7
0.20	0.90	0.407	1.830	0.148	4
0.30	1.35	0.259	1.165	0.094	3
0.40	1.80	0.165	0.743	0.060	2
0.50	2.25	0.105	0.473	0.038	1
0.60	2.70	0.067	0.302	0.024	1
0.70	3.15	0.043	0.194	0.016	0
	Totals		12.415	0.973	28

An approximation is made by considering dx as a constant factor.

$$\sum_{0}^{\infty} \delta e^{-\delta x} \, dx = 1.$$

Therefore

$$dx = 1 / \sum_{0}^{\infty} \delta e^{-\delta x}.$$

In this case $dx = 1/12.415 = 0.805.$

Table of Speeds

$\delta = 4.5$ glissando sounds/measure at 26 MM
$\alpha = 3.88$, quadratic mean of the speeds
v is expressed in semitones/measure at 26 MM
v_m is the mean speed $(v_1 + v_2)/2$
$4.5 \cdot 6.5 = 29$ glissando sounds/cell.

v	$\lambda = v/\alpha$	$\theta(\lambda)$	$P(\lambda) = \theta(\lambda_2) - \theta(\lambda_1)$	$29\,P(\lambda)$	v_m
0	0.000	0.0000			
			0.2869	9	0.5
1	0.258	0.2869			
			0.2510	7	1.5
2	0.516	0.5379			
			0.1859	5	2.5
3	0.773	0.7238			
			0.1310	4	3.5
4	1.032	0.8548			
			0.0771	2	4.5
5	1.228	0.9319			
			0.0397	1	5.5
6	1.545	0.9716			
			0.0179	1	6.5
7	1.805	0.9895			
			0.0071	0	7.5

Table of Intervals

$\delta = 4.5$ glissandi/measure at 26 MM.

$a = 80$ semitones, or 18 times the arbitrary unit of 4.5 semitones.

j is expressed in multiples of 4.5 semitones.

dj is considered to be constant. Therefore $dj = 1/\sum\theta(j)$ or $dj = a/(m + 1)$, and we obtain a step function. For $j = 0$, $\theta(j)dj = 2/(m + 1) = 0.105$; for $j = 18$, $\theta(j)dj = 0$.

$4.5 \cdot 6.5 = 29$ glissando sounds per cell.

We can construct the table of probabilities by means of a straight line.

j	$\theta(j)\, dj = P(j)$	$29\, P(j)$
0	←——— 0.105 ———→	3
1		3
2		3
3		3
4		2
5		2
6		2
7		2
8		2
9		2
10		1
11		1
12		1
13		1
14		1
15		0
16		0
17		0
18		0

We shall not speak of the means of verification of liaisons and correlations between the various values used. It would be too long, complex, and tedious. For the moment let us affirm that the basic matrix was verified by the two formulae:

$$r = \frac{\sum (x - \bar{x})(y - \bar{y})}{\sqrt{\sum (x - \bar{x})^2}\sqrt{\sum (y - \bar{y})^2}},$$

and

$$z = \tfrac{1}{2} \log \frac{1 + r}{1 - r}.$$

Let us now imagine music composed with the aid of matrix (M). An observer who perceived the frequencies of events of the musical sample would deduce a distribution due to chance and following the laws of probability. Now the question is, when heard a number of times, will this music keep its surprise effect? Will it not change into a set of *foreseeable* phenomena through the existence of memory, despite the fact that the law of frequencies has been derived from the laws of chance?

In fact, the data will appear aleatory only at the first hearing. Then, during successive rehearings the relations between the events of the sample ordained by "chance" will form a network, which will take on a definite meaning in the mind of the listener, and will initiate a special "logic," a new cohesion capable of satisfying his intellect as well as his aesthetic sense; that is, if the artist has a certain flair.

If, on the other hand, we wish the sample to be unforeseeable at all times, it is possible to conceive that at each repetition certain data might be transformed in such a way that their deviations from theoretical frequencies would not be significant. Perhaps a programming useful for a first, second, third, etc., performance will give aleatory samples that are not identical in an absolute sense, whose deviations will also be distributed by chance.

Or again a system with electronic computers might permit variations of the parameters of entrance to the matrix and of the clouds, under certain conditions. There would thus arise a music which can be distorted in the course of time, giving the same observer n results apparently due to chance for n performances. In the long run the music will follow the laws of probability and the performances will be *statistically* identical with each other, the identity being defined once for all by the "vector-matrix."

The sonic scheme defined under this form of vector-matrix is consequently capable of establishing a more or less self-determined regulation of the rare sonic events contained in a musical composition sample. It represents a compositional attitude, a fundamentally stochastic behavior, a unity of superior order.   [1956–57].

If the first steps may be summarized by the process vision → rules → works of art, the question concerning the minimum has produced an inverse path: rules → vision. In fact stochastics permits a philosophic vision, as the example of *Achorripsis* bears witness.

CHANCE—IMPROVISATION

Before generalizing further on the essence of musical composition, we must speak of the principle of improvisation which caused a furore among the neo-serialists, and which gives them the right, or so they think, to speak of chance, of the aleatory, which they thus introduce into music. They write scores in which certain combinations of sounds may be freely chosen by the interpreter. It is evident that these composers consider the various possible circuits as equivalent. Two logical infirmities are apparent which deny them the right to speak of chance on the one hand and "composition" on the other (composition in the broad sense, that is):

1. The interpreter is a highly conditioned being, so that it is not possible to accept the thesis of unconditioned choice, of an interpreter acting like a roulette game. The martingale betting at Monte Carlo and the procession of suicides should convince anyone of this. We shall return to this.

2. The composer commits an act of resignation when he admits several possible and equivalent circuits. In the name of a "scheme" the problem of choice is betrayed, and it is the interpreter who is promoted to the rank of composer by the composer himself. There is thus a substitution of authors.

The extremist extension of this attitude is one which uses graphical signs on a piece of paper which the interpreter reads while improvising the whole. The two infirmities mentioned above are terribly aggravated here. I would like to pose a question: If this sheet of paper is put before an interpreter who is an incomparable expert on Chopin, will the result not be modulated by the style and writing of Chopin in the same way that a performer who is immersed in this style might improvise a Chopin-like cadenza to another composer's concerto? From the point of view of the composer there is no interest.

On the contrary, two conclusions may be drawn: first, that serial composition has become so banal that it can be improvised like Chopin's, which confirms the general impression; and second, that the composer resigns his function altogether, that he has nothing to say, and that his function can be taken over by paintings or by cuneiform glyphs.

Chance needs to be calculated

To finish with the thesis of the roulette-musician, I shall add this: Chance is a rare thing and a snare. It can be constructed up to a certain

point with great difficulty, by means of complex reasoning which is summarized in mathematical formulae; it can be constructed a little, but never
improvised or intellectually imitated. I refer to the demonstration of the
impossibility of imitating chance which was made by the great mathemati-
cian Emile Borel, who was one of the specialists in the calculus of probabilities. In any case—to play with sounds like dice—what a truly simplistic
activity! But once one has emerged from this primary field of chance worth-
less to a musician, the calculation of the aleatory, that is to say stochastics,
guarantees first that in a region of precise definition slips will not be made,
and then furnishes a powerful method of reasoning and enrichment of sonic
processes.

STOCHASTIC PAINTING?

In line with these ideas, Michel Philippot introduced the calculus of
probabilities into his painting several years ago, thus opening new directions for investigation in this artistic realm. In music he recently endeavored
to analyze the act of composition in the form of a *flow chart* for an *imaginary
machine*. It is a fundamental analysis of voluntary choice, which leads to a
chain of aleatory or deterministic events, and is based on the work *Composition pour double orchestre* (1960). The term imaginary machine means that the
composer may rigorously define the entities and operating methods, just as
on an electronic computer. In 1960 Philippot commented on his *Composition
pour double orchestre*:

> If, in connection with this work, I happened to use the term
> "experimental music," I should specify in what sense it was meant in
> this particular case. It has nothing to do with concrete or electronic
> music, but with a very banal score written on the usual ruled paper
> and requiring none but the most traditional orchestral instruments.
> However, the experiment of which this composition was in some sense
> a by-product does exist (and one can think of many industries that
> survive only through the exploitation of their by-products).
>
> The end sought was merely to effect, in the context of a work
> which I would have written independent of all experimental ambi-
> tions, an exploration of the processes followed by my own cerebral
> mechanism as it arranged the sonic elements. I therefore devised the
> following steps:
>
> 1. Make the most complete inventory possible of the set of my
> gestures, ideas, mannerisms, decisions, and choices, etc., which were
> mine when I wrote the music.

2. Reduce this set to a succession of simple decisions, binary, if possible; i.e., accept or refuse a particular note, duration, or silence in a situation determined and defined by the context on one hand, and by the conditioning to which I had been subjected and my personal tastes on the other.

3. Establish, if possible, from this sequence of simple decisions, a scheme ordered according to the following two considerations (which were sometimes contradictory): the manner in which these decisions emerged from my imagination in the course of the work, and the manner in which they would have to emerge in order to be most useful.

4. Present this scheme in the form of a flow chart containing the logical chain of these decisions, the operation of which could easily be controlled.

5. Set in motion a mechanism of simulation respecting the rules of the game in the flow chart and note the result.

6. Compare this result with my *musical* intentions.

7. Check the differences between result and intentions, detect their causes, and correct the operating rules.

8. Refer these corrections back to the sequence of experimental phases, i.e., start again at 1. until a satisfactory result has been obtained.

If we confine ourselves to the most general considerations, it would simply be a matter of proceeding to an analysis of the complexity, considered as an accumulation, in a certain order, of single events, and then of reconstructing this complexity, at the same time verifying the nature of the elements and their rules of combination. A cursory look at the flow chart of the first movement specifies quite well by a mere glance the method I used. But to confine oneself to this first movement would be to misunderstand the essentials of musical composition.

In fact the "preludial" character which emerges from this combination of notes (elementary constituents of the orchestra) should remind us of the fact that composition in its ultimate stage is also an assembly of groups of notes, motifs, or themes and their transformations. Consequently the task revealed by the flow charts of the following movements ought to make conspicuous a grouping of a higher order, in which the data of the first movement were used as a sort of "prefabricated" material. Thus appeared the phenomenon, a rather banal one, of autogeneration of complexity by juxtaposition and combination of a large number of single events and operations.

At the end of this experiment I possessed at most some insight into my own musical tastes, but to me, the obviously interesting aspect of

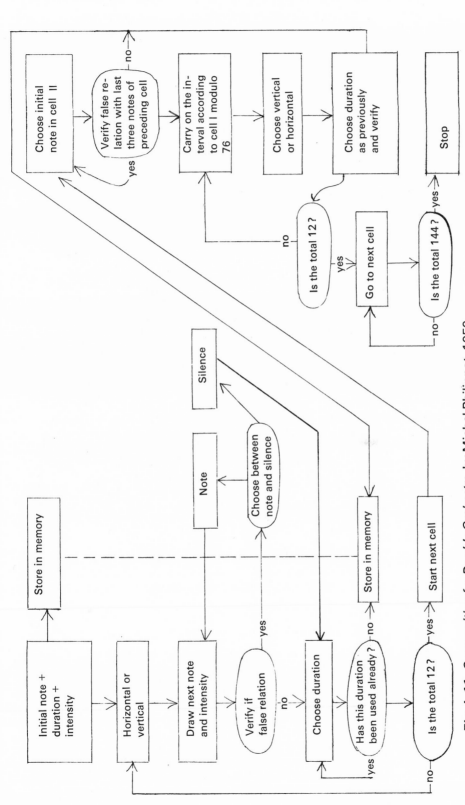

Fig. I–11. *Composition for Double Orchestra*, by Michel Philippot, 1959
Flow Chart of the First Movement

it (as long as there is no error of omission!) was the analysis of the composer, his mental processes, and a certain liberation of the imagination.

The biggest difficulty encountered was that of a conscious and voluntary split in personality. On one hand, was the composer who already had a clear idea and a precise audition of the work he wished to obtain; and on the other was the experimenter who had to maintain a lucidity which rapidly became burdensome in these conditions—a lucidity with respect to his own gestures and decisions. We must not ignore the fact that such experiments must be examined with the greatest prudence, for everyone knows that no observation of a phenomenon exists which does not disturb that phenomenon, and I fear that the resulting disturbance might be particularly strong when it concerns such an ill-defined domain and such a delicate activity. Moreover, in this particular case, I fear that observation might provoke its own disturbance. If I accepted this risk, I did not underestimate its extent. At most, my ambition confined itself to the attempt to project on a marvelous unknown, that of aesthetic creation, the timid light of a dark lantern. (The dark lantern had the reputation of being used especially by housebreakers. On several occasions I have been able to verify how much my thirst for investigation has made me appear in the eyes of the majority as a dangerous housebreaker of inspiration.)

Chapter II

Markovian Stochastic Music—Theory

Now we can rapidly generalize the study of musical composition with the aid of stochastics.

The first thesis is that stochastics is valuable not only in instrumental music, but also in electromagnetic music. We have demonstrated this with several works: *Diamorphoses* 1957–58 (B.A.M. Paris), *Concret PH* (in the Philips Pavilion at the Brussels Exhibition, 1958); and *Orient-Occident*, music for the film of the same name by E. Fulchignoni, produced by UNESCO in 1960.

The second thesis is that stochastics can lead to the creation of new sonic materials and to new forms. For this purpose we must as a preamble put forward a temporary hypothesis which concerns the nature of sound, of all sound [19].

BASIC TEMPORARY HYPOTHESIS (lemma) AND DEFINITIONS

All sound is an integration of grains, of elementary sonic particles, of sonic quanta. Each of these elementary grains has a threefold nature: duration, frequency, and intensity.[1] All sound, even all continuous sonic variation, is conceived as an assemblage of a large number of elementary grains adequately disposed in time. So every sonic complex can be analyzed as a series of pure sinusoidal sounds even if the variations of these sinusoidal sounds are infinitely close, short, and complex. In the attack, body, and decline of a complex sound, thousands of pure sounds appear in a more or less short interval of time, Δt. Hecatombs of pure sounds are necessary for the creation of a complex sound. A complex sound may be imagined as a multi-colored firework in which each point of light appears and instantaneously disappears against a black sky. But in this firework there would be such a quantity of points of light organized in such a way that their rapid and teeming succession would create forms and spirals, slowly unfolding, or conversely, brief explosions setting the whole sky aflame. A line of light would be created by a sufficiently large multitude of points appearing and disappearing instantaneously.

If we consider the duration Δt of the grain as quite small but invariable, we can ignore it in what follows and consider frequency and intensity only. The two physical substances of a sound are frequency and intensity in association. They constitute two sets, F and G, independent by their nature. They have a set product $F \times G$, which is the elementary grain of sound. Set F can be put in any kind of correspondence with G: many-valued, single-valued, one-to-one mapping, ... The correspondence can be given by an extensive representation, a matrix representation, or a canonical representation.

EXAMPLES OF REPRESENTATIONS

Extensive (term by term):

$$
\begin{array}{l}
\text{Frequencies} \quad \Big\downarrow f_1 \quad f_2 \quad f_3 \quad f_4 \quad \cdots \\
\text{Intensities} \quad g_3 \quad g_n \quad g_3 \quad g_h \quad \cdots
\end{array}
$$

Matrix (in the form of a table):

$\downarrow$	f_1	f_2	f_3	f_4	f_5	f_6	f_7	$\cdots$
g_1	+	0	+	0	0	0	+	
g_2	0	+	0	0	0	+	0	
g_3	0	0	0	+	+	0	0	
$\vdots$								

Canonical (in the form of a function):

$$
\begin{array}{l}
\sqrt{f} = Kg \\
f = \text{frequency} \\
g = \text{intensity} \\
K = \text{coefficient.}
\end{array}
$$

The correspondence may also be indeterminate (stochastic), and here the most convenient representation is the matrical one, which gives the transition probabilities.

Example:

$\downarrow$	f_1	f_2	f_3	f_4	$\cdots$
g_1	0.5	0	0.2	0	$\cdots$
g_2	0	0.3	0.3	1	$\cdots$
g_3	0.5	0.7	0.5	0	$\cdots$

The table should be interpreted as follows: for each value f_i of f there are one or several corresponding intensity values g_i, defined by a probability. For example, the two intensities g_2 and g_3 correspond to the frequency f_2, with 30% and 70% chance of occurrence, respectively. On the other hand, each of the two sets F and G can be furnished with a structure—that is to say, internal relations and laws of composition.

Time t is considered as a totally ordered set mapped onto F or G in a lexicographic form.

Examples:

a. f_1 f_2 f_3 $\cdots$
   $t = 1, 2, \cdots$

b. $f_{0.5}$ f_3 $f_{\sqrt{11}}$ f_x $\cdots$
   $t = 0.5, 3, \sqrt{11}, x, \cdots$

c.

$$t = \begin{array}{|c|c|c|c|c|c|c|c|c|c|c|} \hline f_1 & f_1 & f_2 & f_1 & f_2 & f_2 & f_n & f_3 & \cdots & \cdots & \cdots \\ \hline A & B & C & D & E & \cdots & \cdots & \cdots & \cdots & \cdots & \cdots \\ \hline \Delta t & \Delta t & \Delta t & \Delta t & \Delta t & \Delta t & \Delta t & \cdots & \cdots & \cdots & \cdots \\ \hline \end{array}$$

$$\Delta t = \Delta t$$

Example c. is the most general since continuous evolution is sectioned into slices of a single thickness Δt, which transforms it in discontinuity; this makes it much easier to isolate and examine under the magnifying glass.

GRAPHICAL REPRESENTATIONS

We can plot the values of pure frequencies in units of octaves or semitones on the abscissa axis, and the intensity values in decibels on the ordinate axis, using logarithmic scales (see Fig. II–1). This cloud of points is the cylindrical projection on the plane (FG) of the grains contained in a thin slice Δt (see Fig. II–2). The graphical representations Figs. II–2 and II–3 make more tangible the abstract possibilities raised up to this point.

Psychophysiology

We are confronted with a cloud of evolving points. This cloud is the product of the two sets F and G in the slice of time Δt. What are the possible

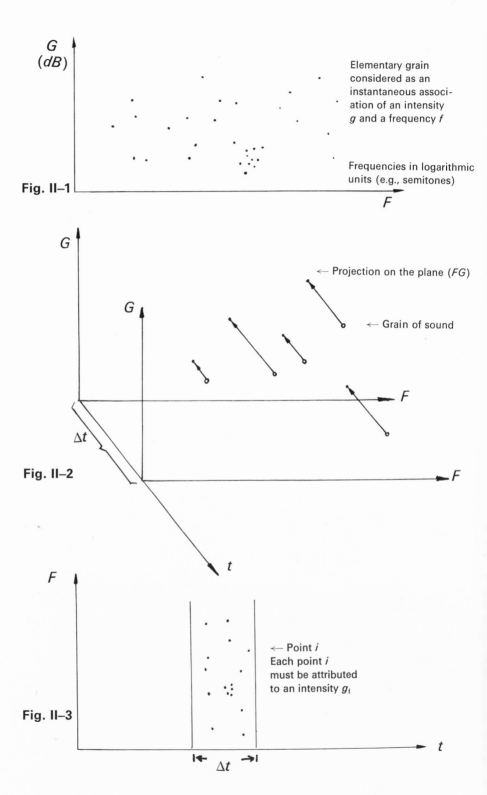

G (*dB*)

Elementary grain
considered as an
instantaneous associ-
ation of an intensity
g and a frequency *f*

Frequencies in logarithmic
units (e.g., semitones)

Fig. II–1

F

G

← Projection on the plane (*FG*)

G

← Grain of sound

Δ*t*

F

Fig. II–2

F

t

F

← Point *i*
Each point *i*
must be attributed
to an intensity *g*ᵢ

Fig. II–3

t

Δ*t*

restrictive limits of human psychophysiology? What are the most general manipulations which may be imposed on the clouds and their transformations within psychophysiological limits?

The basic abstract hypothesis, which is the granular construction of all possible sounds, gives a very profound meaning to these two questions. In fact within human limits, using all sorts of manipulations with these grain clusters, we can hope to produce not only the sounds of classical instruments and elastic bodies, and those sounds generally preferred in concrete music, but also sonic perturbations with evolutions, unparalleled and unimaginable until now. The basis of the timbre structures and transformations will have nothing in common with what has been known until now.

We can even express a more general supposition. Suppose that each point of these clusters represents not only a pure frequency and its satellite intensity, but an already present structure of elementary grains, ordered a priori. We believe that in this way a sonority of a second, third, or higher order can be produced.

Recent work on hearing has given satisfactory answers to certain problems of perception. The basic problems which concern us and which we shall suppose to be resolved, even if some of the solutions are in part lacking, are [2, 3]: 1. What is the minimum perceptible duration (in comfort) of a sinusoidal sound, as a function of its frequency and its intensity? 2. What are the minimum values of intensities in decibels compatible with minimum frequencies and durations of sinusoidal sounds? 3. What are the minimum melodic interval thresholds, as a function of register, intensity, and duration? A good approximation is the Fletcher-Munson diagram of equal loudness contours (see Fig. II–4).

The total number of elementary audible grains is about 340,000. The ear is more sensitive at the center of the audible area. At the extremities it perceives less amplitude and fewer melodic intervals, so that if one wished to represent the audible area in a homogeneous manner using the coordinates F and G, i.e., with each surface element $\Delta F \Delta G$ containing the same density of grains of perceptible sounds, one would obtain a sort of mappa mundi (Fig. II–5).

In order to simplify the reasoning which will follow without altering it, we shall base our argument on Fletcher's diagram and suppose that an appropriate one-to-one transformation applied to this group of coordinates will change this curved space into an ordinary rectangle (Fig. II–6).

All the above experimental results were established in ideal conditions and without reference to the actual complexity of the natural sounds of the orchestra and of elastic bodies in general, not to mention the more complex

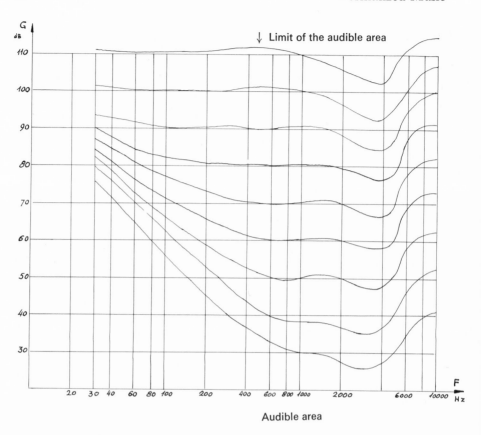

Audible area

Fig. II–4. Fletcher-Munson Diagram

Equal Loudness Contours

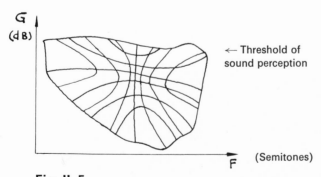

← Threshold of
sound perception

Fig. II–5

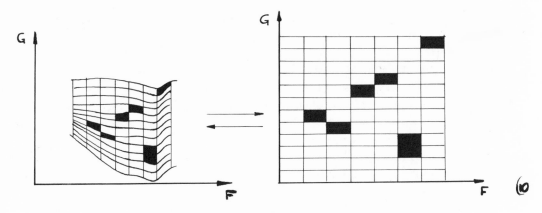

sounds of industry or of chaotic nature [4]. Theoretically [5] a complex sound can only be exhaustively represented on a three-dimensional diagram F, G, t, giving the instantaneous frequency and intensity as a function of time. But in practice this boils down to saying that in order to represent a momentary sound, such as a simple noise made by a car, months of calculations and graphs are necessary. This impasse is strikingly reminiscent of classical mechanics, which claimed that, given sufficient time, it could account for all physical and even biological phenomena using only a few formulae. But just to describe the state of a gaseous mass of greatly reduced volume at one instant t, even if simplifications are allowed at the beginning of the calculation, would require several centuries of human work!

This was a false problem because it is useless; and as far as gaseous masses are concerned, the Maxwell-Boltzmann kinetic theory of gases, with its statistical method, has been very fruitful [6]. This method reestablished the value of scales of observation. For a macroscopic phenomenon it is the massed total result which counts, and each time a phenomenon is to be observed the scale relationship between observer and phenomenon must first be established. Thus if we observe galactic masses, we must decide whether it is the movement of the whole mass, the movement of a single star, or the molecular constitution of a minute region on a star that interests us.

The same thing holds true for complex as well as quite simple sounds. It would be a waste of effort to attempt to account analytically or graphically for the characteristics of complex sounds when they are to be used in an electromagnetic composition. For the manipulation of these sounds macroscopic methods are necessary.

Inversely, and this is what particularly interests us here, to work like architects on the sonic material in order to construct complex sounds and evolutions of these entities means that we must use macroscopic methods of analysis and construction. Microsounds and elementary grains have no importance on the scale which we have chosen. Only groups of grains and the characteristics of these groups have any meaning. Naturally in very particular cases, the single grain will be reestablished in all its glory. In a Wilson chamber it is the elementary particle which carries theoretical and experimental physics on its shoulders, while in the sun it is the mass of particles and their compact interactions which constitute the solar object.

Our field of evolution is therefore the curved space described above, but simplified to a rectilinear space by means of complete one-to-one transformation, which safeguards the validity of the reasoning which we shall pursue.

SCREENS

The graphical representation of a cloud of grains in a slice of time Δt examined earlier brings a new concept, that of the density of grains per unit of volume, $\Delta F \Delta G \Delta t$ (Fig. II–7). Every possible sound may therefore be cut up into a precise quantity of elements $\Delta F \Delta G \Delta t \Delta D$ in four dimensions, distributed in this space and following certain rules defining this sound, which are summarized by a function with four variables: $s(F, G, D, t)$.

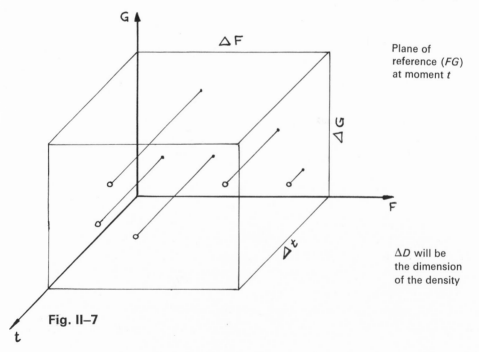

Fig. II–7

The scale of the density will also be logarithmic with its base between 2 and 3.[2] To simplify the explanation we will make an abstraction of this new coordinate of density. It will always be present in our mind but as an entity associated with the three-dimensional element $\Delta F \Delta G \Delta t$.

If time is considered as a procedure of lexicographic ordering, we can, without loss, assume that the Δt are equal constants and quite small. We can thus reason on a two-dimensional space defined by the axes F and G, on condition that we do not lose sight of the fact that the cloud of grains of sound exists in the thickness of time Δt and that the grains of sound are only artificially flattened on the plane (FG).

Definition of the screen. The screen is the audible area (FG) fixed by a sufficiently close and homogeneous grid as defined above, the cells of which may or may not be occupied by grains. In this way any sound and its history may be described by means of a sufficiently large number of sheets of paper carrying a given screen S. These sheets are placed in a fixed lexicographic order (see Fig. II–8).

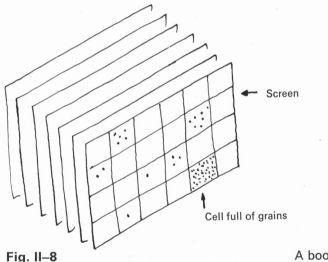

Fig. II–8

Fig. II–8   A book of screens equals
                                 the life of a complex sound

The clouds of grains drawn on the screens will differ from one screen to another by their geographical or topographical position and by their surface density (see Fig. II–9). Screen A contains a small elemental rectangle with a small cluster of density d of mean frequency f and mean amplitude g. It is almost a pure sound. Screen B represents a more complex sound with strong high and low areas but with a weak center. Screen C represents a "white" sound of weak density which may therefore be perceived as a sonic sheen occupying the whole audible area.

What is important in all the statements made up to now is that nothing has been said about the topographic fixity of the grains on the screens. All natural or instrumental sounds are composed of small surface elements filled with grains which fluctuate around a mean frequency and intensity. The same holds for the density. This statement is fundamental, and it is very likely that the failure of electronic music to create new timbres, aside from the inadequacy of the serial method, is largely due to the fixity of the grains, which form structures like packets of spaghetti (Fig. II–10).

Topographic fixity of the grains is a very particular case, the most general case being mobility and the statistical distribution of grains around positions of equilibrium. Consequently in the majority of cases real sounds can be analyzed as quite small rectangles, $\Delta F \Delta G$, in which the topographic positions and the densities vary from one screen to another following more or less well-defined laws.

Thus the sound of example D at this precise instant is formed by the collection of rectangles $(f_2 g_4)$, $(f_2 g_5)$, $(f_4 g_2)$, $(f_4 g_3)$, $(f_5 g_1)$, $(f_5 g_2)$, $(f_6 g_1)$, $(f_6 g_2)$, $(f_6 g_5)$, $(f_7 g_2)$, $(f_7 g_3)$, $(f_7 g_4)$, $(f_7 g_5)$, $(f_8 g_3)$, $(f_8 g_4)$, $(f_8 g_5)$, and in each of the rectangles the grains are disposed in an asymmetric and homogeneous manner (see Fig. II–11).

CONSTRUCTION OF THE ELEMENTS $\Delta F \Delta G$ OF THE SCREENS

1. *By calculation.* We shall examine the means of calculating the elements $\Delta F \Delta G \Delta t \Delta D$.

How should the grains be distributed in an elemental volume? If we fix the mean density of the grains (= number of grains per unit of volume) we have to resolve a problem of probability in a four-dimensional space. A simpler method would be to consider and then calculate the four coordinates independently.

For the coordinate t the law of distribution of grains on the axis of time is:

$$P_x = c\, e^{-cx}\, dx \quad \text{or} \quad P_{x_i} = e^{-civ}\, c\Delta x_i. \quad \text{(r)} \quad \text{(See Appendix I.)}$$

For the coordinates G, F, D the stochastic law will be:

$$f(j)\, dj = \frac{2}{a}\left(1 - \frac{j}{a}\right) dj \qquad \text{(r')}$$

or

$$P_i = \frac{2}{2 \cdot 10^n}\left(1 - \frac{i}{2 \cdot 10^n - 1}\right). \quad \text{(See Appendix I.)}$$

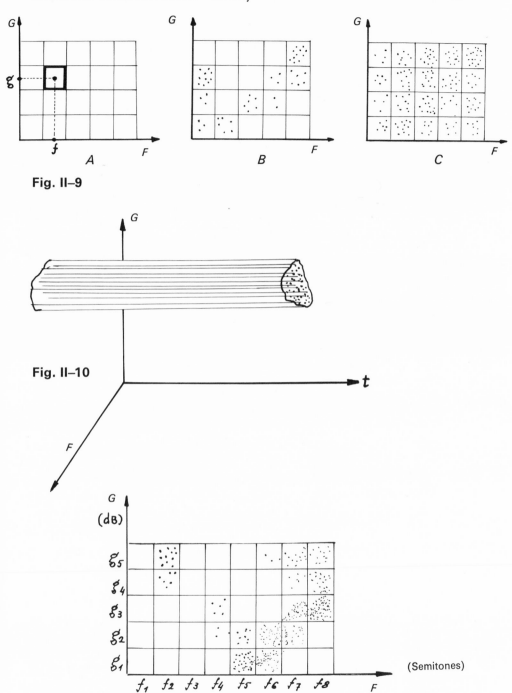

Fig. II–9

Fig. II–10

Fig. II–11

From these formulae we can draw up tables of the frequencies of the values t, G, F, D (see the analogous problem in Chapter I). These formulae are in our opinion privileged, for they arise from very simple reasoning, probably the very simplest; and it is essential to start out with a minimum of terms and constraints if we wish to keep to the principle of the tabula rasa (1st and 3rd rules of Descartes's Discourse on Method).

Let there be one of these elemental volumes $\Delta t \Delta D \Delta F \Delta G$ of the screen at the moment t. This volume has a density D taken from the table derived from formula (r'). Points on Δt are defined with a linear density $D = c$ according to the table defined by formula (r). To each point is attributed a sonic grain of frequency f and intensity g, taken from within the rectangle $\Delta F \Delta G$ by means of the table of frequencies derived from formula (r'). The correspondences are made graphically or by random successive drawings from urns composed according to the above tables.

2. *Mechanically.* a. On the tape recorder: The grains are realized from sinusoidal sounds whose durations are constant, about 0.04 sec. These grains must cover the selected elemental area $\Delta F \Delta G$. Unfolding in time is accomplished by using the table of durations for a minimum density $c = D$. By mixing sections of this tape with itself, we can obtain densities varying geometrically with ratio $1:2:3 \ldots$ according to the number of tracks that we use. b. On computers: The grains are realized from wave forms duly programmed according to Gabor's signals, for a computer to which an analogue converter has been coupled. A second program would provide for the construction of the elemental volumes $\Delta t \Delta D \Delta F \Delta G$ from formulae (r) and (r').

First General Comment

Take the cell $\Delta F \Delta G \Delta t$. Although occupied in a homogeneous manner by grains of sound, it varies in time by fluctuating around a mean density d_m. We can apply another argument which is more synthetic, and admit that these fluctuations will exist in the most general case anyhow (if the sound is long enough), and will therefore obey the laws of chance. In this case, the problem is put in the following manner:

Given a prismatic cloud of grains of density d_m, of cross section $\Delta F \Delta G$ and length $\sum \Delta t$, what is the probability that d grains will be found in an elemental volume $\Delta F \Delta G \Delta t$? If the number d_m is small enough, the probability is given by Poisson's formula:

$$P_k = \frac{(d_m)^k}{K!} e^{-d_m}.$$

For the definition of each grain we shall again use the methods described above.

Second General Comment (Vector Space) [8]

We can construct elemental cells $\Delta F \Delta G$ of the screens not only with points, but with elemental vectors associated with the grains (vector space). The mean density of 0.04 sec/grain really implies a small vector. The particular case of the grain occurs when the vector is parallel to the axis of time, when its projection on the plane (FG) is a point, and when the frequency of the grain is constant. In general, the frequencies and intensities of the grains can be variable and the grain a very short glissando (see Fig. II–12).

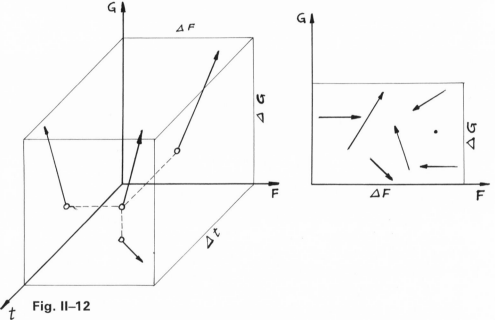

Fig. II–12

In a vector space (FG) thus defined, the construction of screens would perhaps be cumbersome, for it would be necessary to introduce the idea of speed and the statistical distribution of its values, but the interest in the undertaking would be enormous. We could imagine screens as the basis of granular fields which are magnetized or completely neutral (disordered).

In the case of total disorder, we can calculate the probability $f(v)$ of the existence of a vector v on the plane (FG) using Maxwell's formula as applied to two dimensions [11]:

$$f(v) = \frac{2v}{a^2} e^{-v^2/a^2}.$$

For the mean value $v_1 \leq v_m \leq v_2$,

$$P(v_m) = \frac{2\sqrt{\pi}}{a}\left\{\theta(\lambda_1) - \theta(\lambda_2)\right\}$$

in which $\lambda_i = v_i/a$ and

$$\theta(\lambda_i) = \frac{1}{\sqrt{\pi}}\int_{-\lambda_i}^{+\lambda_i} e^{-\lambda^2}\,d\lambda,$$

for $\lambda_1 \leq \lambda \leq \lambda_2$ (normal Gaussian law) [12]. In any case, whether it is a matter of a vector space or a scalar space does not modify the arguments [13].

Summary of the Screens

1. A screen is described by a set of clouds that are themselves a set of elemental rectangles $\Delta F \Delta G$, and which may or may not contain grains of sound. These conditions exist at the moment t in a slice of time Δt, as small as desired.

2. The grains of sound create a density peculiar to each elemental rectangle $\Delta F \Delta G$ and are generally distributed in the rectangles in an ergodic manner. (The ergodic principle states that the capricious effect of an operation that depends on chance is regularized more and more as the operation is repeated. Here it is understood that a very large succession of screens is being considered [14].)

3. The conception of the elemental volume $\Delta F \Delta G \Delta T \Delta D$ is such that no simultaneity of grains is generally admitted. Simultaneity occurs when the density is high enough. Its frequency is bound up with the size of the density. It is all a question of scale and this paragraph refers above all to realization. The temporal dimension of the grain (vector) being of the order of 0.04 sec., no systematic overlapping of two grains (vectors) will be accepted when the elementary density is, for example, $D_0 = 1.5$ grains/sec. And as the surface distribution of the grains is homogeneous, only chance can create this overlapping.

4. The limit for a screen may be only one pure sound (sinusoidal), or even no sound at all (empty screen).

ELEMENTARY OPERATIONS ON SCREENS

Let there be a complex sound. At an instant t of its life during a thickness Δt it can be represented by one or several clouds of grains or vectors on the plane (FG). This is the definition which we gave for the screen. The junction of several of these screens in a given order describes or prescribes the life of this sonic complex. It would be interesting to envisage in all its generality the manner of combining and juxtaposing screens to describe, and above all to construct, sonic evolutions, which may be continuous or discontinuous, with a view to playing with them in a composition. To this end we shall borrow the terminology and symbolism of modern algebra, but in an elementary manner and as a form of introduction to a further development which we shall not undertake at the moment.

Comment: It does not matter whether we place ourselves on the plane of physical phenomena or of perception. In general, on the plane of perception we consider arithmetically that which is geometrical on the physical plane. This can be expressed in a more rigorous manner. Perception constitutes an additive group which is *almost* isomorphic with a physical excitation constituting a multiplicative group. The "almost" is necessary to exorcise approximations.

Grains or vectors on the plane (*FG*) constitute a cloud. A screen can be composed of no grain at all or of several clouds of grains or vectors (see Fig. II–13).

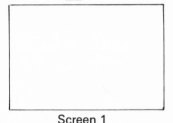 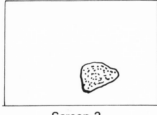 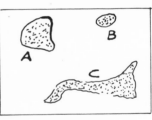

| Screen 1 | Screen 2 | Screen 3 |

Fig. II–13

To notate that a grain or vector *a* belongs to a cloud E, we write $a \in E$ the contrary is written $a \notin E$. If all the grains of a cloud X are grains of another cloud Y, it is said that X is included in Y or that X is a part or sub-cloud of Y. This relation is notated $X \subset Y$ (inclusion).

Consequently we have the following properties:

$$X \subset X \quad \text{for any } X.$$
$$X \subset Y \quad \text{and} \quad Y \subset Z \quad \text{imply} \quad X \subset Z.$$

When $X \subset Y$ and $Y \subset X$, the clouds X and Y consist of the same grains; they are indistinguishable and the relation is written: $X = Y$ (equation).

A cloud may contain as little as a single grain. A cloud X is said to be empty when it contains no grain a, such that $a \in X$. The empty cloud is notated $\varnothing$.

These operations apply equally well to clouds and to screens. We can therefore use the terms "screen" and "cloud" indiscriminately, with cloud and grain as "constitutive elements."

The *intersection* of two screens A and B is the screen of clouds which belong to both A and B. This is notated as $A \cap B$ and read as "A inter B" (Fig. II–14). When $A \cap B = \varnothing$, A and B are said to be *disjoint* (Fig. II–15). The *union* of two screens A and B is the set of clouds which belong to both A and/or B (Fig. II–16). The *complement* of a screen A in relation to a screen E containing A is the set of clouds in E which do *not* belong to A. This is notated $C_E A$ when there is no possible uncertainty about E (Fig. II–17). The *difference* $(A - B)$ of A and B is the set of clouds of A which do not belong to B. The immediate consequence is $A - B = A - (A \cap B) = C_A(A \cap B)$ (Fig. II–18).

We shall stop this borrowing here; however, it will afford a stronger, more precise conception on the whole, better adapted for the manipulations and arguments which follow.

DISTINCTIVE CHARACTERISTICS OF THE SCREENS

In our desire to create sonic complexes from the temporary accepted primary matter of sound, sine waves (or their replacements of the Gabor sort), and to create sonic complexes as rich as but more extraordinary than natural sounds (using scientifically controlled evolutions on very general abstract planes), we have implicitly recognized the importance of three basic factors which seem to be able to dominate both the theoretical construction of a sonic process and its sensory effectiveness: 1. the density of the elementary elements, 2. the topographic situation of events on the screens, and 3. the order or disorder of events.

At first sight then the density of grains or vectors, their topography, and their degree of order are the indirect entities and aspects perceived by our macroscopic ears. It is wonderful that the ear and the mind follow objective reality and react directly in spite of gross inherent or cultural imperfections. Measurement has been the foundation of the experimental sciences. Man voluntarily treats himself as a sensory invalid, and it is for this reason that he has armed himself, justifiably, with machines that measure other machines. His ears and eyes do measure entities or physical phenomena, but they are transformed as if a distorting filter came between immediate perception and consciousness. About a century ago the logarithmic

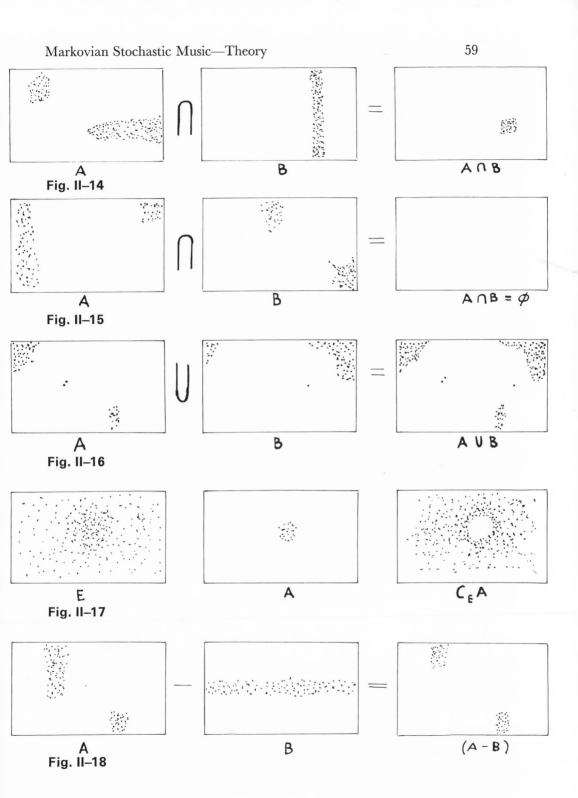

A   ∩   B   =   A ∩ B
Fig. II–14

A   ∩   B   =   A ∩ B = ∅
Fig. II–15

A   ∪   B   =   A ∪ B
Fig. II–16

E   A   C_E A
Fig. II–17

A   —   B   =   (A − B)
Fig. II–18

law of sensation was discovered; until now it has not been contradicted. But as knowledge never stops in its advance, tomorrow's science will without doubt find not only a greater flexibility and exactitude for this law, but also the beginnings of an explanation of this distorting filter, which is so astonishing.

This statistical, but none the less quasi–one-to-one transformation of excitation into perception has up to now allowed us to argue about physical entities, such as screens, all the while thinking "perceived events." A reciprocity of the same kind between perception and its comprehension permits us to pass from the screens to the consequent distinctive characteristics. Thus the arguments which we shall pursue apply equally well to pure concepts and to those resulting from perception or sensory events, and we may take the attitude of the craftsman or the listener.

We have already remarked on the density and the topography of grains and cells and we have acknowledged the concepts of order and disorder in the homogeneous superficial distribution or grains.

We shall examine closely the concept of order, for it is probably hidden behind the other two. That is to say, density and topography are rather palpably simplified embodiments of this fleeting and many-sided concept of disorder.

When we speak of order or disorder we imply first of all "objects" or "elements." Then, and this is already more complex, we define the very "elements" which we wish to study and from which we wish to construct order or disorder, and their scale in relation to ours. Finally we qualify and endeavor to measure this order or disorder. We can even draw up a list of all the orders and disorders of these entities on all scales, from all aspects, for all measurements, even the characteristics of order or disorder of this very list, and establish anew aspects and measurements.

Take the example of the gases mentioned above. On the molecular scale (and we could have descended to the atomic level), the absolute values of the speeds, directions, and distributions in space are of all sorts. We can distinguish the "elements" which carry order or disorder. Thus if we could theoretically isolate the element "directions" and assume that there is an obligation to follow certain privileged directions and not all directions, we could impose a certain degree of order which would be independent of the other elements constituting the concept "gas." In the same way, given enough time, the values of the speeds of a single molecule will be distributed around a mean value and the size of the deviations will follow Gauss's law. There we will have a certain order since these values are vastly more numerous in the neighborhood of their mean than anywhere else, from infinitely small to infinitely large.

Let us take another example, more obvious and equally true. A crowd of 500,000 persons is assembled in a town square. If we examine the group displacement of this crowd we can prove that it does not budge. However, each individual moves his limbs, his head, his eyes, and displaces his center of gravity by a few centimeters in every direction. If the displacements of the centers of gravity were very large the crowd would break up with yells of terror because of the multiple collisions between individuals. The statistical values of these displacements normally lie between very narrow limits which vary with the density of the crowd, From the point of view of these values as they affect immobility, the disorder is weak.

Another characteristic of the crowd is the orientation of the faces. If an orator on a balcony were to speak with a calming effect, 499,000 faces would look at the balcony and 998,000 ears would listen to the honeyed words. A thousand or so faces and 2000 ears would be distracted for various reasons: fatigue, annoyance, imagination, sexuality, contempt, theft, etc. We could confirm, along with the mass media, without any possible dispute, that crowd and speaker were in complete accord, that 500,001 people, in fact, were unanimous. The degree of order that the speaker was after would attain a maximum for a few minutes at least, and if unanimity were expressed equally strongly at the conclusion of the meeting, the orator could be persuaded that the ideas were as well ordered in the heads of the crowd as in his own.

We can establish from these two extreme examples that the concept of order and disorder is basic to a very large number of phenomena, and that even the definition of a phenomenon or an object is very often attributable to this concept. On the other hand, we can establish that this concept is founded on precise and distinct groups of elements; that the scale is important in the choice of elements; and finally, that the concept of order or disorder implies the relationship between effective values over all possible values that the elements of a group can possess. This introduces the concept of probability in the quantitative estimate of order or disorder.

We shall call the number of distinct elements in a group its *variety*. We shall call the degree of order or disorder definable in a group of elements its *entropy*. Entropy is linked with the concept of variety, and for that very reason, it is linked to the probability of an element in the group. These concepts are those of the theory of communications, which itself borrows from the second law of thermodynamics (Boltzmann's theorem H) [15].

Variety is expressed as a pure number or as its logarithm to the base 2. Thus human sex has two elements, male and female, and its variety is 2, or 1 bit: 1 bit $= \log_2 2$.

Let there be a group of probabilities (a group of real numbers p, positive or zero, whose sum is 1). The entropy H of this group is defined as

$$H = -K \sum p_i \log p_i.$$

If the logarithmic base is 2, the entropy is expressed in bits. Thus if we have a sequence of heads and tails, the probability of each is $\frac{1}{2}$, and the entropy of this sequence, i.e., its uncertainty at each throw, will be 1 bit. If both sides of the coin were heads, the uncertainty would be removed and the entropy H would be zero.

Let us suppose that the advent of a head or a tail is not controlled by tossing the coin, but by a fixed, univocal law, e.g., heads at each even toss and tails at each odd toss. Uncertainty or disorder is always absent and the entropy is zero. If the law becomes very complex the appearance of heads or tails will seem to a human observer to be ruled by the law of chance, and disorder and uncertainty will be reestablished. What the observer could do would be to count the appearances of heads and tails, add up their respective frequencies, deduce their probabilities, and then calculate the entropy in bits. If the frequency of heads is equal to that of tails the uncertainty will be maximum and equal to 1 bit.

This typical example shows roughly the passage from order to disorder and the means of calibrating this disorder so that it may be compared with other states of disorder. It also shows the importance of scale. The intelligence of the observer would assimilate a deterministic complexity up to a certain limit. Beyond that, in his eyes, the complexity would swing over into unforeseeability and would become chance or disorder; and the visible (or macroscopic would slide into the invisible (or microscopic). Other methods and points of view would be necessary to observe and control the phenomena.

At the beginning of this chapter we admitted that the mind and especially the ear were very sensitive to the order or disorder of phenomena. The laws of perception and judgment are probably in a geometrical or logarithmic relation to the laws of excitation. We do not know much about this, and we shall again confine ourselves to examining general entities and to tracing an overall orientation of the poetic processes of a very general kind of music, without giving figures, moduli, or determinisms. We are still optimistic enough to think that the interdependent experiment and action of abstract hypotheses can cut biologically into the living conflict between ignorance and reality(if there is any reality).

Study of Ataxy (order or disorder) on the Plane of a Cloud of Grains or Vectors

Axis of time: The degree of ataxy, or the entropy, is a function of the simultaneity of the grains and of the distinct intervals of time between the emission of each grain. If the *variety* of the durations of the emissions is weak, the entropy is also weak. If, for example, in a given Δt each grain is emitted at regular intervals of time, the temporal variety will be 1 and the entropy zero. The cloud will have zero ataxy and will be completely ordered. Conversely, if in a fairly long succession of Δt the grains are emitted according to the law $P_x = \delta e^{-\delta x}\, dx$, the degree of ataxy will be much larger. The limit of entropy is infinity, for we can imagine all possible values of time intervals with an equal probability. Thus, if the variety is $n \to \infty$, the probability for each time interval is $p_i = 1/n$, and the entropy is

$$H = -K \sum_{i=0}^{n} p_i \log p_i$$

$$H = -K \sum_{i=0}^{n} \frac{1}{n} \log \frac{1}{n} = -K\, n\, \frac{1}{n} \log \frac{1}{n} = -K \log \frac{1}{n} = K \log n$$

for $n \to \infty$, $H \to \infty$.

This is less true in practice, for a Δt will never offer a very great variety of durations and its entropy will be weak. Furthermore a sonic composition will rarely have more than 100,000 Δt's, so that $H \leq \log 100,000$ and $H \leq 16.6$ bits.

Axis of frequencies (*melodic*): The same arguments are valid here but with greater restriction on the variety of melodic intervals and on the absolute frequencies because of the limits of the audible area.

Entropy is zero when the variety of frequencies of grains is 1, i.e., when the cloud contains only one pure sound.

Axis of intensity and density: The above observations are valid. Therefore, if at the limit, the entropies following the three axes of an element $\Delta F \Delta G \Delta t \Delta D$ are zero, this element will only contain one pure sound of constant intensity emitted at regular intervals.

In conclusion, a cloud may contain just one single pure sound emitted at regular intervals of time (see Fig. II–19), in which case its mean entropy (arithmetic mean of the three entropies) would be zero. It may contain chaotically distributed grains, with maximum ataxy and maximum mean entropy (theoretically ∞). Between these two limits the grains may be distributed in an infinite number of ways with mean entropies between 0 and the maximum and able to produce both the Marseillaise and a raw, dodecaphonic series.

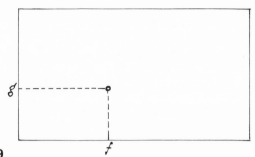

Fig. II–19

A single grain emitted at regular intervals of time

Parentheses

GENERAL OBSERVATIONS ON ATAXY

Taking this last possibility as a basis, we shall examine the very general formal processes in all realms of thought, in all physical and psychic realities.

To this end we shall imagine a "Primary Thing," malleable at will; capable of deforming instantaneously, progressively, or step-by-step; extendible or retractable; unique or plural; as simple as an electron (!) or as complex as the universe (as compared to man, that is).

It will have a given mean entropy. At a defined time we will cause it to undergo a transformation. From the point of view of ataxy this transformation can have one of three effects:

1. The degree of complexity (variety) does not change; the transformation is neutral; and the overall entropy does not change.

2. The degree of complexity increases and so does the entropy.

3. The transformation is a simplifying one, and the entropy diminishes.

Thus the neutral transformation may act on and transform: perfect disorder into perfect disorder (fluctuations), partial disorder into partial disorder, and perfect order into perfect order.

Multiplicative transformation transforms: perfect disorder into perfect disorder, partial disorder into greater disorder, and perfect order into partial disorder.

And simplifying transformation transforms: perfect disorder into partial disorder, partial order into greater order, and partial order into perfect order. Fig. II–20 shows these transformations in the form of a kinematic diagram.

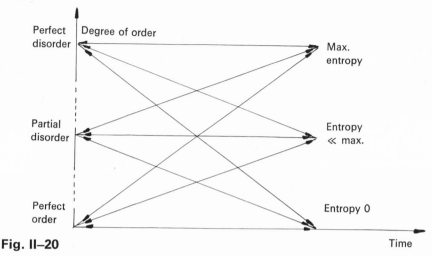

Fig. II–20

STUDY OF ATAXY AT THE LEVEL OF SCREENS (SET OF CLOUDS)

From the above discussion, a screen which is composed of a set of cells $\Delta F \Delta G$ associated with densities during a slice of time Δt, may be dissociated according to the two characters of the grains, frequency and amplitude, and affected by a mean entropy. Thus we can classify screens according to the criterion of ataxy by means of two parameters of disorder: the variety of the frequencies and the variety of the intensities. We shall make an abstraction of the temporal distribution of the grains in Δt and of the density, which is implicitly bound up with the varieties of the two fundamental sizes of the grain. In symbolic form:

$$\text{Perfect disorder} = \infty$$
$$\text{Partial disorder} = n \ \text{ or } \ m$$
$$\text{Partial order} \quad = m \ \text{ or } \ n$$
$$\text{Perfect order} \quad = 0.$$

From the point of view of ataxy a screen is formulated by a pair of entropy values ascribed to a pair of frequencies and intensities of its grains. Thus the pair (n, ∞) means a screen whose frequencies have quite a small entropy (partial order or disorder) and whose intensities have maximum entropy (more or less perfect disorder).

CONSTRUCTION OF THE SCREENS

We shall quickly survey some of the screens in the entropy table in Fig. II–21.

Perfect disorder		Partial disorder		Perfect order		Symbol	Description	Diagram	Diagram
F	G	F	G	F	G				
F	G					∞, ∞	Unique screen	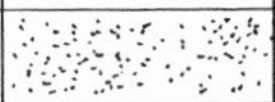	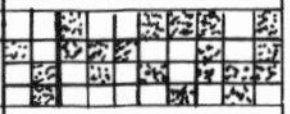
F			G			∞, n	Infinite number of screens	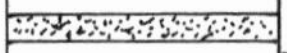	
F					G	∞, 0	Unique screen		
	G	F				n, ∞	Infinite number of screens		
	G			F		0, ∞	Unique screen, pure sounds		
		F	G			n, m	Infinite number of screens		
		F			G	n, 0	Infinite number of screens		
			G	F		0, n	Infinite number of screens		
				F	G	0, 0	Unique screen, pure sound		

Fig. II–21. Screen Entropy Table

SCREEN (∞, ∞)

Let there be a very large number of grains distributed at random over the whole range of the audible area and lasting an interval of time equal to Δt. Let there also be a grid fine enough so that the average density will not be more than 30 grains per cell. The distribution law is then given by Poisson's formula

$$P_k = \frac{(d_m)^k}{K!} e^{-d_m},$$

where d_m is the mean density and P_k the probability that there will be k grains in a cell. If d_m becomes greater than about 30, the distribution law will become *normal*.

Fig. II–22 is an example of a Poisson distribution for a mean density $d_m = 0.6$ grains/cell in a grid of 196 cells for a screen (∞, ∞).

Thus we may construct the (∞, ∞) screens by hand, according to the distributions for the rows and columns, or with suitable computer programs.

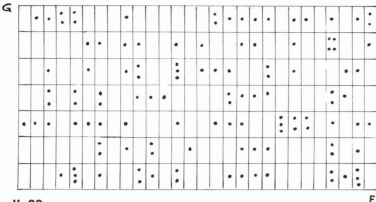

Fig. II–22

For a very high mean density the screens in which disorder is perfect (maximum) will give a very rich sound, almost a white sound, which will never be identical throughout time. If the calculation is done by hand we can construct a large number of (∞, ∞) screens from the first (∞, ∞) screen in order to avoid work and numerical calculation for each separate screen. To this end we permute the cells by column and row (see Fig. II–23).

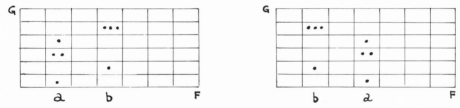

Fig. II–23. Example of Permutation by Columns

Discussion. It is obvious that for a high mean density, the greater the number of cells, the more the distribution of grains in one region of the screen tends to regularize (ergodism) and the weaker are the fluctuations from one cell or cloud to another. But the absolute limits of the density in the cells in the audible area will be a function of the technical means available: slide rules, tables, calculating machines, computers, ruled paper, orchestral instruments, tape recorders, scissors, programmed impulses of pure sounds, automatic splicing devices, programmed recordings, analogue converters, etc.

If each cell is considered as a symbol defined by the number of grains k, the entropy of the screen (for a given fineness of grid) will naturally be affected by the mean density of the grains per cell and will grow at the same time. It is here that a whole series of statistical experiments will have to circumscribe the perceptible limits of ataxy for these screens (∞, ∞) and even express the color nuances of white sound. It is very possible that the ear classifies in the same file a great number of screens whose entropies vary tremendously. There would result from this an impoverishment and a simplification of the communication: physical information $\rightarrow$ perception, but at least there will be the advantage that the work involved in constructing screens will be considerably reduced.

ALL SCREENS

Starting from a few screens and applying the *elementary operations* we can construct all the screens of the entropy table. See Fig. II–24 for a few examples. In practice, frequency and intensity filters imitate these elementary operations perfectly.

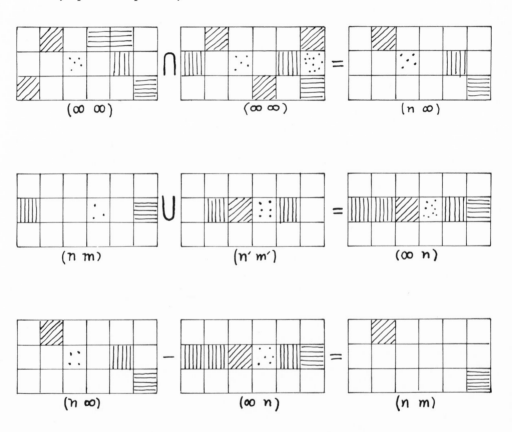

Fig. II–24

LINKING THE SCREENS

Up to now we have admitted that any sound or music could be described by a number of screens arranged in the lexicographic order of the pages of a book. If we represent each screen by a specific symbol (one-to-one coding), the sound or the music can be translated by a succession of symbols called a protocol:

$$a \; b \; g \; k \; a \; b \cdots b \; g \cdots$$

each letter identifying screens and moments t for isochronous Δt's.

Without seeking the causes of a particular succession of screens, i.e., without entering into either the physical structure of the sound or the logical structure of the composition, we can disengage certain modes of succession and species of protocols [16]. We shall quickly review the elementary definitions.

Any matter or its unique symbol is called a *term*. Two successive terms cause a *transition* to materialize. The second term is called the *transform* and the change effected is represented by term $A \to$ term B, or $A \to B$.

A *transformation* is a collection of transitions. The following example is drawn from the above protocol:

$$\left\downarrow \begin{matrix} a & b & g & k & \cdots \\ b & g & k & a & \cdots \end{matrix} \right. ,$$

another transformation with musical notes:

$$\left\downarrow \begin{matrix} C & D & E & \cdots \\ B & G & A & \cdots \end{matrix} \right.$$

A transformation is said to be *closed* when the collection of transforms contains only elements belonging to the collection of terms, for example:

the alphabet,

$$\left\downarrow \begin{matrix} a & b & c & \cdots & z \\ b & c & d & \cdots & a \end{matrix} \right.$$

musical notes,

$$\left\downarrow\begin{array}{ccccccccccc} C & D\flat & D & E\flat & E & F & G\flat & G & A & B\flat & B \\ D & G\flat & G & C & F & B & A & D\flat & E\flat & E & B\flat \end{array}\right.$$

musical sounds,

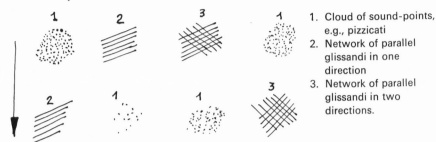

1. Cloud of sound-points, e.g., pizzicati
2. Network of parallel glissandi in one direction
3. Network of parallel glissandi in two directions.

an infinity of terms,

$$\left\downarrow\begin{array}{cccccccc} 1 & 2 & 3 & 4 & 5 & 6 & \cdots \\ 6 & 7 & 4 & 100 & 1 & 2 & \cdots \end{array}\right.$$

A transformation is *univocal* or single-valued (mapping) when each term has a single transform, for example:

$$\left\downarrow\begin{array}{cccc} b & a & c & e & \cdots \\ a & b & c & d & \cdots \end{array}\right.$$

The following are examples of transformations that are not univocal:

$$a.\quad\left\downarrow\begin{array}{ccc} a & b & c \\ b, c & d & m, n, p \end{array}\right.$$

b.

c. timbre change of a group of values

Timbres	clarinets	oboes	strings	timpani	brass
	timpani, strings	timpani, bassoon	brass	oboes	strings, oboes

and d. concrete music characteriology [4, 5]

	nil	vibrated	trembled	cyclical	irregular
"Manner"	cyclical or trembled	irregular	nil or irregular	trembled	nil or vibrated or cyclical

A transformation is a one-to-one mapping when each term has a single transform and when each transform is derived from a single term, for example:

$$\begin{array}{ccccc} a & b & c & d & \cdots \\ b & a & d & c & \cdots \end{array}$$

MATRICAL REPRESENTATION

A transformation:

$$\begin{array}{ccc} a & b & c \\ a & c & c \end{array}$$

can be represented by a table as follows:

↓	a	b	c
a	+	0	0
b	0	0	0
c	0	+	+

or

↓	a	b	c
a	1	0	0
b	0	0	0
c	0	1	1

This table is a matrix of the transitions of the collection of terms to a collection of transforms.

PRODUCT

Let there be two transformations T and U:

$$T: \begin{array}{cccc} a & b & c & d \\ b & d & a & b \end{array} \qquad \text{and} \qquad U: \begin{array}{cccc} a & b & c & d \\ d & c & d & b \end{array}$$

In certain cases we can apply to a term n of T a transformation T, then a transformation U. This is written: $U[T(n)]$, and is the product of the two transformations T and U, on condition that the transforms of T are terms of U. Thus, first $T: a \rightarrow b$, then $U: b \rightarrow c$, which is summarized as $V = UT: a \rightarrow c$.

To calculate the product applied to all the terms of T we shall use the following matrical representation:

<table>
<tr><td></td><td>↓</td><td>a</td><td>b</td><td>c</td><td>d</td><td></td><td>↓</td><td>a</td><td>b</td><td>c</td><td>d</td></tr>
<tr><td></td><td>a</td><td>0</td><td>0</td><td>1</td><td>0</td><td></td><td>a</td><td>0</td><td>0</td><td>0</td><td>0</td></tr>
<tr><td>T:</td><td>b</td><td>1</td><td>0</td><td>0</td><td>1</td><td>U:</td><td>b</td><td>0</td><td>0</td><td>0</td><td>1</td></tr>
<tr><td></td><td>c</td><td>0</td><td>0</td><td>0</td><td>0</td><td></td><td>c</td><td>0</td><td>1</td><td>0</td><td>0</td></tr>
<tr><td></td><td>d</td><td>0</td><td>1</td><td>0</td><td>0</td><td></td><td>d</td><td>1</td><td>0</td><td>1</td><td>0</td></tr>
</table>

the total transformation V equals the product of the two matrices T and U in the order U,T.

$$
\begin{matrix} U \\ \begin{vmatrix} 0 & 0 & 0 & 0 \\ 0 & 0 & 0 & 1 \\ 0 & 1 & 0 & 0 \\ 1 & 0 & 1 & 0 \end{vmatrix} \end{matrix}
\times
\begin{matrix} T \\ \begin{vmatrix} 0 & 0 & 1 & 0 \\ 1 & 0 & 0 & 1 \\ 0 & 0 & 0 & 0 \\ 0 & 1 & 0 & 0 \end{vmatrix} \end{matrix}
=
\begin{matrix} V \\ \begin{vmatrix} 0 & 0 & 0 & 0 \\ 0 & 1 & 0 & 0 \\ 1 & 0 & 0 & 1 \\ 0 & 0 & 1 & 0 \end{vmatrix} \end{matrix}
$$

KINEMATIC DIAGRAM

The kinematic or transition diagram is a graphical expression of transformation. To draw it each term is connected to its transform by an arrow pointed at the transform. The *representative point* of a kinematic diagram is an imaginary point which moves in jumps from term to term following the arrows of the diagram; for an example see Fig. II–25.

$$
T: \quad \begin{vmatrix} A & C & D & I & L & N & P & A \\ D & D & I & A & N & A & N & N \end{vmatrix}
$$

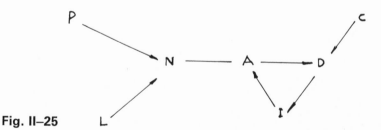

Fig. II–25

A transformation is really a mechanism and theoretically all the mechanisms of the physical or biological universes can be represented by transformations under five conditions of correspondence:

1. Each state of the mechanism (continuity is broken down into discrete states as close together as is desired) is in a one-to-one correspondence with a term of the transformation.

2. Each sequence of states crossed by the mechanism by reason of its internal structure corresponds to an uninterrupted sequence of the terms of the transformation.

3. If the mechanism reaches a state and remains there (absorbing or stationary state), the term which corresponds to this state has no transform.

4. If the states of a mechanism reproduce themselves in the same manner without end, the transformation has a kinematic diagram in closed circuit.

5. A halt of the mechanism and its start from another state is represented in the diagram by a displacement of the representative point, which is not due to an arrow but to an arbitrary action on the paper.

The mechanism is determined when the corresponding transformation is univocal and closed. The mechanism is not determined when the corresponding transformation is many-valued. In this case the transformation is said to be *stochastic*. In a stochastic mechanism the numbers 0 and 1 in the transformation matrix must be replaced by relative frequencies. These are the alternative probabilities of various transformations. The determined mechanism is a particular case of the stochastic mechanism, in which the probabilities of transition are 0 and 1.

Example: All the harmonic or polyphonic rules of classical music could be represented by mechanisms. The fugue is one of the most accomplished and determined mechanisms. One could even generalize and say that the avant-garde composer is not content with following the mechanisms of his age but proposes new ones, for both detail and general form.

If these probabilities are constant over a long period of time, and if they are independent of the states of origin, the stochastic sequence is called, more particularly, a Markov chain.

Let there be two screens A and B and a protocol of 50 transitions:

ABABBBABAABABABABBBBABAABABBAABABBABAAABABBA
ABBABBA.

The real frequencies of the transitions are:

$A \to B$	17 times		$B \to A$	17 times
$A \to A$	6 times		$B \to B$	10 times
	23 times			27 times

The matrix of the frequencies of real transitions is:

↓	A	B
A	6	17
B	17	10

The matrix of transition probabilities (relative frequencies) (MTP) is:

↓	A	B
A	0.26	0.63
B	0.74	0.37
	1.00	1.00

If the preceding matrix were:

↓	A	B
A	0.5	0.5
B	0.5	0.5

the unpredictability of the succession of A and B would be maximum and so would the entropy. Inversely, the constraint would be zero.

If the preceding matrix were:

↓	A	B
A	0	1
B	1	0

the transformation would be absolutely determined and the entropy of the sequence zero. The constraint would be maximum.

It may be that the symbols of a protocol depend in a certain way on the preceding terms, e.g., digram, trigram, etc., protocols. In this case, the matrix of transition probabilities (MTP) may be made independent by using an appropriate coding.

We can have (MTP) with a, b, and c as parameters, e.g.:

	↓	A	B		↓	A	B		↓	A	B
a.	A	0.26	0.63	b.	A	0.5	0.5	c.	A	1	0
	B	0.74	0.37		B	0.5	0.5		B	0	1

We can couple two or several (MTP) of different symbols on condition that we introduce a determined or stochastic transformation between the various parameters. Thus a protocol of timbres may be coupled with a protocol of intensity and a protocol of frequencies, etc., and each of the protocols may be linked in pairs with all the others. Isolated or coupled mechanisms can have one or several stationary or absorbing states towards which they tend in a manner which may or may not be unique. The stochastic mechanism may be a completely closed one on the same grounds as a determined mechanism.

If a Matrix of Transition Probabilities (MTP) is regular, that is, if all the entries of some power of this matrix are positive, the (MTP) has a unique *fixed* probability vector t; and in the long run, the sequence of increasing powers of (MTP) approaches the matrix T, whose rows are each the *fixed point t*. This T matrix is called the *stationary distribution* of the Markov chain represented by the stochastic (MTP) matrix. In the next chapter we shall see two methods of calculating this stationary distribution, or state of stability, from one (MTP) and the definition of a mean entropy. It is with the aid of this mean entropy that we shall be able to define and then compare the degrees of ataxy of a particular mechanism that we have applied to a set of screens.

In this way all that has been said about the ataxy of grains and clouds may be generalized and transposed to the sets (books) of screens. A fundamental criterion of the evolution of a piece of music can be shaped by the transformations of ataxy over time.

For example, it is very common in musical composition not to unleash at one go all the riches of which one is capable but to reserve them and introduce them little by little. It is also possible to imagine a piece of music which would give, at one stroke in the beginning, all the variety available and then break it into its separate elements in time.

The elementary evolutions of ataxy are diagrammed in Fig. II–26. Diagram F can be given in the form of a protocol. Ataxy can therefore be put in a matrical form with parameters, etc., and all the logical rules of transformation which we have allowed so far are applicable to the (MTP) of entropy.

How is this ataxy perceived? In many ways. If the grains of a given surface of a screen are distributed in a homogeneous manner, increasing the density will increase the richness, unpredictability, and entropy. In the same ergodic distribution of grains, if certain symmetries in the disposition of the grains appear and are discernible, a constraint is felt, and consequently a diminution of the entropy. If melodic or harmonic liaisons are effected and perceived in the same distribution, unpredictability and entropy are both diminished.

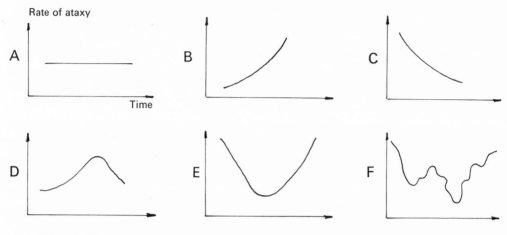

Fig. II–26

A. The evolution is nil.   B. The rate of disorder and the richness increase.   C. Ataxy decreases.   D. Ataxy increases and then decreases.   E. Ataxy decreases and then increases.   F. The evolution of the ataxy is very complex, but it may be analyzed from the first three diagrams.

Thus after the first unfolding of a series of twelve sounds of the tempered scale, the unpredictability has fallen to zero, the constraint is maximum, the choice is nil, and the entropy is zero. Richness and hence interest are displaced to other fields, such as harmonies, timbres, and durations, and many other compositional wiles are aimed at reviving entropy. In fact sonic discourse is nothing but a perpetual fluctuation of entropy in all its forms [17].

However, human sensitivity does not necessarily follow the variation in entropy even if it is logarithmic to an appropriate base. It is rather a succession or a protocol of strains and relaxations of every degree that often excites the listener in a direction contrary to that of entropy. Thus Ravel's *Bolero*, in which the only variation is in the dynamics, has a virtually zero entropy after the third or fourth repetition of the fundamental idea. However, the interest, or rather the psychological agitation, grows with time through the very fact of this immobility and banality.

All incantatory manifestations aim at an effect of maximum tension with minimum entropy. The inverse is equally true, and seen from a certain angle, white noise with its maximum entropy is soon tiresome. It would seem that there is no correspondence aesthetics ↔ entropy. These two entities are linked in quite an independent manner at each occasion. This statement still leaves some respite for the free will of the composer even if this free will is buried under the rubbish of culture and civilization and is only a shadow, at the least a tendency, a simple stochasm.

The great obstacle to a too hasty generalization is chiefly one of logical order; for an object is only an object as a function of its definition, and there is, especially in art, a near-infinity of definitions and hence a near-infinity of entropies, for the notion of entropy is an epiphenomenon of the definition. Which of these is valid? The ear, the eye, and the brain unravel sometimes inextricable situations with what is called intuition, taste, and intelligence. Two definitions with two different entropies can be perceived as identical, but it is also true that the set of definitions of an object has its own degree of disorder. We are not concerned here with investigating such a difficult, complex, and unexplored situation, but simply with looking over the possibilities that connected realms of contemporary thought promise, with a view to action.

To conclude briefly, since the applications which follow are more eloquent than explanatory texts, we shall accept that a collection or book of screens can be expressed by matrices of transition probabilities having parameters. They are affected by a degree of ataxy or entropy which is calculable under certain conditions. However, in order to render the analysis and then the synthesis of a sonic work within reach of understanding and the slide rule, we shall establish three criteria for a screen:

1. TOPOGRAPHIC CRITERION

The position of the cells $\Delta F \Delta G$ on the audible area is qualitatively important, and an enumeration of their possible combinations is capable of creating a group of well defined terms to which we can apply the concept of entropy and its calculation.

2. DENSITY CRITERION

The superficial density of the grains of a cell $\Delta F \Delta G$ also constitutes a quality which is immediately perceptible, and we could equally well define terms to which the concept and calculation of entropy would be applicable.

3. CRITERION OF PURE ATAXY (defined in relation to the grains of a screen)

A cell has three variables: mean frequency, mean amplitude, and mean density of the grains. For a screen we can therefore establish three independent or connected protocols, then three matrices of transition probabilities which may or may not be coupled. Each of the matrices will have its entropy and the three coupled matrices will have a mean entropy. In the procession of sound we can establish several series of three matrices and hence several series of mean entropies, their variations constituting the criterion of ataxy.

The first two criteria, which are general and on the scale of screens or cells, will not concern us in what follows. But the third, more conventional criterion will be taken up in detail in the next chapter.

Chapter III

Markovian Stochastic Music— Applications

In this chapter we will discuss two musical applications: *Analogique A*, for string orchestra, and *Analogique B*, for sinusoidal sounds, both composed in 1958–59.

We shall confine ourselves to a simple case in which each of the components G, F, D of the screen take only two values, following matrices of transition probability which will be coupled by means of parameters. In addition, the choice of probabilities in the matrices will be made in such a way that we shall have only the regular case, conforming to the chain of events theory as it has been defined in the work of Maurice Fréchet [14].

It is obvious that richer and more complex stochastic mechanisms are highly interesting to construct and to put in work, but in view of the considerable volume of calculations which they necessitate it would be useless to undertake them by hand, but very desirable to program them for the computer.

Nevertheless, despite the structural simplicity of what follows, the stochastic mechanism which will emerge will be a model, a standard subjacent to any others that are far more complex, and will serve to catalyze further studies of greater elaboration. For although we confine ourselves here to the study of screens as they have been defined in this study (sets of elementary grains), it goes without saying that nothing prevents the generalization of this method of structuralization (composition) for definitions of sonic entities of more than three dimensions. Thus, let us no longer suppose screens, but *criteria* of definitions of a sonic entity, such that for the timbre, degree of order, density, variation, and even the *criteria* of more or less

79

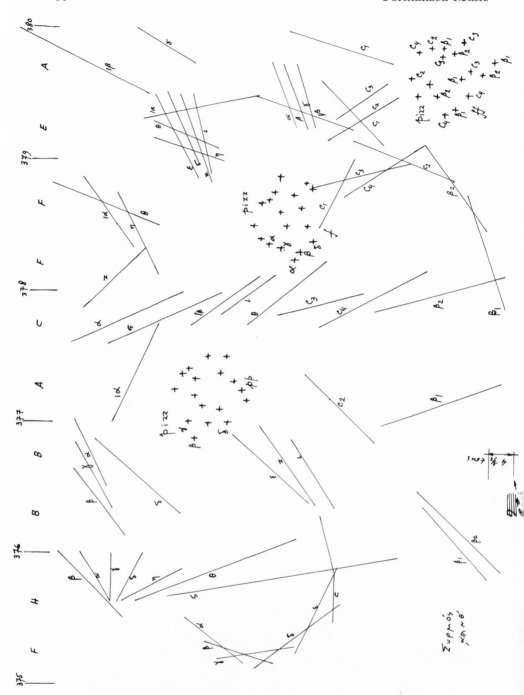

Fig. III–1. *Syrmos* for 18 strings

complex elementary structures (e.g., melodic and temporal structures of groups of sounds, and instrumental, spatial, and kinematic structures) the same stochastic scheme is adaptable. It is enough to define the variations well and to be able to classify them even in a rough manner.

The sonic result thus obtained is not guaranteed a priori by calculation. Intuition and experience must always play their part in guiding, deciding, and testing.

ANALYSIS
(definition of the scheme of a mechanism)

We shall define the scheme of a mechanism as the "analogue" of a stochastic process. It will serve for the production of sonic entities and for their transformations over time. These sonic entities will have screens which will show the following characteristics freely chosen:

1. They will permit two distinct combinations of frequency regions f_0 and f_1 (see Fig. III–2).

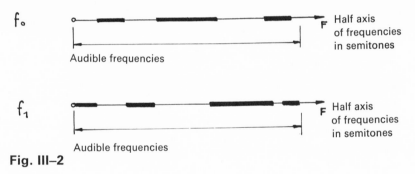

Fig. III–2

Syrmos, written in 1959, is built on stochastic transformations of eight basic textures : parallel horizontal bowed notes, parallel ascending bowed glissandi, parallel descending bowed glissandi, crossed (ascending and descending) parallel bowed notes, pizzicato clouds, atmospheres made up of col legno struck notes with short col legno glissandi, geometric configurations of convergent or divergent glissandi, and glissando configurations treated as undevelopable ruled surfaces. The mathematical structure of this work is the same as that of *Analogique A* and *Analogique B*.

2. They will permit two distinct combinations of intensity regions (see Fig. III–3).

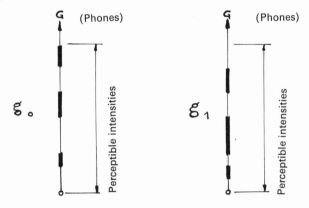

Fig. III–3

3. They will permit two distinct combinations of density regions (see Fig. III–4).

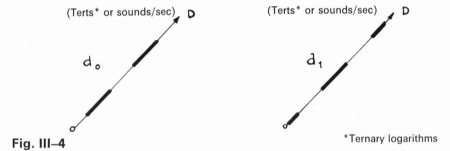

Fig. III–4   *Ternary logarithms

4. Each of these three variables will present a protocol which may be summarized by two matrices of transition probabilities (MTP).

(ρ) ↓	X	Y		(σ) ↓	X	Y
X	0.2	0.8		X	0.85	0.4
Y	0.8	0.2		Y	0.15	0.6

The letters (ρ) and (σ) constitute the parameters of the (MTP).

MTPF (of frequencies)

(α) ↓	f_0	f_1		(β) ↓	f_0	f_1
f_0	0.2	0.8		f_0	0.85	0.4
f_1	0.8	0.2		f_1	0.15	0.6

MTPG (of intensities)

(γ)	$\downarrow$	g_0	g_1
	g_0	0.2	0.8
	g_1	0.8	0.2

(ε)	$\downarrow$	g_0	g_1
	g_0	0.85	0.4
	g_1	0.15	0.6

MTPD (of densities)

(λ)	$\downarrow$	d_0	d_1
	d_0	0.2	0.8
	d_1	0.8	0.2

(μ)	$\downarrow$	d_0	d_1
	d_0	0.85	0.4
	d_1	0.15	0.6

5. The transformations of the variables are indeterminate at the interior of each (MTP) (digram processes), but on the other hand their (MTP) will be connected by means of a determined coupling of parameters. The coupling is given by the following transformations:

$$(e_0) \quad \downarrow \begin{array}{cccccccccccc} f_0 & f_1 & d_0 & d_1 & g_0 & g_1 & g_0 & g_1 & f_0 & f_1 & d_0 & d_1 \\ \lambda & \mu & \alpha & \beta & \lambda & \mu & \beta & \alpha & \gamma & \varepsilon & \gamma & \varepsilon \end{array}$$

By these rules we have described the structure of a mechanism. It is thus constituted by three pairs of (MTP): (MTPF), (MTPG), (MTPD), and by the group (e_0) of the six couplings of these (MTP).

Significance of the coupling. Let f_0 be the state of the frequencies of the screen at an instant t of the sonic evolution of the mechanism during a slice of time Δt. Let g_1 and d_1 be the values of the other variables of the screen at the moment t. At the next moment, $t + \Delta t$, the term f_0 is bound to change, for it obeys one of the two (MTPF), (α) or (β). The choice of (α) or (β) is conditioned by the values g_1 and d_1 of the moment t, conforming to the transformation of the coupling. Thus g_1 proposes the parameter (α) and d_1 the parameter (β) simultaneously. In other words the term f_0 must either remain f_0 or yield its place to f_1 according to mechanism (α) or mechanism (β). Imagine the term f_0 standing before two urns (α) and (β), each containing two colors of balls, red for f_0 and blue for f_1, in the following proportions:

Urn (α)
red balls (f_0), 0.2
blue balls (f_1), 0.8

Urn (β)
red balls (f_0), 0.85
blue balls (f_1), 0.15

The choice is free and the term f_0 can take its successor from either urn (α)

or urn (β) with a probability equal to $\frac{1}{2}$ (total probabilities).

Once the urn has been chosen, the choice of a blue or a red ball will have a probability equal to the proportion of colors in the chosen urn. Applying the law of compound probabilities, the probability that f_0 from moment t will remain f_0 at the moment $t + \Delta t$ is $(0.20 + 0.85)/2 = 0.525$, and the probability that it will change to f_1 is $(0.80 + 0.15)/2 = 0.475$.

The five characteristics of the composition of the screens have established a stochastic mechanism. Thus in each of the slices Δt of the sonic evolution of the created mechanism, the three variables f_i, g_i, d_i follow a round of unforeseeable combinations, always changing according to the three (MTP) and the coupling which connects terms and parameters.

We have established this mechanism without taking into consideration any of the screen criteria. That is to say, we have implied a topographic distribution of grain regions at the time of the choice of f_0, f_1 and g_0, g_1, but without specifying it. The same is true for the density distribution. We shall give two examples of very different realizations in which these two criteria will be effective. But before setting them out we shall pursue further the study of the criterion of ataxy.

We shall neglect the entropies of the three variables at the grain level, for what matters is the macroscopic mechanism at the screen level. The fundamental questions posed by these mechanisms are, "Where does the transformation summarized by an (MTP) go? What is its destiny?"

Let us consider the (MTP):

$\downarrow$	X	Y
X	0.2	0.8
Y	0.8	0.2

and suppose one hundred mechanisms identified by the law of this single (MTP). We shall allow them all to set out from X and evolve freely. The preceding question then becomes, "Is there a general tendency for the states of the hundred mechanisms, and if so, what is it?" (See Appendix II.)

After the first stage the $100X$ will be transformed into $0.2\ (100X) \rightarrow 20X$, and $0.8\ (100X) \rightarrow 80Y$. At the third stage 0.2 of the X's and 0.8 of the Y's will become X's. Conversely 0.8 of the X's will become Y's and 0.2 of the Y's will remain Y's. This general argument is true for all stages and can be written:

$$X' = 0.2X + 0.8Y$$
$$Y' = 0.8X + 0.2Y.$$

If this is to be applied to the 100 mechanisms X as above, we shall have:

Stage	Mechanisms X	Mechanisms Y
0	100	0
1	20	80
2	68	32
3	39	61
4	57	43
5	46	54
6	52	48
7	49	51
8	50	50
9	50	50
$\vdots$	$\vdots$	$\vdots$

We notice oscillations that show a general tendency towards a stationary state at the 8th stage. We may conclude, then, that of the 100 mechanisms that leave from X, the 8th stage will in all probability send 50 to X and 50 to Y. The same stationary probability distribution of the Markov chain, or the fixed probability vector, is calculated in the following manner:

At equilibrium the two probability values X and Y remain unchanged and the preceding system becomes

$$X = 0.2X + 0.8Y$$
$$Y = 0.8Y + 0.2Y$$

or

$$0 = -0.8X + 0.8Y$$
$$0 = +0.8X - 0.8Y.$$

Since the number of mechanisms is constant, in this case 100 (or 1), one of the two equations may be replaced at the stationary distribution by $1 = X + Y$. The system then becomes

$$0 = 0.8X - 0.8Y$$
$$1 = X + Y$$

and the stationary probability values X, Y are $X = 0.50$ and $Y = 0.50$.

The same method can be applied to the $(\text{MTP})(\sigma)$, which will give us stationary probabilities $X = 0.73$ and $Y = 0.27$.

Another method, particularly interesting in the case of an (MTP) with many terms, which forces us to resolve a large system of linear equations in order to find the stationary probabilities, is that which makes use of matrix calculus.

Thus the first stage may be considered as the matrix product of the (MTP) with the unicolumn matrix $\begin{vmatrix} 100 \\ 0 \end{vmatrix}$

$$X: \begin{vmatrix} 0.2 & 0.8 \\ 0.8 & 0.2 \end{vmatrix} \times \begin{vmatrix} 100 \\ 0 \end{vmatrix} = \begin{vmatrix} 20 \\ 80 \end{vmatrix}.$$

The second stage will be

$$\begin{vmatrix} 0.2 & 0.8 \\ 0.8 & 0.2 \end{vmatrix} \times \begin{vmatrix} 20 \\ 80 \end{vmatrix} = \begin{vmatrix} 4 + 64 \\ 16 + 16 \end{vmatrix} = \begin{vmatrix} 68 \\ 32 \end{vmatrix},$$

and the nth stage

$$\begin{vmatrix} 0.2 & 0.8 \\ 0.8 & 0.2 \end{vmatrix}^n \times \begin{vmatrix} 100 \\ 0 \end{vmatrix}.$$

Now that we know how to calculate the stationary probabilities of a Markov chain we can easily calculate its mean entropy. The definition of the entropy of a system is

$$H = -\sum p_i \log p_i.$$

The calculation of the entropy of an (MTP) is made first by columns ($\sum p_i = 1$), the p_i being the probability of the transition for the (MTP); then this result is weighted with the corresponding stationary probabilities. Thus for the (MTP)(σ):

$\downarrow$	X	Y
X	0.85	0.4
Y	0.15	0.6

The entropy of the states of X will be $-0.85 \log 0.85 - 0.15 \log 0.15 = 0.611$ bits; the entropy of the states of Y, $-0.4 \log 0.4 - 0.6 \log 0.6 = 0.970$ bits; the stationary probability of $X = 0.73$; the stationary probability of $Y = 0.27$; the mean entropy at the stationary stage is

$$H\sigma = 0.611(0.73) + 0.970(0.27) = 0.707 \text{ bits};$$

and the mean entropy of the (MTP)(ρ) at the stationary stage is

$$H\rho = 0.722 \text{ bits.}$$

The two entropies do not differ by much, and this is to be expected, for if we look at the respective (MTP) we observe that the great contrasts of probabilities inside the matrix (ρ) are compensated by an external equality of stationary probabilities, and conversely in the (MTP)(σ) the interior quasi-equality, 0.4 and 0.6, succeeds in counteracting the interior contrast, 0.85 and 0.15, and the exterior contrast, 0.73 and 0.27.

At this level we may modify the (MTP) of the three variables f_i, g_i, d_i in such a way as to obtain a new pair of entropies. As this operation is repeatable we can form a protocol of pairs of entropies and therefore an (MTP) of pairs of entropies. These speculations and investigations are no doubt interesting, but we shall confine ourselves to the first calculation made above and we shall pursue the investigation on an even more general plane.

MARKOV CHAIN EXTENDED SIMULTANEOUSLY FOR f_i, g_i, d_i

On p. 83 we analyzed the mechanism of transformation of f_0 to f_0 or f_1 when the probabilities of the two variables g_i and d_i are given. We can apply the same arguments for each of the three variables f_i, g_i, d_i when the two others are given.

Example for g_i. Let there be a screen at the moment t whose variables have the values (f_0, g_1, d_1). At the moment $t + \Delta t$ the value of g_1 will be transformed into g_1 or g_0. From f_0 comes the parameter (γ), and from d_1 comes the parameter (ε).

With (MTP)(γ) the probability that g_1 will remain g_1 is 0.2. With (MTP)(ε) the probability that g_1 will remain g_1 is 0.6. Applying the rules of compound probabilities and/or probabilities of mutually exclusive events as on p. 83, we find that the probability that g_1 will remain g_1 at the moment $t + \Delta t$ under the simultaneous effects of f_0 and d_1 is equal to $(0.2 + 0.6)/2 = 0.4$. The same holds for the calculation of the transformation from g_1 into g_0 and for the transformations of d_1.

We shall now attempt to emerge from this jungle of probability combinations, which is impossible to manage, and look for a more general viewpoint, if it exists.

In general, each screen is constituted by a triad of specific values of the variables F, G, D so that we can enumerate the different screens emerging from the mechanism that we are given (see Fig. III–5). The possible

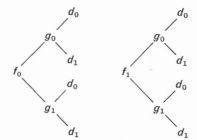

Fig. III–5

combinations are: $(f_0 g_0 d_0)$, $(f_0 g_0 d_1)$, $(f_0 g_1 d_0)$, $(f_0 g_1 d_1)$, $(f_1 g_0 d_0)$, $(f_1 g_0 d_1)$, $(f_1 g_1 d_0)$, $(f_1 g_1 d_1)$; i.e., eight different screens, which, with their protocols, will make up the sonic evolution. At each moment t of the composition we shall encounter one of these eight screens and no others.

What are the rules for the passage from one combination to another? Can one construct a matrix of transition probabilities for these eight screens?

Let there be a screen $(f_0 g_1 d_1)$ at the moment t. Can one calculate the probability that at the moment $t + \Delta t$ this screen will be transformed into $(f_1 g_1 d_0)$? The above operations have enabled us to calculate the probability that f_0 will be transformed into f_1 under the influence of g_1 and d_1 and that g_1 will remain g_1 under the influence of f_0 and d_1. These operations are schematized in Fig. III–6, and the probability that screen $(f_0 g_1 d_1)$ will be transformed into $(f_1 g_1 d_0)$ is 0.114.

	f_0	g_1	d_1
Screen at the moment t :			
Parameters derived from the coupling transformations :	α β	ε γ	μ λ
Screen at the moment $t + \Delta t$:	f_1	g_1	d_0
Values of probabilities taken from the (MTP) corresponding to the coupling parameters :	0.80 0.15	0.6 0.2	0.4 0.8
Compound probabilities :	0.475	0.4	0.6
Compound probabilities for independent events :	0.475 · 0.4 · 0.6 = 0.114		

Fig. III–6

We can therefore extend the calculation to the eight screens and construct the matrix of transition probabilities. It will be square and will have eight rows and eight columns.

MTPZ

↓	A $(f_0 g_0 d_0)$	B $(f_0 g_0 d_1)$	C $(f_0 g_1 d_0)$	D $(f_0 g_1 d_1)$	E $(f_1 g_0 d_0)$	F $(f_1 g_0 d_1)$	G $(f_1 g_1 d_0)$	H $(f_1 g_1 d_1)$
$A(f_0 g_0 d_0)$	0.021	0.357	0.084	0.189	0.165	0.204	0.408	0.096
$B(f_0 g_0 d_1)$	0.084	0.089	0.076	0.126	0.150	0.136	0.072	0.144
$C(f_0 g_1 d_0)$	0.084	0.323	0.021	0.126	0.150	0.036	0.272	0.144
$D(f_0 g_1 d_1)$	0.336	0.081	0.019	0.084	0.135	0.024	0.048	0.216
$E(f_1 g_0 d_0)$	0.019	0.063	0.336	0.171	0.110	0.306	0.102	0.064
$F(f_1 g_0 d_1)$	0.076	0.016	0.304	0.114	0.100	0.204	0.018	0.096
$G(f_1 g_1 d_0)$	0.076	0.057	0.084	0.114	0.100	0.054	0.068	0.096
$H(f_1 g_1 d_1)$	0.304	0.014	0.076	0.076	0.090	0.036	0.012	0.144

Does the matrix have a region of stability? Let there be 100 mechanisms Z whose scheme is summarized by (MTPZ). At the moment t, d_A mechanisms will have a screen A, d_B a screen B, . . ., d_H a screen H. At the moment $t + \Delta t$ all 100 mechanisms will produce screens according to the probabilities written in (MTPZ). Thus,

$0.021\ d_A$ will stay in A,
$0.357\ d_B$ will be transformed to A,
$0.084\ d_C$ will be transformed to A,
. . .
$0.096\ d_H$ will be transformed to A.

The d_A screens at the moment t will become d'_A screens at the moment $t + \Delta t$, and this number will be equal to the sum of all the screens that will be produced by the remaining mechanisms, in accordance with the corresponding probabilities.
Therefore:

$$(e_1) \quad \begin{cases} d'_A = 0.021 d_A + 0.357 d_B + 0.084 d_C + \cdots + 0.096 d_H \\ d'_B = 0.084 d_A + 0.089 d_B + 0.076 d_C + \cdots + 0.144 d_H \\ d'_C = 0.084 d_A + 0.323 d_B + 0.021 d_C + \cdots + 0.144 d_H \\ \cdots \\ d'_H = 0.304 d_A + 0.014 d_B + 0.076 d_C + \cdots + 0.144 d_H. \end{cases}$$

At the stationary state the frequency of the screens $A, B, C, . . ., H$ will remain constant and the eight preceding equations will become:

$$(d'_A = d_A,\ d'_B = d_B,\ d'_C = d_C,\ \cdots,\ d'_H = d_H)$$

$$(e_2) \begin{cases} 0 = -0.979d_A + 0.357d_B + 0.084d_C + \cdots + 0.096d_H \\ 0 = 0.084d_A - 0.911d_B + 0.076d_C + \cdots + 0.144d_H \\ 0 = 0.084d_A + 0.323d_B - 0.979d_C + \cdots + 0.144d_H \\ \cdots \\ 0 = 0.304d_A + 0.014d_B + 0.076d_C + \cdots - 0.856d_H \end{cases}$$

On the other hand

$$d_A + d_B + d_C + \cdots + d_H = 1.$$

If we replace one of the eight equations by the last, we obtain a system of eight linear equations with eight unknowns. Solution by the classic method of determinants gives the values:

$$(e_3) \quad \begin{cases} d_A = 0.17, d_B = 0.13, d_C = 0.13, d_D = 0.11, d_E = 0.14, d_F = 0.12, \\ d_G = 0.10, d_H = 0.10, \end{cases}$$

which are the probabilities of the screens at the stationary stage. This method is very laborious, for the chance of error is very high (unless a calculating machine is available).

The second method (see p. 85), which is more approximate but adequate, consists in making all 100 mechanisms Z set out from a single screen and letting them evolve by themselves. After several more or less long oscillations, the stationary state, if it exists, will be attained and the proportions of the screens will remain invariable.

We notice that the system of equations (e_1) may be broken down into:

1. Two vectors V' and V which may be represented by two unicolumn matrices:

$$V' = \begin{vmatrix} d'_A \\ d'_B \\ \vdots \\ d'_G \\ d'_H \end{vmatrix}$$

$$\text{and } V = \begin{vmatrix} d_A \\ d_B \\ \vdots \\ d_G \\ d_H \end{vmatrix}$$

2. A linear operator, the matrix of transition probabilities Z. Consequently system (e_1) can be summarized in a matrix equation:

$$(e_4) \qquad V' = ZV.$$

To cause all 100 mechanisms Z to leave screen X and evolve "freely" means allowing a linear operator:

$$Z = \begin{vmatrix} 0.021 & 0.357 & 0.084 & 0.189 & 0.165 & 0.204 & 0.408 & 0.096 \\ 0.084 & 0.089 & 0.076 & 0.126 & 0.150 & 0.136 & 0.072 & 0.144 \\ 0.084 & 0.323 & 0.021 & 0.126 & 0.150 & 0.036 & 0.272 & 0.144 \\ 0.336 & 0.081 & 0.019 & 0.084 & 0.135 & 0.024 & 0.048 & 0.216 \\ 0.019 & 0.063 & 0.336 & 0.171 & 0.110 & 0.306 & 0.102 & 0.064 \\ 0.076 & 0.016 & 0.304 & 0.114 & 0.100 & 0.204 & 0.018 & 0.096 \\ 0.076 & 0.057 & 0.084 & 0.114 & 0.100 & 0.054 & 0.068 & 0.096 \\ 0.304 & 0.014 & 0.076 & 0.076 & 0.090 & 0.036 & 0.012 & 0.144 \end{vmatrix}$$

to perform on the column vector

$$V = \begin{vmatrix} 0 \\ 0 \\ \vdots \\ 100 \\ \vdots \\ 0 \\ 0 \end{vmatrix}$$

in a continuous manner at each moment t. Since we have broken down continuity into a discontinuous succession of thickness in time Δt, the equation (e_4) will be applied to each stage Δt.

Thus at the beginning (moment $t = 0$) the population vector of the mechanisms will be V^0. After the first stage (moment $0 + \Delta t$) it will be $V' = ZV^0$; after the second stage (moment $0 + 2\Delta t$), $V'' = ZV' = Z^2 V^0$; and at the nth stage (moment $n\Delta t$), $V^{(n)} = Z^n V^0$. In applying these data to the vector

$$V_H^0 = \begin{vmatrix} 0 \\ 0 \\ 0 \\ 0 \\ 0 \\ 0 \\ 0 \\ 100 \end{vmatrix}$$

after the first stage at the
moment Δt:

$$V'_H = ZV^0_H = \begin{vmatrix} 9.6 \\ 14.4 \\ 14.4 \\ 21.6 \\ 6.4 \\ 9.6 \\ 9.6 \\ 14.4 \end{vmatrix}$$

after the second stage at the
moment $2\Delta t$:

$$V''_H = ZV'_H = \begin{vmatrix} 18.941 \\ 10.932 \\ 14.477 \\ 11.148 \\ 15.156 \\ 11.955 \\ 8.416 \\ 8.959 \end{vmatrix}$$

after the third stage at the
moment $3\Delta t$:

$$V'''_H = ZV''_H = \begin{vmatrix} 16.860 \\ 10.867 \\ 13.118 \\ 13.143 \\ 14.575 \\ 12.257 \\ 8.145 \\ 11.046 \end{vmatrix}$$

and after the fourth stage at the
moment $4\Delta t$:

$$V''''_H = ZV'''_H = \begin{vmatrix} 17.111 \\ 11.069 \\ 13.792 \\ 12.942 \\ 14.558 \\ 12.111 \\ 8.238 \\ 10.716 \end{vmatrix}$$

Thus after the fourth stage, an average of 17 out of the 100 mechanisms will have screen A, 11 screen B, 14 screen C, . . ., 11 screen H.

If we compare the components of the vector V'''' with the values (e_3) we notice that by the fourth stage we have almost attained the stationary state. Consequently the mechanism we have built shows a very rapid abatement of the oscillations, and a very great convergence towards final stability, the goal (stochos). The perturbation P_H, which was imposed on the mechanism (MPTZ) when we considered that all the mechanisms (here 100) left from a single screen, was one of the strongest we could create.

Let us now calculate the state of the 100 mechanisms Z after the first stage with the maximal perturbations P applied.

$$P_A$$

$$V_A^0 = \begin{vmatrix} 100 \\ 0 \\ 0 \\ 0 \\ 0 \\ 0 \\ 0 \\ 0 \end{vmatrix} \quad V_A' = \begin{vmatrix} 2.1 \\ 8.4 \\ 8.4 \\ 33.6 \\ 1.9 \\ 7.6 \\ 7.6 \\ 30.4 \end{vmatrix}$$

$$P_B$$

$$V_B^0 = \begin{vmatrix} 0 \\ 100 \\ 0 \\ 0 \\ 0 \\ 0 \\ 0 \\ 0 \end{vmatrix} \quad V_B' = \begin{vmatrix} 35.7 \\ 8.9 \\ 32.3 \\ 8.1 \\ 6.3 \\ 1.6 \\ 5.7 \\ 1.4 \end{vmatrix}$$

$$P_C$$

$$V_C^0 = \begin{vmatrix} 0 \\ 0 \\ 100 \\ 0 \\ 0 \\ 0 \\ 0 \\ 0 \end{vmatrix} \quad V_C' = \begin{vmatrix} 8.4 \\ 7.6 \\ 2.1 \\ 1.9 \\ 33.6 \\ 30.4 \\ 8.4 \\ 7.6 \end{vmatrix}$$

$$P_D$$

$$V_D^0 = \begin{vmatrix} 0 \\ 0 \\ 0 \\ 100 \\ 0 \\ 0 \\ 0 \\ 0 \end{vmatrix} \quad V_D' = \begin{vmatrix} 18.9 \\ 12.6 \\ 12.6 \\ 8.4 \\ 17.1 \\ 11.4 \\ 11.4 \\ 7.6 \end{vmatrix}$$

$$P_E$$

$$V_E^0 = \begin{vmatrix} 0 \\ 0 \\ 0 \\ 0 \\ 100 \\ 0 \\ 0 \\ 0 \end{vmatrix} \quad V_E' = \begin{vmatrix} 16.5 \\ 15.0 \\ 15.0 \\ 13.5 \\ 11.0 \\ 10.0 \\ 10.0 \\ 9.0 \end{vmatrix}$$

$$P_F$$

$$V_F^0 = \begin{vmatrix} 0 \\ 0 \\ 0 \\ 0 \\ 0 \\ 100 \\ 0 \\ 0 \end{vmatrix} \quad V_F' = \begin{vmatrix} 20.4 \\ 13.6 \\ 3.6 \\ 2.4 \\ 30.6 \\ 20.4 \\ 5.4 \\ 3.6 \end{vmatrix}$$

$$P_G$$

$$V_G^0 = \begin{vmatrix} 0 \\ 0 \\ 0 \\ 0 \\ 0 \\ 0 \\ 100 \\ 0 \end{vmatrix} \quad V_G' = \begin{vmatrix} 40.8 \\ 7.2 \\ 27.2 \\ 4.8 \\ 10.2 \\ 1.8 \\ 6.8 \\ 1.2 \end{vmatrix}$$

Recapitulation of the Analysis

Having arrived at this stage of the analysis we must take our bearings. On the level of the screen cells we now have: 1. partial mechanisms of transformation for frequency, intensity, and density ranges, which are expressed by the (MTPF), (MTPG), (MTPD); and 2. an interaction between the three fundamental variables F, G, D of the screen (transformations of the coupling (e_0)).

On the level of the screens we now have: 1. eight different screens, A, B, C, D, E, F, G, H; 2. a general mechanism, the (MTPZ), which summarizes all the partial mechanisms and their interactions; 3. a final state of equilibrium (the goal, stochos) of the system Z towards which it tends quite quickly, the stationary distribution; and 4. a procedure of disequilibrium in system Z with the help of the perturbations P which are imposed on it.

SYNTHESIS

Mechanism Z which we have just constructed does not imply a real evolution of the screens. It only establishes a dynamic situation and a potential evolution. The natural process is that provoked by a perturbation P imposed on the system Z and the advancement of this system towards its goal, its stationary state, once the perturbation has ceased its action. We can therefore act on this mechanism through the intermediary of a perturbation such as P, which is stronger or weaker as the case may be. From this it is only a brief step to imagining a whole series of successive perturbations which would force the apparatus Z to be displaced towards exceptional regions at odds with its behavior at equilibrium.

In effect the intrinsic value of the organism thus created lies in the fact that it must manifest itself, be. The perturbations which apparently change its structure represent so many negations of this existence. And if we create a succession of perturbations or negations, on the one hand, and stationary states or existences on the other, we are only *affirming* mechanism Z. In other words, at first we argue positively by proposing and offering as evidence the existence itself; and then we confirm it negatively by opposing it with perturbatory states.

The bi-pole of being a thing and not being this thing creates the whole —the object which we intended to construct at the beginning of Chapter III. A dual dialectics is thus at the basis of this compositional attitude, a dialectics that sets the pace to be followed. The "experimental" sciences are an expression of this argument on an analogous plane. An experiment establishes a body of data, a web which it disentangles from the magma of objective reality with the help of negations and transformations imposed on this body. The repetition of these dual operations is a fundamental condition on which the whole universe of knowledge rests. To state something once is not to define it; the causality is confounded with the repetition of phenomena considered to be identical.

In conclusion, this dual dialectics with which we are armed in order to compose within the framework of our mechanism is homothetic with that of the experimental sciences; and we can extend the comparison to the dialectics of biological beings or to nothing more than the dialectics of being. This brings us back to the point of departure.

Thus an entity must be proposed and then a modification imposed on it. It goes without saying that to propose the entity or its modification in our particular case of musical composition is to give a human observer the means to perceive the two propositions and to compare them. Then the antitheses, entity and modification, are repeated enough times for the entity to be identified.

What does identification mean in the case of our mechanism Z?

Parenthesis. We have supposed in the course of the analysis that 100 mechanisms Z were present simultaneously, and that we were following the rules of the game of these mechanisms at each moment of an evolution created by a displacement beyond the stationary zone. We were therefore comparing the states of 100 mechanisms in a Δt with the states of these 100 mechanisms in the next t, so that in comparing two successive stages of the group of 100 simultaneous states, we *enumerate* 100 states twice. Enumeration, that is, insofar as abstract action implies ordered operations, means to observe the 100 mechanisms one by one, classify them, and test them; then start again with 100 at the following stage, and finally compare the classes number by number. And if the observation of each mechanism necessitates a fraction of time x, it would take $200x$ of time to enumerate 200 mechanisms.

This argument therefore allows us to transpose abstractly a simultaneity into a lexicographic (temporal) succession without subtracting anything, however little, from the definition of transformations engendered by scheme Z. Thus to compare two successive stages of the 100 mechanisms Z comes down to comparing 100 states produced in an interval of time $100x$ with 100 others produced in an equal interval of time $100x$ (see Fig. III–7).

MATERIAL IDENTIFICATION OF MECHANISM Z

Identification of mechanism Z means essentially a comparison between

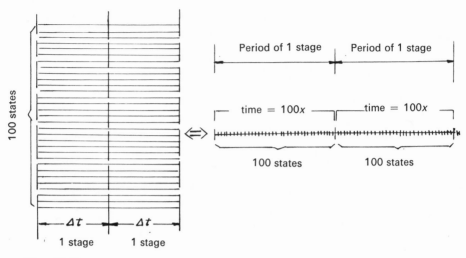

Fig. III–7

all its possibilities of being: perturbed states compared to stationary states, independent of order.

Identification will be established over equal periods of time $100x$ following the diagram:

Phenomenon: $P_N \to \quad E \to \quad P_M \to \quad E \quad \cdots$
Time: $\qquad 100x \quad 100x \quad 100x \quad 100x \quad \cdots$

in which P_N and P_M represent any perturbations and E is the state of Z at equilibrium (stationary state).

An alternation of P and E is a protocol in which $100x$ is the unit of time ($100x$ = period of the stage), for example:

$$P_A \quad P_A \quad E \quad E \quad E \quad P_H \quad P_G \quad P_G \quad E \quad P_C \quad \cdots.$$

A new mechanism W may be constructed with an (MTP), etc., which would control the identification and evolution of the composition over more general time-sets. We shall not pursue the investigation along these lines for it would lead us too far afield.

A realization which will follow will use a very simple kinematic diagram of perturbations P and equilibrium E, conditioned on one hand by the degrees of perturbation P, and on the other by a freely agreed selection.

$$(e_5) \qquad E \to P_A^0 \to P_A' \to E \to P_C' \to P_C^0 \to P_B^0 \to P_B' \to E \to P_A'$$

Definition of State *E* and of the Perturbations *P*

From the above, the stationary state *E* will be expressed by a sequence of screens such as:

Protocol E(Z)

ADFFECBDBCFEFADGCHCCHBEDFEFFECFEHBFFFBC
    HDBABADDBADADAHHBGADGAHDADGFBEBGABEBB····.

To carry out this protocol we shall utilize eight urns [*A*], [*B*], [*C*], [*D*], [*E*], [*F*], [*G*], [*H*], each containing balls of eight different colors, whose proportions are given by the probabilities of (MTPZ). For example, urn [*G*] will contain 40.8% red balls *A*, 7.2% orange balls *B*, 27.2% yellow balls *C*, 4.8% maroon balls *D*, 10.2% green balls *E*, 1.8% blue balls *F*, 6.8% white balls *G*, and 1.2% black balls *H*. The composition of the other seven urns can be read from (MTPZ) in similar fashion.

We take a yellow ball *C* at random from urn [*G*]. We note the result and return the ball to urn [*G*]. We take a green ball *E* at random from urn [*C*]. We note the result and return the ball to urn [*C*]. We take a black ball *H* at random from urn [*E*], note the result, and return the ball to urn [*E*]. From urn [*H*] we take . . .. The protocol so far is: *GCEH* . . ..

Protocol P_A^0 (V_A^0) is obviously

$$AAAA \quad ····.$$

Protocol P_A' (V_A'). Consider an urn [*Y*] in which the eight colors of balls are in the following proportions: 2.1% color *A*, 8.4% color *B*, 8.4% color *C*, 33.6% color *D*, 1.9% color *E*, 7.6% color *F*, 7.6% color *G*, and 30.4% color *H*. After each draw return the ball to urn *Y*. A likely protocol might be the following:

GFFGHDDCBHGGHDDHBBHCDDDCGDDDDFDDHHHBF
    FHDBHDHHCHHECHDBHHDHHFHDDGDAFHHHDFDG····.

Protocol P_C' (V_C'). The same method furnishes us with a protocol of *P'*:

EEGFGEFEEFADFEBECGEEAEFBFBEADEFAAEEFH
    ABFECHFEBEFEEFHFAEBFFFEFEEAFHFBEFEEB····.

Protocol P_C^0 (V_C^0):

$$CCCC····.$$

Protocol P_B^0 (V_B^0):

$$BBBB····.$$

Protocol P_C' (V_C'):

AAADCCECDAACEBAFGBCAAADGCDDCGCADGAAGEC
CAACAAHAACGCDAACDAABDCCCGACACAACACB····.

REALIZATION OF *ANALOGIQUE A* FOR ORCHESTRA

The instrumental composition follows the preceding exposition point
by point, within the limits of orchestral instruments and conventional
execution and notation. The mechanism which will be used is system *Z*,
which has already been treated numerically. The choice of variables for the
screens are shown in Figs. III–8, 9, 10.

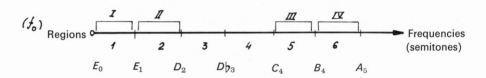

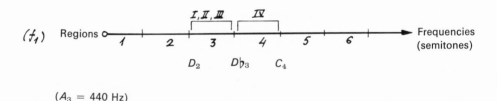

(A_3 = 440 Hz)

Fig. III–8. Frequencies

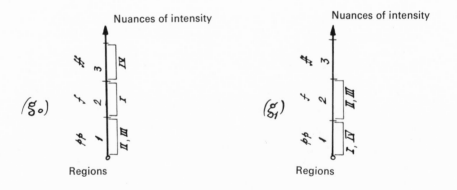

Fig. III–9. Intensities

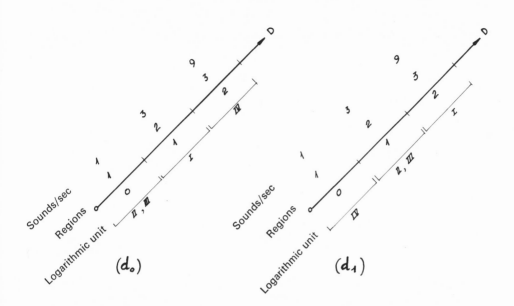

Fig. III–10. Densities

This choice gives us the partial screens *FG* (Fig. III–11) and *FD* (Fig. III–12), the partial screens *GD* being a consequence of *FG* and *FD*. The Roman numerals are the liaison agents between all the cells of the three planes of reference, *FG*, *FD*, and *GD*, so that the different combinations (f_i, g_j, d_k) which are perceived theoretically are made possible.

For example, let there be a screen (f_1, g_1, d_0) and the sonic entity C_3 corresponding to frequency region no. 3. From the partial screens above, this entity will be the arithmetic sum in three dimensions of the grains of cells I, II, and III, lying on frequency region no. 3. $C_3 = I + II + III$.

The dimensions of the cell corresponding to I are: ΔF = region 3, ΔG = region 1, ΔD = region 2. The dimensions of the cell corresponding to II are: ΔF = region 3, ΔG = region 2, ΔD = region 1. The dimensions of the cell corresponding to III are: ΔF = region 3, ΔG = region 2, ΔD = region 1. Consequently in this sonic entity the grains will have frequencies included in region 3, intensities included in regions 1 and 2, and they will form densities included in regions 1 and 2, with the correspondences set forth above.

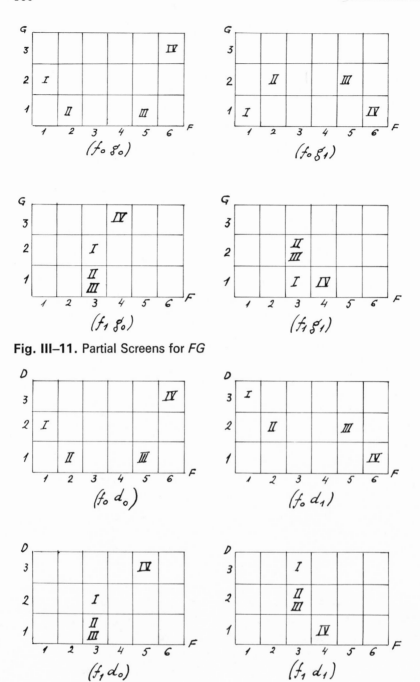

Fig. III–11. Partial Screens for *FG*

Fig. III–12. Partial Screens for *FD*

The eight principal screens A, B, C, D, E, F, G, H which derive from the combinations in Fig. III–5 are shown in Fig. III–13. The duration Δt of each screen is 1.11 sec. (1 half note = 54 MM). Within this duration the densities of the occupied cells must be realized. The period of time necessary for the exposition of the protocol of each stage (of the protocol at the stationary stage, and of the protocols for the perturbations) is $30\Delta t$, which becomes 15 whole notes (1 whole note = 27 MM).

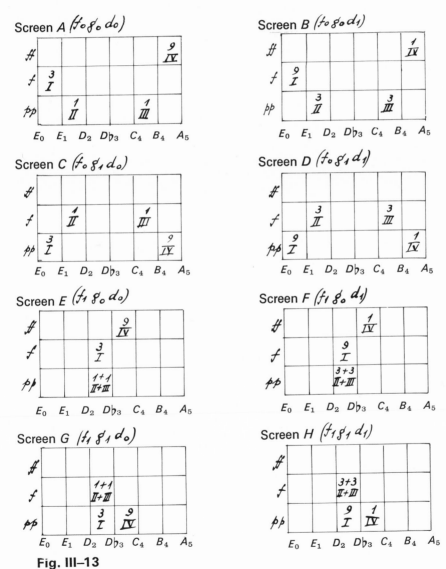

Fig. III–13

NOTE: The numbers written in the cells are the mean densities in grains/sec.

The linkage of the perturbations and the stationary state of (MTPZ) is given by the following kinematic diagram, which was chosen for this purpose:

$$(e_5) \qquad E \to P_A^0 \to P_A' \to E \to P_C' \to P_C^0 \to P_B^0 \to P_B' \to E \to P_A'$$

Fig. III–14. Bars 105–15 of *Analogique A*

Fig. III–14, bars 105–15 of the score of *Analogique A*, comprises a section of perturbations P_B^0 and P_B'. The change of period occurs at bar 109. The disposition of the screens is given in Fig. III–15. For technical reasons screens E, F, G, and H have been simplified slightly.

105   109   115

$\cdots$ | BB | BB | BB | BB | AA | GE | CC | AA | CA | AH | $\cdots$

End of the period of →|← Beginning of return to equi-
perturbation P_B^0 librium (perturbation P_B')

Fig. III–15

Analogique A replaces elementary sinusoidal sounds by very ordered clouds of elementary grains, restoring the string timbres. In any case a realization with classical instruments could not produce screens having a timbre other than that of strings because of the limits of human playing. The hypothesis of a sonority of a second order cannot, therefore, be confirmed or invalidated under these conditions.

On the other hand, a realization using electromagnetic devices as mighty as computers and adequate converters would enable one to prove the existence of a second order sonority with elementary sinusoidal grains or grains of the Gabor type as a base.

While anticipating some such technique, which has yet to be developed, we shall demonstrate how more complex screens are realizable with the resources of an ordinary electroacoustic studio equipped with several magnetic tapes or synchronous recorders, filters, and sine-wave generators.

ELECTROMAGNETIC MUSIC (sinusoidal sounds)—EXAMPLE TAKEN FROM *ANALOGIQUE B*

We choose: 1. Two groups of frequency regions f_0, f_1, as in Fig. III–16. The protocols of these two groups will be such that they will obey the preceding (MTP)'s:

	↓	f_0	f_1
(α)	f_0	0.2	0.8
	f_1	0.8	0.2

	↓	f_0	f_1
(β)	f_0	0.85	0.4
	f_1	0.15	0.6

in which (α) and (β) are the parameters.

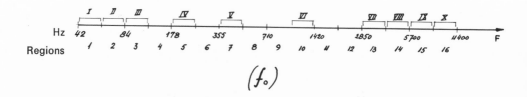

$$(f_0)$$

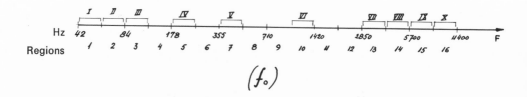

$$(f_1)$$

Fig. III–16

2. Two groups of intensity regions g_0, g_1, as in Fig. III–17. The protocols of this group will again obey the same (MTP)'s with their parameters (γ) and (ε):

(γ)	$\downarrow$	g_0	g_1
	g_0	0.2	0.8
	g_1	0.8	0.2

(ε)	$\downarrow$	g_0	g_1
	g_0	0.85	0.4
	g_1	0.15	0.6

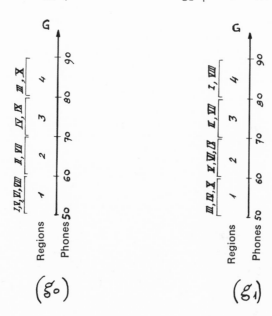

$$(g_0)$$ $$(g_1)$$

Fig. III–17

3. Two groups of density regions d_0, d_1, as in Fig. III–18. The protocols of this group will have the same (MTP)'s with parameters (λ) and (μ):

$$(\lambda) \quad \begin{array}{c|cc} \downarrow & d_0 & d_1 \\ \hline d_0 & 0.2 & 0.8 \\ d_1 & 0.8 & 0.2 \end{array} \qquad (\mu) \quad \begin{array}{c|cc} \downarrow & d_0 & d_1 \\ \hline d_0 & 0.85 & 0.4 \\ d_1 & 0.15 & 0.6 \end{array}$$

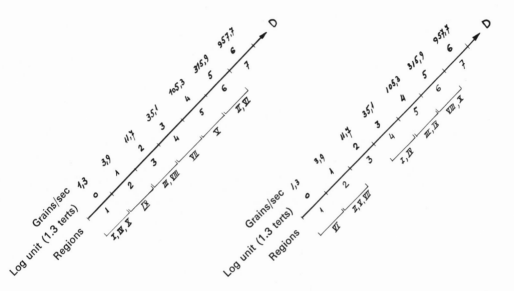

Fig. III–18

This choice gives us the principal screens A, B, C, D, E, F, G, H, as shown in Fig. III–19. The duration Δt of each screen is about 0.5 sec. The period of exposition of a perturbation or of a stationary state is about 15 sec.

We shall choose the same protocol of exchanges between perturbations and stationary states of (MTPZ), that of *Analogique A*.

$$(e_5) \qquad E \to P_A^0 \to P_A' \to E \to P_C' \to P_C^0 \to P_B^0 \to P_B' \to E \to P_A'$$

The screens of *Analogique B* calculated up to now constitute a special choice. Later in the course of this composition other screens will be used more particularly, but they will always obey the same rules of coupling and the same (MTPZ). In fact, if we consider the combinations of regions of the variable f_i of a screen, we notice that without tampering with the name of the variable f_i its structure may be changed.

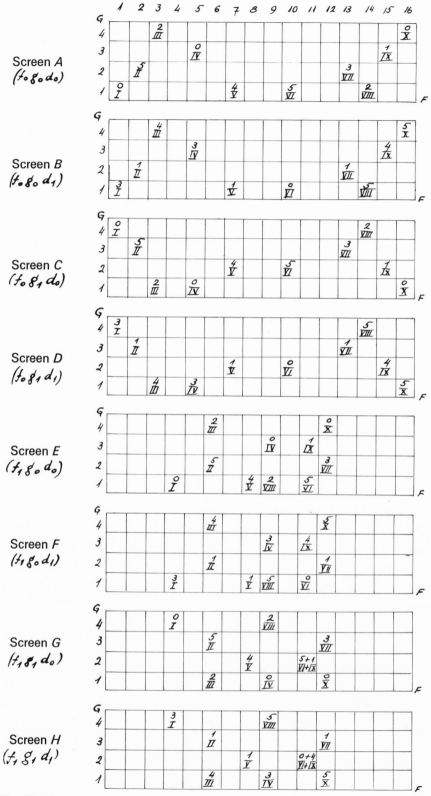

Screen A
$(f_0 g_0 d_0)$

Screen B
$(f_0 g_0 d_1)$

Screen C
$(f_0 g_1 d_0)$

Screen D
$(f_0 g_1 d_1)$

Screen E
$(f_1 g_0 d_0)$

Screen F
$(f_1 g_0 d_1)$

Screen G
$(f_1 g_1 d_0)$

Screen H
$(f_1 g_1 d_1)$

Fig. III–19

Thus for f_0 we may have the regions shown in Fig. III–20. The Roman numerals establish the liaison with the regions of the other two variables.

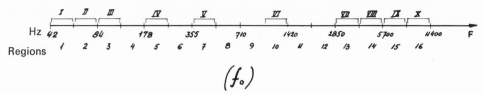

$$(f_0)$$

Fig. III–20

But we could have chosen another combination f_0, as in Fig. III–21.

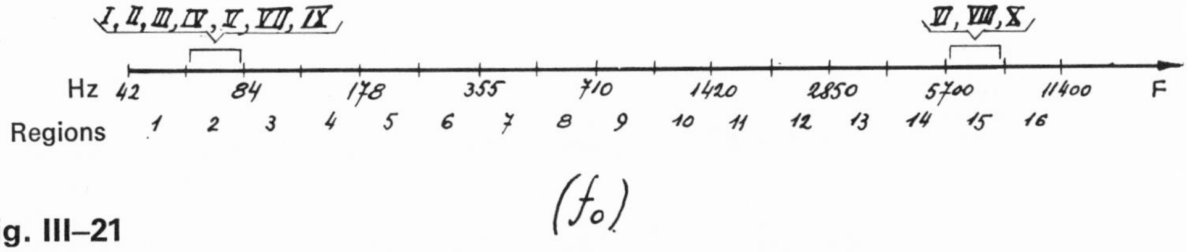

$$(f_0)$$

Fig. III–21

This prompts the question: "Given n divisions ΔF (regions on F) what is the total number of possible combinations of ΔF regions?

1st case. None of the n areas is used. The screen corresponding to this combination is silent. The number of these combinations will be

$$\frac{n!}{(n-0)!\,0!}\ (=1).$$

2nd case. One of the n areas is occupied. The number of combinations will be

$$\frac{n!}{(n-1)!\,1!}.$$

3rd case. Two of the n areas are occupied. The number of combinations will be

$$\frac{n!}{(n-2)!\,2!}.$$

mth case. m of the n areas are occupied. The number of combinations will be

$$\frac{n!}{(n-m)!\,m!}.$$

FIG. III–19: The Arabic numbers above the Roman numerals in the cells indicate the density in logarithmic units. Thus cell (10,1) will have a density of [(log 1.3/log 3) +5] terts, which is 315.9 grains/sec on the average.

nth case. n of the areas are occupied. The number of the combinations will be

$$\frac{n!}{(n-n)!n!}.$$

The total number of combinations will be equal to the sum of all the preceding:

$$\frac{n!}{(n-0)!0!} + \frac{n!}{(n-1)!1!} + \frac{n!}{(n-2)!2!} + \cdots$$

$$+ \frac{n!}{[n-(n-1)]!(n-1)!} + \frac{n!}{(n-n)!n!} = 2^n$$

The same argument operates for the other two variables of the screen. Thus for the intensity, if k is the number of available regions ΔG, the total number of variables g_i will be 2^k; and for the density, if r is the number of available regions ΔD, the total number of variables d_i will be 2^r.

Consequently the total number of possible screens will be

$$T = 2^{(n+k+r)}.$$

In the case of *Analogique B* we could obtain $2^{(16+4+7)} = 2^{27} = 134,217,728$ different screens.

Important comment. At the start of this chapter we would have accepted the richness of a musical evolution, an evolution based on the method of stochastic protocols of the coupled screen variables, as a function of the transformations of the entropies of these variables. From the preceding calculation, we now see that without modifying the entropies of the (MTPF), (MTPG), and (MTPD) we may obtain a supplementary subsidiary evolution by utilizing the different combinations of regions (topographic criterion).

Thus in *Analogique B* the (MTPF), (MTPG), and (MTPD) will not vary. On the contrary, in time the f_i, g_i, d_i will have new structures, corollaries of the changing combinations of their regions.

Complementary Conclusions about Screens and Their Transformations

1. *Rule.* To form a screen one may choose any combination of regions on F, G, and D, the f_i, g_j, d_k.

2. *Fundamental Criterion.* Each region of one of the variables F, G, D must be associable with a region corresponding to the other two variables in all the chosen couplings. (This is accomplished by the Roman numerals.)

3. The preceding association is arbitrary (free choice) for two pairs, but obligatory for the third pair, a consequence of the first two. For example, the associations of the Roman numerals of f_i with those of g_j and with those of d_k are both free; the association of the Roman numerals of g_j with those of d_k is obligatory, because of the first two associations.

4. The components f_i, g_j, d_k of the screens generally have stochastic protocols which correspond, stage by stage.

5. The (MTP) of these protocols will, in general, be coupled with the help of parameters.

6. If F, G, D are the "variations" (number of components f_i, g_i, d_i, respectively) the maximum number of couplings between the components and the parameters of (MTPF), (MTPG), (MTPD) is the sum of the products $GD + FG + FD$. In an example from *Analogique A* or *B*:

$$F = 2 \ (f_0 \text{ and } f_1) \quad \text{the parameters of the (MTP)'s are: } \alpha, \beta$$
$$G = 2 \ (g_0 \text{ and } g_1) \qquad\qquad\qquad\qquad\qquad\qquad \gamma, \varepsilon$$
$$D = 2 \ (d_0 \text{ and } d_1) \qquad\qquad\qquad\qquad\qquad\qquad \lambda, \mu$$

and there are 12 couplings:

$$\downarrow \begin{array}{cccccccccccc} f_0 & f_1 & f_0 & f_1 & g_0 & g_1 & g_0 & g_1 & d_0 & d_1 & d_0 & d_1 \\ \gamma & \varepsilon & \lambda & \mu & \beta & \alpha & \lambda & \mu & \alpha & \beta & \gamma & \varepsilon \end{array}$$

Indeed, $FG + FD + GD = 4 + 4 + 4 = 12$.

7. If F, G, D are the "variations" (number of components f_i, g_j, d_k, respectively), the number of possible screens T is the product FGD. For example, if $F = 2 \ (f_0$ and $f_1)$, $G = 2 \ (g_0$ and $g_1)$, $D = 2 \ (d_0$ and $d_1)$, $T = 2 \times 2 \times 2 = 8$.

8. The protocol of the screens is stochastic (in the broad sense) and can be summarized when the chain is ergodic (tending to regularity), by an (MTPZ). This matrix will have FGD rows and FGD columns.

SPATIAL PROJECTION

No mention at all has been made in this chapter of the spatialization of sound. The subject was confined to the fundamental concept of a sonic complex and of its evolution in itself. However nothing would prevent broadening of the technique set out in this chapter and "leaping" into space. We can, for example, imagine protocols of screens attached to a particular point in space, with transition probabilities, space-sound couplings, etc. The method is ready and the general application is possible, along with the reciprocal enrichments it can create.

Chapter IV

Musical Strategy—Strategy, Linear Programming, and Musical Composition

Before passing to the problem of the mechanization of stochastic music by the use of computers, we shall take a stroll in a more enjoyable realm, that of games, their theory, and application in musical composition.

AUTONOMOUS MUSIC

The musical composer establishes a scheme or pattern which the conductor and the instrumentalists are called upon to follow more or less rigorously. From the final details—attacks, notes, intensities, timbres, and styles of performance—to the form of the whole work, virtually everything is written into the score. And even in the case where the composer leaves a margin of improvisation to the conductor, the instrumentalist, the machine, or to all three together, the unfolding of the sonic discourse follows an open line without *loops*. The score-model which is presented to them once and for all does not give rise to any *conflict* other than that between a "good" performance in the technical sense, and its "musical expression" as desired or suggested by the writer of the score. This opposition between the sonic realization and the symbolic schema which plots its course might be called *internal conflict*; and the role of the conductors, instrumentalists, and their machines is to control the output by feedback and comparison with the input signals, a role analogous to that of servo-mechanisms that reproduce profiles by such means as grinding machines. In general we can state that

110

the nature of the technical oppositions (instrumental and conductorial) or even those relating to the aesthetic logic of the musical discourse, is *internal* to the works written until now. The tensions are shut up in the score even when more or less defined stochastic processes are utilized. This traditional class of *internal conflict* might be qualified as *autonomous music*.

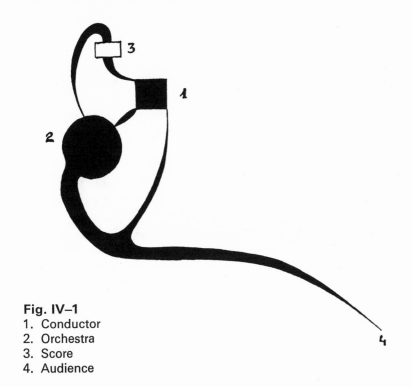

Fig. IV–1
1. Conductor
2. Orchestra
3. Score
4. Audience

HETERONOMOUS MUSIC

It would be interesting and probably very fruitful to imagine another class of musical discourse, which would introduce a concept of *external conflict* between, for instance, two opposing orchestras or instrumentalists. One party's move would influence and condition that of the other. The sonic discourse would then be identified as a very strict, although often stochastic, succession of sets of acts of sonic opposition. These acts would derive from both the will of the two (or more) conductors as well as from the will of the composer, all in a higher dialectical harmony.

Let us imagine a competitive situation between two orchestras, each having one conductor. Each of the conductors directs sonic operations *against* the operations of the other. Each operation represents a *move* or a *tactic* and the encounter between two moves has a numerical and/or a qualitative value which benefits one and harms the other. This value is written in a grid or matrix at the intersection of the row corresponding to move *i* of conductor *A* and the column corresponding to move *j* of conductor *B*. This is the partial score *ij*, representing the payment one conductor gives the other. This game, a *duel*, is defined as a *two-person zero-sum game*.

The external conflict, or *heteronomy*, can take all sorts of forms, but can always be summarized by a *matrix of payments ij*, conforming to the mathematical theory of games. The theory demonstrates that there is an optimum way of playing for *A*, which, in the long run, guarantees him a minimum advantage or gain over *B* whatever *B* might do; and that conversely there exists for *B* an optimum way of playing, which guarantees that his disadvantage or loss under *A* whatever *A* might do will not exceed a certain maximum. *A*'s minimum gain and *B*'s maximum loss coincide in absolute value; this is called the *game value*.

The introduction of an external conflict or *heteronomy* into music is not entirely without precedent. In certain traditional folk music in Europe and other continents there exist competitive forms of music in which two instrumentalists strive to confound one another. One takes the initiative and attempts either rhythmically or melodically to uncouple their tandem arrangement, all the while remaining within the musical context of the tradition which permits this special kind of improvisation. This contradictory virtuosity is particularly prevalent among the Indians, especially among tabla and sarod (or sitar) players.

A *musical heteronomy* based on modern science is thus legitimate even to the most conformist eye. But the problem is not the historical justification of a new adventure; quite the contrary, it is the enrichment and the leap forward that count. Just as stochastic processes brought a beautiful generalization to the complexity of linear polyphony and the deterministic logic of musical discourse, and at the same time disclosed an unsuspected opening on a totally asymmetric aesthetic form hitherto qualified as nonsense; in the same way *heteronomy* introduces into stochastic music a complement of dialectical structure.

We could equally well imagine setting up conflicts between two or more instrumentalists, between one player and what we agree to call natural environment, or between an orchestra or several orchestras and the public. But the fundamental characteristic of this situation is that there exists a gain and a loss, a victory and a defeat, which may be expressed by a moral or material reward such as a prize, medal, or cup for one side, and by a penalty for the other.

A *degenerate* game is one in which the parties play arbitrarily following a more or less improvised route, without any conditioning for conflict, and therefore without any new compositional argument. This is a false game.

A gambling device with sound or lights would have a *trivial* sense if it were made in a gratuitous way, like the usual slot machines and juke boxes, that is, without a new competitive inner organization inspired by any heteronomy. A sharp manufacturer might cash in on this idea and produce new sound and light devices based on heteronomic principles. A less trivial use would be an educational apparatus which would require children (or adults) to react to sonic or luminous combinations. The aesthetic interest, and hence the rules of the game and the payments, would be determined by the players themselves by means of special input signals.

In short the fundamental interest set forth above lies in the mutual conditioning of the two parties, a conditioning which respects the greater diversity of the musical discourse and a certain liberty for the players, but which involves a strong influence by a single composer. This point of view may be generalized with the introduction of a spatial factor in music and with the extension of the games to the art of light.

In the field of calculation the problem of games is rapidly becoming difficult, and not all games have received adequate mathematical clarification, for example, games for several players. We shall therefore confine ourselves to a relatively simple case, that of the two-person zero-sum game.

ANALYSIS OF *DUEL*

This work for two conductors and two orchestras was composed in 1958–59. It appeals to relatively simple concepts: sonic constructions put into mutual correspondence by the will of the conductors, who are themselves conditioned by the composer. The following events can occur:

Event I: A cluster of sonic grains such as pizzicati, blows with the wooden part of the bow, and very brief arco sounds distributed stochastically.

Event II: Parallel sustained strings with fluctuations.

Event III: Networks of intertwined string glissandi.

Event IV: Stochastic percussion sounds.

Event V: Stochastic wind instrument sounds.
Event VI: Silence.

Each of these events is written in the score in a very precise manner and with sufficient length, so that at any moment, following his instantaneous choice, the conductor is able to cut out a slice without destroying the identity of the event. We therefore imply an overall homogeneity in the writing of each event, at the same time maintaining local fluctuations.

We can make up a list of couples of simultaneous events x, y issuing from the two orchestras X and Y, with our subjective evaluations. We can also write this list in the form of a qualitative matrix (M_1).

Table of Evaluations

Couple $(x, y) = (y, x)$	Evaluation	
(I, I)	passable	(p)
(I, II) = (II, I)	good	(g)
(I, III) = (III, I)	good$^+$	(g^+)
(I, IV) = (IV, I)	passable$^+$	(p^+)
(I, V) = (V, I)	very good	(g^{++})
(II, II)	passable	(p)
(II, III) = (III, II)	passable	(p)
(II, IV) = (IV, II)	good	(g)
(II, V) = (V, II)	passable$^+$	(p^+)
(III, III)	passable	(p)
(III, IV) = (IV, III)	good$^+$	(g^+)
(III, V) = (V, III)	good	(g)
(IV, IV)	passable	(p)
(IV, V) = (V, IV)	good	(g)
(V, V)	passable	(p)

Conductor Y

		I	II	III	IV	V	Minimum per row	
	I	p	g	g^+	p^+	g^{++}	p	
	II	g	p	p	g	p^+	p	
Conductor X	III	g^+	p	p	g^+	g	p	(M_1)
	IV	p^+	g	g^+	p	g	p	
	V	g^{++}	p^+	g	g	p	p	
Maximum per column		g^{++}	g	g^+	g^+	g^{++}		

In (M_1) the largest minimum per row and the smallest maximum per column do not coincide $(g \neq p)$, and consequently the game has no saddle point and no pure strategy. The introduction of the move of silence (VI) modifies (M_1), and matrix (M_2) results.

Conductor Y

		I	II	III	IV	V	VI		
	I	p	g	g^{++}	g^+	g^+	p	p	
	II	g	p	p	g	p^+	p	p	
	III	g^{++}	p	p	g^+	g	p	p	
Conductor X	IV	g^+	g	g^+	p	g	p	p	(M_2)
	V	g^+	p^+	g	g	p	p	p	
	VI	p	p	p	p	p	p^-	p^-	
		g^{++}	g	g^{++}	g^+	g^+	p		

This time the game has several saddle points. All tactics are possible, but a closer study shows that the conflict is still too slack: Conductor Y is interested in playing tactic VI only, whereas conductor X can choose freely among I, II, III, IV, and V. It must not be forgotten that the rules of this matrix were established for the benefit of conductor X and that the game in this form is not fair. Moreover the rules are too vague. In order to pursue our study we shall attempt to specify the qualitative values by ordering them on an axis and making them correspond to a rough numerical scale:

$$p^- \quad p \quad p^+ \quad g \quad g^+ \quad g^{++}$$

0	1	2	3	4	5

If, in addition, we modify the value of the couple (VI, VI) the matrix becomes (M_3).

Conductor Y

	I	II	III	IV	V	VI	
I	1	3	5	4	4	1	1
II	3	1	1	3	2	1	1
III	5	1	1	4	3	1	1
IV	4	3	4	1	3	1	1
V	4	2	3	3	1	1	1
VI	1	1	1	1	1	3	1
	5	3	5	4	4	3	

Conductor X (M_3)

(M_3) has no saddle point and no recessive rows or columns. To find the solution we apply an approximation method, which lends itself easily to computer treatment but modifies the relative equilibrium of the entries as little as possible. The purpose of this method is to find a mixed strategy; that is to say, a weighted multiplicity of tactics of which none may be zero. It is not possible to give all the calculations here [21], but the matrix that results from this method is (M_4), with the two unique strategies for X and for Y written in the margin of the matrix. Conductor X must therefore play

Conductor Y

		I	II	III	IV	V	VI	
	I	2	3	4	2	3	2	18
	II	3	2	2	3	3	2	4
	III	4	2	1	4	3	1	5
Conductor X	IV	2	4	4	2	2	2	5
	V	3	2	3	3	2	2	11
	VI	2	2	1	2	2	4	15
		9	6	8	12	9	14	58 Total

(M_4)

tactics I, II, III, IV, V, VI in proportions 18/58, 4/58, 5/58, 5/58, 11/58, 15/58, respectively; while conductor Y plays these six tactics in the proportions 9/58, 6/58, 8/58, 12/58, 9/58, 14/58, respectively. The game value from this method is about 2.5 in favor of conductor X (game with zero-sum but still not fair).

We notice immediately that the matrix is no longer symmetrical about its diagonal, which means that the tactic couples are not commutative, e.g., (IV, II = 4) $\neq$ (II, IV = 3). There is an orientation derived from the adjustment of the calculation which is, in fact, an enrichment of the game.

The following stage is the experimental control of the matrix.

Two methods are possible:

1. Simulate the game, i.e., mentally substitute oneself for the two conductors, X and Y, by following the matrix entries stage by stage, without memory and without bluff, in order to test the least interesting case.

Stages:	1	2	3	4	5	6	7	8	9	10	11	12	13	14	15	16	17	18	19	20	21
Cond. X	I	III		I		VI		I		III		VI		IV		III		III		IV	
Cond. Y	IV		III		VI		III		I		VI		III		V		II		III		IV
Scores:	2	4	1	4	2	4	1	4	2	4	1	4	1	4	2	3	2	2	1	4	2

Game value: 52/20 = 2.6 points in X's favor.

2. Choose tactics at random, but with frequencies proportional to the marginal numbers in (M_4).

Stages:	1	2	3	4	5	6	7	8	9	10	11	12	13	14	15	16	17	18	19	20	21
Cond. X	I	VI		VI		II		I		II		V		IV		I		V		V	
Cond. Y	VI		VI		V		III		I		IV		VI		V		IV		VI		III
Scores:	2	4	4	4	2	3	2	4	2	3	3	3	2	2	2	3	2	3	2	2	3

Game value: $57/21 = 2.7$ points in X's favor.

We now establish that the experimental game values are very close to the value calculated by approximation. The sonic processes derived from the two experiments are, moreover, satisfactory.

We may now apply a rigorous method for the definition of the optimum strategies for X and Y and the value of the game by using methods of linear programming, in particular the simplex method [22]. This method is based on two theses:

1. The fundamental theorem of game theory (the "minimax theorem") is that the minimum score (maximin) corresponding to X's optimum strategy is always equal to the maximum score (minimax) corresponding to Y's optimum strategy.

2. The calculation of the maximin or minimax value, just as the probabilities of the optimum strategies of a two-person zero-sum game, comes down to the resolution of a pair of dual problems of linear programming (dual simplex method).

Here we shall simply state the system of linear equations for the player of the minimum, Y. Let $y_1, y_2, y_3, y_4, y_5, y_6$ be the probabilities corresponding to tactics I, II, III, IV, V, VI of Y; $y_7, y_8, y_9, y_{10}, y_{11}, y_{12}$ be the "slack" variables; and v be the game value which must be minimized. We then have the following liaisons:

$$y_1 + y_2 + y_3 + y_4 + y_5 + y_6 = 1$$
$$2y_1 + 3y_2 + 4y_3 + 2y_4 + 3y_5 + 2y_6 + y_7 = v$$
$$3y_1 + 2y_2 + 2y_3 + 2y_4 + 3y_5 + 2y_6 + y_8 = v$$
$$2y_1 + 4y_2 + 4y_3 + 2y_4 + 2y_5 + 2y_6 + y_9 = v$$
$$3y_1 + 2y_2 + 3y_3 + 3y_4 + 2y_5 + 2y_6 + y_{10} = v$$
$$2y_1 + 2y_2 + y_3 + 2y_4 + 2y_5 + 4y_6 + y_{11} = v$$
$$4y_1 + 2y_2 + y_3 + 4y_4 + 3y_5 + y_6 + y_{12} = v.$$

To arrive at a unique strategy, the calculation leads to the modification of the score (III, IV = 4) into (III, IV = 5). The solution gives the following optimum strategies:

For X		For Y	
Tactics	Probabilities	Tactics	Probabilities
I	2/17	I	5/17
II	6/17	II	2/17
III	0	III	2/17
IV	3/17	IV	1/17
V	2/17	V	2/17
VI	4/17	VI	5/17

and for the game value, $v = 42/17 \approx 2.47$. We have established that X must completely abandon tactic III (probability of III = 0), and this we must avoid.

Modifying score (II, IV = 3) to (II, IV = 2), we obtain the following optimum strategies:

For X		For Y	
Tactics	Probabilities	Tactics	Probabilities
I	14/56	I	19/56
II	6/56	II	7/56
III	6/56	III	6/56
IV	6/56	IV	1/56
V	8/56	V	7/56
VI	16/56	VI	16/56

and for the game value, $v = 138/56 \approx 2.47$ points.

Although the scores have been modified a little, the game value has, in fact, not moved. But on the other hand the optimum strategies have varied widely. A rigorous calculation is therefore necessary, and the final matrix accompanied by its calculated strategies is (M_5).

Conductor Y

		I	II	III	IV	V	VI	
	I	2	3	4	2	3	2	14
	II	3	2	2	2	3	2	6
	III	4	2	1	5	3	1	6
Conductor X	IV	2	4	4	2	2	2	6
	V	3	2	3	3	2	2	8
	VI	2	2	1	2	2	4	16
		19	7	6	1	7	16	56 Total

(M_5)

By applying the elementary matrix operations to the rows and columns in such a way as to make the game fair (game value = 0), we obtain the equivalent matrix (M_6) with a zero game value.

Conductor Y

		I	II	III	IV	V	VI	
	I	-13	15	43	-13	15	-13	$\frac{14}{56}$
	II	15	-13	-13	-13	15	-13	$\frac{6}{56}$
	III	43	-13	-41	71	15	-41	$\frac{6}{56}$
Conductor X	IV	-13	43	43	-13	-13	-13	$\frac{6}{56}$
	V	15	-13	15	15	-13	-13	$\frac{8}{56}$
	VI	-13	-13	-41	-13	-13	43	$\frac{16}{56}$
		$\frac{19}{56}$	$\frac{7}{56}$	$\frac{6}{56}$	$\frac{1}{56}$	$\frac{7}{56}$	$\frac{16}{56}$	

(M_6)

As this matrix is difficult to read, it is simplified by dividing all the scores by $+13$. It then becomes (M_7) with a game value $v = -0.07$, which

Conductor Y

	I	II	III	IV	V	VI	
I	-1	$+1$	$+3$	-1	$+1$	-1	$\frac{14}{56}$
II	$+1$	-1	-1	-1	$+1$	-1	$\frac{6}{56}$
III	$+3$	-1	-3	$+5$	$+1$	-3	$\frac{6}{56}$
IV	-1	$+3$	$+3$	-1	-1	-1	$\frac{6}{56}$
V	$+1$	-1	$+1$	$+1$	-1	-1	$\frac{8}{56}$
VI	-1	-1	-3	-1	-1	$+3$	$\frac{16}{56}$
	$\frac{19}{56}$	$\frac{7}{56}$	$\frac{6}{56}$	$\frac{1}{56}$	$\frac{7}{56}$	$\frac{16}{56}$	

Conductor X (on left of rows) (M_7)

means that at the end of the game, at the final score, conductor Y should give $0.07m$ points to conductor X, where m is the total number of moves.

If we convert the numerical matrix (M_7) into a qualitative matrix according to the correspondence:

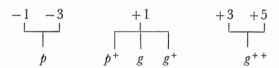

we obtain (M_8), which is not very different from (M_2), except for the silence couple, VI, VI, which is the opposite of the first value. The calculation is now finished.

p	p^+	g^{++}	p	g	p
p^+	p	p	p	p^+	p
g^{++}	p	p	g^{++}	p^+	p
p	g^{++}	g^{++}	p	p	p
p^+	p	p^+	p^+	p	p
p	p	p	p	p	g^{++}

(M_8)

Mathematical manipulation has brought about a refinement of the duel and the emergence of a paradox: the couple VI, VI, characterizing total silence. Silence is to be avoided, but to do this it is necessary to augment its potentiality.

It is impossible to describe in these pages the fundamental role of the mathematical treatment of this problem, or the subtle arguments we are forced to make on the way. We must be vigilant at every moment and over every part of the matrix area. It is an instance of the kind of work where detail is dominated by the whole, and the whole is dominated by detail. It was to show the value of this intellectual labor that we judged it useful to set out the processes of calculation.

The conductors direct with their backs to each other, using finger or light signals that are invisible to the opposing orchestra. If the conductors use illuminated signals operated by buttons, the successive partial scores can be announced automatically on lighted panels in the hall, the way the score is displayed at football games. If the conductors just use their fingers, then a referee can count the points and put up the partial scores manually so they are visible in the hall. At the end of a certain number of exchanges or minutes, as agreed upon by the conductors, one of the two is declared the winner and is awarded a prize.

Now that the principle has been set out, we can envisage the intervention of the public, who would be invited to evaluate the pairs of tactics of conductors X and Y and vote immediately on the make-up of the game matrix. The music would then be the result of the conditioning of the composer who established the musical score, conductors X and Y, and the public who construct the matrix of points.

RULES OF THE WORK *STRATÉGIE*

The two-headed flow chart of *Duel* is shown in Fig. IV–2. It is equally valid for *Stratégie*, composed in 1962. The two orchestras are placed on either side of the stage, the conductors back-to-back (Fig. IV–3), or on platforms on opposite sides of the auditorium. They may choose and play one of six sonic constructions, numbered in the score from I to VI. We call them tactics and they are of stochastic structure. They were calculated on the IBM-7090 in Paris. In addition, each conductor can make his orchestra play simultaneous combinations of two or three of these fundamental tactics. The six fundamental tactics are:

    I. Winds
   II. Percussion
  III. String sound-box struck with the hand
  IV. String pointillistic effects
   V. String glissandi
  VI. Sustained string harmonics.

The following are 13 compatible and simultaneous combinations of these tactics:

I & II = VII	II & III = XII	I & II & III = XVI
I & III = VIII	II & IV = XIII	I & II & IV = XVII
I & IV = IX	II & V = XIV	I & II & V = XVIII
I & V = X	II & VI = XV	I & II & VI = XIX
I & VI = XI		

Thus there exist in all 19 tactics which each conductor can make his orchestra play, 361 (19 × 19) possible pairs that may be played simultaneously.

The Game

    1. *Choosing tactics.* How will the conductors choose which tactics to play?

    a. A first solution consists of arbitrary choice. For example, conductor X chooses tactic I. Conductor Y may then choose any one of the 19 tactics including I. Conductor X, acting on Y's choice, then chooses a new tactic (see Rule 7 below). X's second choice is a function of both his taste and Y's choice. In his turn, conductor Y, acting on X's choice and his own taste, either chooses a new tactic or keeps on with the old one, and plays it for a certain optional length of time. And so on. We thus obtain a continuous succession of couplings of the 19 structures.

    b. The conductors draw lots, choosing a new tactic by taking one card from a pack of 19; or they might make a drawing from an urn containing balls numbered from I to XIX in different proportions. These operations can be carried out before the performance and the results of the successive draws set down in the form of a sequential plan which each of the conductors will have before him during the performance.

    c. The conductors get together in advance and choose a fixed succession which they will direct.

    d. Both orchestras are directed by a single conductor who establishes the succession of tactics according to one of the above methods and sets them down on a master plan, which he will follow during the performance.

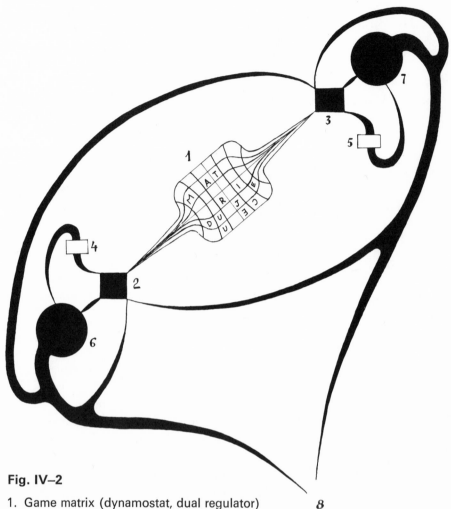

Fig. IV–2

1. Game matrix (dynamostat, dual regulator)
2. Conductor *A* (device for comparison and decision)
3. Conductor *B* (device for comparison and decision)
4. Score *A* (symbolic excitation)
5. Score *B* (symbolic excitation)
6. Orchestra *A* (human or electronic trans-forming device)
7. Orchestra *B* (human or electronic trans-forming device)
8. Audience

Fig. IV–3. Strategy

Placement of the Orchestras on a Single Stage

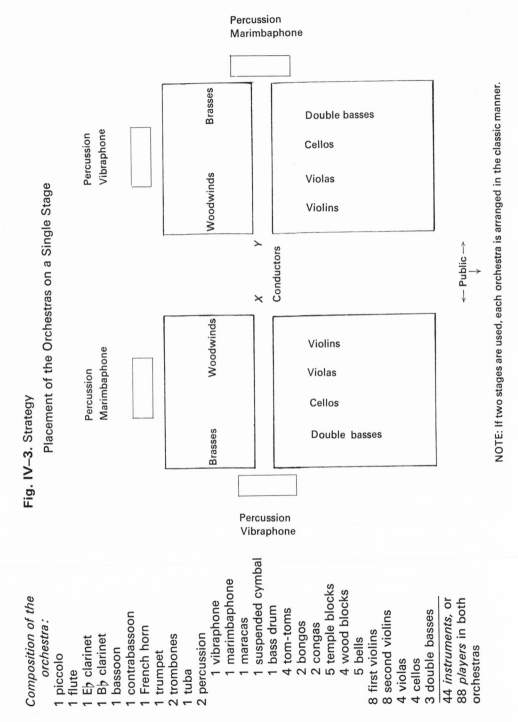

Composition of the orchestra:

1 piccolo
1 flute
1 E♭ clarinet
1 B♭ clarinet
1 bassoon
1 contrabassoon
1 French horn
1 trumpet
2 trombones
1 tuba
2 percussion
   1 vibraphone
   1 marimbaphone
   1 maracas
   1 suspended cymbal
   1 bass drum
   4 tom-toms
   2 bongos
   2 congas
   5 temple blocks
   4 wood blocks
   5 bells
8 first violins
8 second violins
4 violas
4 cellos
3 double basses
_____
44 *instruments,* or
88 *players* in both
orchestras

NOTE: If two stages are used, each orchestra is arranged in the classic manner.

e. Actually all these ways constitute what one may call "degenerate" competitive situations. The only worthwhile setup, which adds something new in the case of more than one orchestra, is one that introduces dual conflict between the conductors. In this case the pairs of tactics are performed simultaneously without interruption from one choice to the next (see Fig. IV–4), and the decisions made by the conductors are conditioned by the winnings or losses contained in the game matrix.

CONDUCTOR X	GAINS	78	72	46	36	
	TACTICS	IX	XVIII	XIV	XV	VII

CONDUCTOR Y	GAINS	52	40	48	28	48
	TACTICS	VII	XIX	XV	V	

Fig. IV–4

2. *Limiting the game.* The game may be limited in several ways: *a.* The conductors agree to play to a certain number of points, and the first to reach it is the winner. *b.* The conductors agree in advance to play *n* engagements. The one with more points at the end of the *n*th engagement is the winner. *c.* The conductors decide on the duration for the game, *m* seconds (or minutes), for instance. The one with more points at the end of the *m*th second (or minute) is the winner.

3. *Awarding points.*

a. One method is to have one or two referees counting the points in two columns, one for conductor *X* and one for conductor *Y*, both in positive numbers. The referees stop the game after the agreed limit and announce the result to the public.

b. Another method has no referees, but uses an automatic system that consists of an individual board for each conductor. The board has the *n* × *n* cells of the game matrix used. Each cell has the corresponding partial score and a push button. Suppose that the game matrix is the large one of 19 × 19 cells. If conductor *X* chooses tactic XV against *Y*'s IV, he presses the button at the intersection of row XV and column IV. Corresponding to this intersection is the cell containing the partial score of 28 points for *X* and the button that *X* must push. Each button is connected to a small adding machine which totals up the results on an electric panel so that they can be seen by the public as the game proceeds, just like the panels in the football stadium, but on a smaller scale.

4. *Assigning of rows or columns* is made by the conductors tossing a coin.

5. *Deciding who starts* the game is determined by a second toss.

6. *Reading the tactics.* The orchestras perform the tactics cyclically on a closed loop. Thus the cessation of a tactic is made instantaneously at a bar line, at the discretion of the conductor. The subsequent eventual resumption of this tactic can be made either by: *a.* reckoning from the bar line defined above, or *b.* reckoning from a bar line identified by a particular letter. The conductor will usually indicate the letter he wishes by displaying a large card to the orchestra. If he has a pile of cards bearing the letters *A* through *U*, he has available 22 different points of entry for each one of the tactics. In the score the tactics have a duration of at least two minutes. When the conductor reaches the end of a tactic he starts again at the beginning, hence the "da capo" written on the score.

7. *Duration of the engagements.* The duration of each engagement is optional. It is a good idea, however, to fix a lower limit of about 10 seconds; i.e., if a conductor engages in a tactic he must keep it up for at least 10 seconds. This limit may vary from concert to concert. It constitutes a wish on the part of the composer rather than an obligation, and the conductors have the right to decide the lower limit of duration for each engagement before the game. There is no upper limit, for the game itself conditions whether to maintain or to change the tactic.

8. *Result of the contest.* To demonstrate the dual structure of this composition and to honor the conductor who more faithfully followed the conditions imposed by the composer in the game matrix, at the end of the combat one might *a.* proclaim a victor, or *b.* award a prize, bouquet of flowers, cup, or medal, whatever the concert impresario might care to donate.

9. *Choice of matrix.* In *Stratégie* there exist three matrices. The large one, 19 rows × 19 columns (Fig. IV–5), contains all the partial scores for pairs of the fundamental tactics I to VI and their combinations. The two smaller matrices, 3 × 3, also contain these but in the following manner: Row 1 and column 1 contain the fundamental tactics from I to VI without discrimination; row 2 and column 2 contain the two-by-two compatible combinations of the fundamental tactics; and row 3 and column 3 contain the three-by-three compatible combinations of these tactics. The choice between the large 19 × 19 matrix and one of the 3 × 3 matrices depends on the ease with which the conductors can read a matrix. The cells with positive scores mean a gain for conductor *X* and automatically a symmetrical loss for conductor *Y*. Conversely, the cells with negative scores mean a loss for conductor *X* and automatically a symmetrical gain for conductor *Y*. The two simpler, 3 × 3 matrices with different strategies are shown in Fig. IV–6.

MATRIX OF THE GAME

Conductor Y (columns)

	I	II	III	IV	V	VI	VII	VIII	IX	X	XI	XII	XIII	XIV	XV	XVI	XVII	XVIII	XIX	
I°	116	10	84	-48	4	-52	-60	-40	132	-44	-8	-36	-22	24	-46	102	138	-38	32	2
II	-56	96	-44	-22	-24	52	-50	-14	12	28	6	-48	-20	-16	-10	-24	-36	-20	44	3
III	-110	-2	96	96	24	0	4	-56	-32	-24	4	-52	-48	-40	-16	-44	-16	20	72	1
IV	0	-20	24	84	4	-12	12	-12	-28	8	-8	-24	-40	4	22	-10	-16	28	-16	11
V	-110	-204	-86	4	104	-8	44	20	-8	4	8	-8	-38	-24	-16	40	8	20	-24	1
VI	24	44	12	-14	-6	64	24	-8	24	4	-24	-40	-52	-44	24	44	4	4	-48	7
VII	-56	-52	20	16	36	44	44	4	-52	-48	0	-46	-36	-12	-20	-40	-44	16	40	4
VIII	-32	-8	-52	-8	12	4	4	48	-44	-12	8	-52	-4	8	32	-36	-40	-16	24	3
IX	-36	10	-16	-32	2	4	-44	-52	52	44	2	48	-18	64	24	22	-36	-28	-52	6
X	-48	22	-22	4	-4	32	-46	-16	8	-36	-24	-4	8	32	24	4	-8	20	-32	4
XI	4	24	26	-4	4	-28	-36	-12	20	4	64	68	4	40	-12	-2	-24	-27	-32	10
XII	-36	-196	-188	-28	-34	-42	36	32	24	0	-32	74	76	-4	4	-32	-28	40	76	7
XIII	166	-20	-42	-40	-52	-44	14	-16	4	22	-14	80	72	-26	-58	40	-18	78	42	2
XIV	32	-14	-34	0	-32	-52	36	12	-12	36	24	-28	42	76	-48	-64	-30	-29	72	5
XV	-20	8	4	28	-28	14	0	20	2	-4	-32	14	26	-56	46	-36	12	-8	14	4
XVI	88	88	104	-28	20	16	-2	-16	20	-20	-50	-26	-8	-36	-40	108	-24	-33	60	9
XVII	32	92	52	-28	16	8	-44	-48	-32	0	-16	-16	-20	-32	24	-30	96	52	-36	8
XVIII	-36	-24	8	4	0	-2	52	78	-12	-4	36	-8	28	-24	-16	-14	42	-12	-40	9
XIX	-52	-52	-66	4	6	-6	-4	44	-66	-4	44	12	44	40	16	-46	44	-42	-32	4
	1	1	2	3	7	11	3	3	4	6	9	2	5	7	10	4	4	8	10	100

Conductor X (rows)

Fig. IV–5. Strategy

Two-person Game. Value of the Game = 0.

◢ Woodwinds
● Normal percussion
⊢ Strings striking sound-boxes
∵ Strings pizzicato
Strings glissando
☰ Strings sustained

● Combinations
of two and three
different tactics

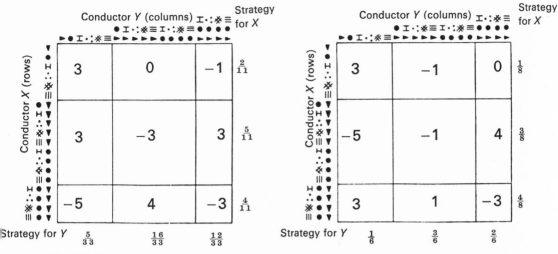

Fig. IV–6

Two-person Zero-sum Game.
Value of the Game = 1/11.
This game is not fair for Y.

Two-person Zero-sum Game.
Value of the Game = 0.
This game is fair for both
conductors.

▼ Woodwinds
● Normal percussion
H Strings striking sound-boxes
∴ Strings pizzicato
⚹ Strings glissando
III Strings sustained

Combinations
of two dis-
tinct tactics

Combinations
of three dis-
tinct tactics

Simplification of the 19 × 19 Matrix

To make first performances easier, the conductors might use an equivalent 3 × 3 matrix derived from the 19 × 19 matrix in the following manner:

Let there be a fragment of the matrix containing row tactics $r + 1, \ldots, r + m$ and column tactics $s + 1, \ldots, s + n$ with the respective probabilities $q_{r+1}, \ldots, q_{r+m}$ and $k_{s+1}, \ldots, k_{s+n}$.

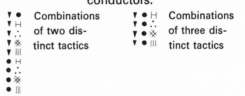

	k_{s+1}		k_{s+j}		k_{s+n}
q_{r+1}	$a_{r+1,s+1}$	$\cdots$	$a_{r+1,s+j}$	$\cdots$	$a_{r+1,s+n}$
q_{r+i}	$a_{r+i,s+1}$	$\cdots$	$a_{r+i,s+j}$	$\cdots$	$a_{r+i,s+n}$
q_{r+m}	$a_{r+m,s+1}$	$\cdots$	$a_{r+m,s+j}$	$\cdots$	$a_{r+m,s+n}$

This fragment can be replaced by the single score

$$A_{r+m,s+n} = \frac{\sum_{i,j=1}^{i=m,j=n} (a_{r+i,s+j})(q_{r+i})(k_{s+j})}{\sum_i^m q_{r+i} \sum_j^n k_{s+j}}$$

and by the probabilities

$$Q = \sum_{i=1}^{m} q_{r+i}$$

and

$$K = \sum_{j=i}^{n} k_{s+j}.$$

Operating in this way with the 19×19 matrix we obtain the following matrix (the tactics will be the same as in the matrices in Fig. IV–6):

$\dfrac{7704}{25 \times 25}$	$-\dfrac{8296}{49 \times 25}$	$\dfrac{592}{25 \times 26}$	25
$-\dfrac{14522}{25 \times 45}$	$\dfrac{17610}{49 \times 45}$	$-\dfrac{3088}{45 \times 26}$	45
$\dfrac{6818}{25 \times 30}$	$-\dfrac{9314}{49 \times 30}$	$\dfrac{2496}{30 \times 26}$	30
25	49	26	

or

2465	-1354	182	25
-2581	1597	-528	45
1818	-1267	640	30
25	49	26	

Chapter V

Free Stochastic Music by Computer

After this interlude, we return to the treatment of composition by machines.

The theory put forward by *Achorripsis* had to wait four years before being realized mechanically. This realization occurred thanks to M. François Génuys of IBM-France and to M. Jacques Barraud of the Régie Autonome des Transports Parisiens.

THE PARADOX: MUSIC AND COMPUTERS

A STOCHASTIC WORK EXECUTED BY THE IBM-7090

The general public has a number of different reactions when faced by the alliance of the machine with artistic creation. They fall into three categories:

"It is impossible to obtain a *work of art*, since by definition it is a handicraft and requires moment-by-moment "creation" for each detail and for the entire structure, while a machine is an inert thing and cannot invent."

"Yes, one may play games with a machine or use it for speculative purposes, but the result will not be "finished": it will represent only an experiment—interesting, perhaps, but no more."

The enthusiasts who at the outset accept without flinching the whole frantic brouhaha of science fiction. "The moon? Well, yes, it's within our reach. Prolonged life will also be with us tomorrow—why not a creative machine?" These people are among the credulous, who, in their idiosyncratic optimism, have replaced the myths of Icarus and the fairies, which have decayed, by the scientific civilization of the twentieth century, and science partly agrees with them. In reality, science is neither all paradox nor all animism, for it progresses in limited stages that are not foreseeable at too great a distance.

131

There exists in all the arts what we may call rationalism in the etymological sense: the search for proportion. The *artist* has always called upon it out of *necessity*. The rules of construction have varied widely over the centuries, but there have always been rules in every epoch because of the necessity of making oneself understood. Those who believe the first statement above are the first to refuse to apply the qualification *artistic* to a product which they do not *understand* at all.

Thus the musical scale is a convention which circumscribes the area of potentiality and permits construction within those limits in its own particular symmetry. The rules of Christian hymnography, of harmony, and of counterpoint in the various ages have allowed artists to construct and to make themselves understood by those who adopted the same constraints—through traditions, through collective taste or imitation, or through sympathetic resonance. The rules of serialism, for instance, those that banned the traditional octave doublings of tonality, imposed constraints which were partly new but none the less real.

Now everything that is rule or repeated constraint is part of the mental machine. A little "imaginary machine," Philippot would have said—a choice, a set of decisions. A musical work can be analyzed as a multitude of mental machines. A melodic theme in a symphony is a mold, a mental machine, in the same way as its structure is. These mental machines are something very restrictive and deterministic, and sometimes very vague and indecisive. In the last few years we have seen that this idea of mechanism is really a very general one. It flows through every area of human knowledge and action, from strict logic to artistic manifestations.

Just as the wheel was once one of the greatest products of human intelligence, a mechanism which allowed one to travel farther and faster with more luggage, so is the computer, which today allows the transformation of man's ideas. Computers resolve logical problems by heuristic methods. But computers are not really responsible for the introduction of mathematics into music; rather it is mathematics that makes use of the computer in composition. Yet if people's minds are in general ready to recognize the usefulness of geometry in the plastic arts (architecture, painting, etc.), they have only one more stream to cross to be able to conceive of using more abstract, non-visual mathematics and machines as aids to musical composition, which is more abstract than the plastic arts.

To summarize:

1. The creative thought of man gives birth to mental mechanisms,

which, in the last analysis, are merely sets of constraints and choices. This process takes place in all realms of thought, including the arts.

2. Some of these mechanisms can be expressed in mathematical terms.

3. Some of them are physically realizable: the wheel, motors, bombs, digital computers, analogue computers, etc.

4. Certain mental mechanisms may correspond to certain mechanisms of nature.

5. Certain mechanizable aspects of artistic creation may be simulated by certain physical mechanisms or machines which exist or may be created.

6. It happens that computers can be useful in certain ways.

Here then is the theoretical point of departure for a utilization of electronic computers in musical composition.

We may further establish that the role of the living composer seems to have evolved, on the one hand, to one of inventing schemes (previously forms) and exploring the limits of these schemes, and on the other, to effecting the scientific synthesis of the new methods of construction and of sound emission. In a short while these methods must comprise all the ancient and modern means of musical instrument making, whether acoustic or electronic, with the help, for example, of digital-to-analogue converters; these have already been used in communication studies by N. Guttman, J. R. Pierce, and M. V. Mathews of Bell Telephone Laboratories in New Jersey. Now these explorations necessitate impressive mathematical, logical, physical, and psychological impedimenta, especially computers that accelerate the mental processes necessary for clearing the way for new fields by providing immediate experimental verifications at all stages of musical construction.

Music, by its very abstract nature, is the first of the arts to have attempted the conciliation of artistic creation with scientific thought. Its industrialization is inevitable and irreversible. Have we not already seen attempts to industrialize serial and popular music by the Parisian team of P. Barbaud, P. Blanchard, and Jeanine Charbonnier, as well as by the musicological research of Hiller and Isaacson at the University of Illinois?

In the preceding chapters we demonstrated some new areas of musical creation: Poisson, Markov processes, musical games, the thesis of the minimum of constraints, etc. They are all based on mathematics and especially on the theory of probability. They therefore lend themselves to being treated and explored by computers. The simplest and most meaningful scheme is one of minimum constraints in composition, as exemplified by *Achorripsis*.

Thanks to my friend Georges Boudouris of the C.N.R.S. I made the acquaintance of Jacques Barraud, Engineer of the Ecole des Mines, then director of the Ensemble Electroniques de Gestion de la Société des Petroles Shell-Berre, and François Génuys, agrégé in mathematics, and head of the Etudes Scientifiques Nouvelles at IBM-France. All three are scientists, yet they consented to attempt an experiment which seemed at first far-fetched— that of a marriage of music with one of the most powerful machines in the world.

In most human relations it is rarely pure logical persuasion which is important; usually the paramount consideration is material interest. Now in this case it was not logic, much less self-interest, that arranged the betrothal, but purely experiment for experiment's sake, or game for game's sake, that induced collaboration. Stochastically speaking, my venture should have encountered failure. Yet the doors were opened, and at the end of a year and a half of contacts and hard work "the most unusual event witnessed by the firm or by this musical season [in Paris]" took place on 24 May 1962 at the headquarters of IBM-France. It was a live concert presenting a work of stochastic instrumental music entitled *ST/10–1, 080262*, which had been calculated on the IBM-7090. It was brilliantly performed by the conductor C. Simonovic and his Ensemble de Musique Contemporaine de Paris. By its passage through the machine, this work made tangible a stochastic method of composition, that of the minimum of constraints and rules.

Position of the Problem

The first working phase was the drawing up of the flow chart, i.e., writing down clearly and in order the stages of the operations of the scheme of *Achorripsis*,[1] and adapting it to the machine structure. In the first chapter we set out the entire synthetic method of this minimal structure. Since the machine is an iterative apparatus and performs these iterations with extraordinary speed, the thesis had to be broken down into a sequential series of operations reiterated in loops. An excerpt from the first flow chart is shown in Fig. V–1.

The statement of the thesis of *Achorripsis* receives its first machine-oriented interpretation in the following manner:

1. *The work consists of a succession of sequences or movements each a_i seconds long.* Their durations are totally independent (asymmetric) but have a fixed mean duration, which is introduced in the form of a parameter. These durations and their stochastic succession are given by the formula

$$P_{a_i} = ce^{-ca_i} \, da_i. \qquad \text{(See Appendix I.)}$$

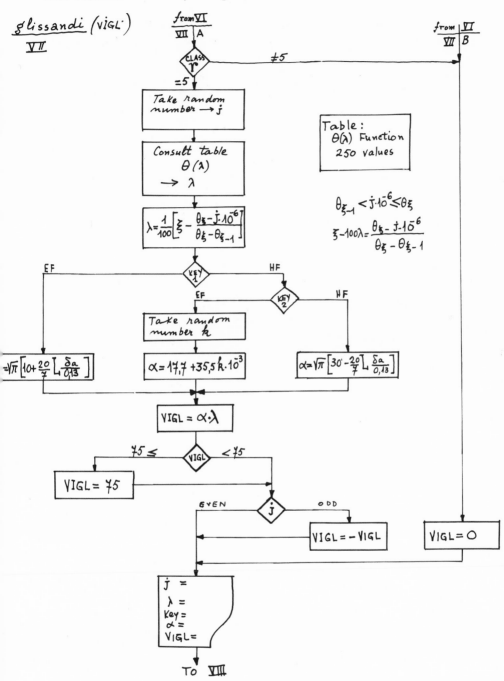

Fig. V–1. Excerpt from the First Flow Chart of *Achorripsis*

2. *Definition of the mean density of the sounds during a_i.* During a sequence sounds are emitted from several sonic sources. If the total number of these sounds or points during a sequence is N_{a_i}, the mean density of this point-cluster is N_{a_i}/a_i sounds/sec. In general, for a given instrumental ensemble this density has limits that depend on the number of instrumentalists, the nature of their instruments, and the technical difficulties of performance. For a large orchestra the upper limit is of the order of 150 sounds/sec. The lower limit $(V3)$ is arbitrary and positive. We choose $(V3) = 0.11$ sounds/sec. Previous experiments led us to adopt a logarithmic progression for the density sensation with a number between 2 and 3 as its base. We adopted $e = 2.71827$. Thus the densities are included between $(V3)e^0$ and $(V3)e^R$ sounds/sec., which we can draw on a line graduated logarithmically (base e).[2] As our purpose is total independence, we attribute to each of the sequences a_i calculated in 1. a density represented by a point drawn at random from the portion of the line mentioned above. However a certain concern for continuity leads us to temper the independence of the densities among sequences a_i; to this end we introduce a certain "memory" from sequence to sequence in the following manner:

Let a_{i-1} be a sequence of duration a_{i-1}, $(DA)_{i-1}$ its density, and a_i the next sequence with duration a_i and density $(DA)_i$. Density $(DA)_i$ will be given by the formula:

$$(DA)_i = (DA)_{i-1}e^{\pm x},$$

in which x is a segment of line drawn at random from a line segment s of length equal to $(R - 0)$. The probability of x is given by

$$P_x = \frac{2}{s}\left(1 - \frac{x}{s}\right)dx \qquad \text{(see Appendix I)}$$

and finally,

$$N_{a_i} = (DA)_{i}a_i.$$

3. *Composition Q of the orchestra during sequence a_i.* First the instruments are divided into r classes of timbres, e.g., flutes and clarinets, oboes and bassoons, brasses, bowed strings, pizzicati, col legno strokes, glissandi, wood, skin, and metal percussion instruments, etc. (See the table for *Atrées*.) The composition of the orchestra is stochastically conceived, i.e., the distribution of the classes is not deterministic. Thus during a sequence of duration a_i it may happen that we have 80% pizzicati, 10% percussion, 7% keyboard, and 3% flute class. Under actual conditions the determining factor which would condition the composition of the orchestra is density. We therefore

Composition of the Orchestra for *Atrées* (ST/10–3,060962)
Timbre classes and instruments as on present input data

Class	Timbre	Instrument	Instrument No.
1	Percussion	Temple-blocks	1—5
		Tom-toms	6—9
		Maracas	10
		Susp. cymbal	11
		Gong	12
2	Horn	French horn	1
3	Flute	Flute	1
4	Clarinet	Clarinet $B\flat$	1
		Bass clar. $B\flat$	2
5	Glissando	Violin	1
		Cello	2
		Trombone	3
6	Tremolo	Flute	1
	or	Clarinet $B\flat$	2
	flutter-	Bass clar. $B\flat$	3
	tongue	French horn	4
		Trumpet	5
		Trombone a	6
		Trombone b	7
		(pedal notes)	
		Violin	8
		Cello	9
7	Plucked	Violin	1
	strings	Cello	2
8	Struck	Violin	1
	strings*	Cello	2
9	Vibraphone	Vibraphone	1
10	Trumpet	Trumpet	1
11	Trombone	Trombone a	1
		Trombone b	2
		(pedal notes)	
12	Bowed	Violin	1
	strings	Cello	2

* col legno

connect the orchestral composition with density by means of a special diagram. An example from *ST/10–1, 080262* is shown in Fig. V–2.

Fig. V–2 is expressed by the formula

$$Q_r = (n - x)(e_{n,r} - e_{n+1,r}) + e_{n,r}$$

in which r = the number of the class, $x = \log_e[(DA)_i/(V3)]$, $n = 0, 1, 2, \ldots, R$, such that $n \leq x \leq n + 1$, and $e_{n,r}$ and $e_{n+1,r}$ are the probabilities of class r as a function of n. It goes without saying that the composition of this table is a precise task of great complexity and delicacy. Once these preliminaries have been completed, we can define, one after the other, the N_{a_i} sounds of sequence a_i.

4. *Definition of the moment of occurrence of the sound N within the sequence a_i.* The mean density of the points or sounds to be distributed within a_i is $k = N_{a_i}/a_i$. The formula which gives the intervals separating the sound attacks is

$$P_t = ke^{-kt}\, dt. \qquad \text{(See Appendix I.)}$$

5. *Attribution to the above sound of an instrument belonging to orchestra Q, which has already been calculated.* First class r is drawn at random with probability q_r from the orchestra ensemble calculated in 3. (Consider an urn with balls of r colors in various proportions.) Then from within class r the number of the instrument is drawn according to the probability p_n given by an arbitrary table (urn with balls of n colors). Here also the distribution of instruments within a class is delicate and complex.

6. *Attribution of a pitch as a function of the instrument.* Taking as the zero point the lowest $B\flat$ of the piano, we establish a chromatic scale in semitones of about 85 degrees. The range s of each instrument is thus expressed by a natural number (distance). But the pitch h_u of a sound is expressed by a decimal number of which the whole number part is related to a note of the chromatic scale within the instrument's range.

Just as for the density in 2., we accept a certain memory of or dependence on the preceding pitch played by the same instrument, so that we have

$$h_u = h_{u-1} \pm z,$$

where z is given by the probability formula

$$P_z = \frac{2}{s}\left(1 - \frac{z}{s}\right) dz. \qquad \text{(See Appendix I.)}$$

P_z is the probability of the interval z taken at random from the range s, and

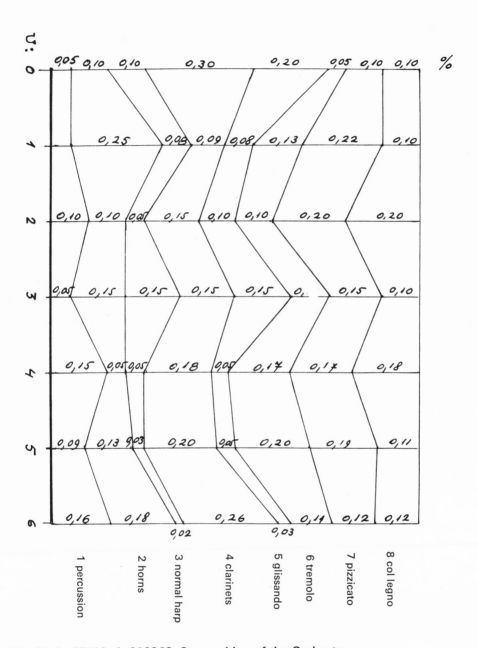

Fig. V–2. *ST/10–1, 080262*, Composition of the Orchestra

Density $= (DA)_i = 0.11e^U$, $U = \log_e (DA/0.11)$

s is expressed as the difference between the highest and lowest pitches that can be played on the instrument.

7. *Attribution of a glissando speed if class r is characterized as a glissando.* The homogeneity hypotheses in Chap. **I** led us to the formula

$$f(v) = \frac{2}{a\sqrt{\pi}} e^{-v^2/a^2},$$

and by the transformation $v/a = u$ to its homologue:

$$T(u) = \frac{2}{\sqrt{\pi}} \int_0^u e^{-u^2} \, du,$$

for which there are tables. $f(v)$ is the probability of occurrence of the speed v (which is expressed in semitones/sec.); it has a parameter a, which is proportional to the standard deviation s ($a = s\sqrt{2}$).

a is defined as a function of the logarithm of the density of sequence a_i by: an inversely proportional function

$$a = \sqrt{\pi}\left(30 - \frac{20}{R} L[(DA)_i/(V3)]\right),$$

or a directly proportional function

$$a = \sqrt{\pi}\left(10 + \frac{20}{R} L[(DA)_i/(V3)]\right),$$

or a function independent of density

$$a = 17.7 + 35k,$$

where k is a random number between 0 and 1.

The constants of the preceding formulae derive from the limits of the speeds that string glissandi may take.

Thus for $(DA)_i = 145$ sounds/sec.

$$a = 53.2 \text{ semitones/sec.}$$
$$2s = 75 \quad \text{semitones/sec.,}$$

and for $(DA)_i = 0.13$ sounds/sec.

$$a = 17.7 \text{ semitones/sec.}$$
$$2s = 25 \quad \text{semitones/sec.}$$

8. *Attribution of a duration x to the sounds emitted.* To simplify we establish a mean duration for each instrument, which is independent of tessitura and

nuance. Consequently we reserve the right to modify it when transcribing into traditional notation. The following is the list of constraints that we take into account for the establishment of duration x:

G, the maximum length of respiration
or desired duration
$(DA)_i$, the density of the sequence
q_r, the probability of class r
p_n, the probability of the instrument n

Then if we define z as a parameter of a sound's duration, z could be inversely proportional to the probability of the occurrence of the instrument, so that

$$z = \frac{1}{(DA)_i p_n q_r}.$$

z will be at its maximum when $(DA)_i p_n q_r$ is at its minimum, and in this case we could choose $z_{max} = G$.

Instead of letting $z_{max} = G$, we shall establish a logarithmic law so as to freeze the growth of z. This law applies for any given value of z.

$$z' = G \ln z / \ln z_{max}$$

Since we admit a total independence, the distribution of the durations x will be Gaussian:

$$f(x) = \frac{1}{s\sqrt{2\pi}} e^{-(x-m)^2/2s^2},$$

where m is the arithmetic mean of the durations, s the standard deviation, and

$$m - 4.25s = 0$$

$$m + 4.25s = z'$$

the linear system which furnishes us with the constants m and s. By assuming $u = (x - m)/s\sqrt{2}$ we find the function $T(u)$, for which we consult the tables.

Finally, the duration x of the sound will be given by the relation

$$x = \pm us\sqrt{2} + m.$$

We do not take into account incompatibilities between instruments, for this would needlessly burden the machine's program and calculation.

9. *Attribution of dynamic forms to the sounds emitted.* We define four zones of mean intensities: ppp, p, f, ff. Taken three at a time they yield $4^3 = 64$

permutations, of which 44 are different (an urn with 44 colors); for example,
$ppp \mathord{<} f \mathord{>} p$.

10. *The same operations are begun again for each sound of the cluster N_{a_i}.*

11. *Recalculations of the same sort are made for the other sequences.*

An extract from the sequential statement was reproduced in Fig. V–1.
Now we must proceed to the transcription into Fortran IV, a language
"understood" by the machine (see Fig. V–3).

It is not our purpose to describe the transformation of the flow chart
into Fortran. However, it would be interesting to show an example of the
adaptation of a mathematical expression to machine methods.

Let us consider the elementary law of probability (density function)

$$f(x)\, dx = ce^{-cx}\, dx. \tag{20}$$

How shall we proceed in order for the computer to give us lengths x with
the probability $f(x)\, dx$? The machine can only draw random numbers y_0
with equiprobability between 0 and 1. We shall "modulate" this probability: Assume some length x_0; then we have

$$\text{prob. } (0 \le x \le x_0) = \int_0^{x_0} f(x)\, dx = 1 - e^{-cx_0} = F(x_0),$$

where $F(x_0)$ is the distribution function of x. But

$$F(x_0) = \text{prob. } (0 \le y \le y_0) = y_0$$

then

$$1 - e^{-cx_0} = y_0$$

and

$$x_0 = -\frac{\ln(1 - y_0)}{c}$$

for all $x_0 \ge 0$.

Once the program is transcribed into language that the machine's
internal organization can assimilate, a process that can take several months,
we can proceed to punching the cards and setting up certain tests. Short
sections are run on the machine to detect errors of logic and orthography
and to determine the values of the entry parameters, which are introduced
in the form of variables. This is a very important phase, for it permits us to
explore all parts of the program and determine the modalities of its operation. The final phase is the decoding of the results into traditional notation,
unless an automatic transcriber is available.

Table of the 44 Intensity Forms Derived from 4 Mean Intensity
Values, ppp, p, f, ff

Conclusions

A large number of compositions of the same kind as *ST/10-1, 080262* is possible for a large number of orchestral combinations. Other works have already been written: *ST/48-1, 240162*, for large orchestra, commissioned by RTF (France III); *Atrées* for ten soloists; and *Morisma-Amorisima*, for four soloists.

Although this program gives a satisfactory solution to the minimal structure, it is, however, necessary to jump to the stage of pure composition by coupling a digital-to-analogue converter to the computer. The numerical calculations would then be changed into sound, whose internal organization had been conceived beforehand. At this point one could bring to fruition and generalize the concepts described in the preceding chapters.

The following are several of the advantages of using electronic computers in musical composition:

1. The long laborious calculation made by hand is reduced to nothing. The speed of a machine such as the IBM-7090 is tremendous—of the order of 500,000 elementary operations/sec.

2. Freed from tedious calculations the composer is able to devote himself to the general problems that the new musical form poses and to explore the nooks and crannies of this form while modifying the values of the input data. For example, he may test all instrumental combinations from soloists to chamber orchestras, to large orchestras. With the aid of electronic computers the composer becomes a sort of pilot: he presses the buttons, introduces coordinates, and supervises the controls of a cosmic vessel sailing in the space of sound, across sonic constellations and galaxies that he could formerly glimpse only as a distant dream. Now he can explore them at his ease, seated in an armchair.

3. The program, i.e., the list of sequential operations that constitute the new musical form, is an objective manifestation of this form. The program may consequently be dispatched to any point on the earth that possesses computers of the appropriate type, and may be exploited by any composer pilot.

4. Because of certain uncertainties introduced in the program, the composer-pilot can instill his own personality in the sonic result he obtains.

Fig. V–3. Stochastic Music Rewritten in Fortran IV

```
C      PROGRAM FREE STOCHASTIC MUSIC   (FORTRAN IV)                    XEN    6
C                                                                      XEN    7
C      GLOSSARY OF THE PRINCIPAL ABBREVIATIONS                         XEN    8
C                                                                      XEN
C      A - DURATION OF EACH SEQUENCE IN SECONDS                        XEN    9
C      A10,A20,A17,A35,A30 - NUMBERS FOR GLISSANDO CALCULATION         XEN   10
C      ALEA - PARAMETER USED TO ALTER THE RESULT OF A SECOND RUN WITH THEXEN 11
C      SAME INPUT DATA                                                 XEN   12
C      ALFA(3) - THREE EXPRESSIONS ENTERING INTO THE THREE SPEED VALUES XEN  13
C      OF THE SLIDING TONES ( GLISSANDI )                              XEN   14
C      ALIM - MAXIMUM LIMIT OF SEQUENCE DURATION A                     XEN   15
C      (AMAX(I),I=1,KTR) TABLE OF AN EXPRESSION ENTERING INTO THE       XEN   16
C      CALCULATION OF THE NOTE LENGTH IN PART 8                        XEN   17
C      BF - DYNAMIC FORM NUMBER. THE LIST IS ESTABLISHED INDEPENDENTLY XEN   18
C      OF THIS PROGRAM AND IS SUBJECT TO MODIFICATION                  XEN   19
C      DELTA - THE RECIPROCAL OF THE MEAN DENSITY OF SOUND EVENTS DURING XEN 20
C      A SEQUENCE OF DURATION A                                        XEN   21
C      (E(I,J),I=1,KTR,J=1,KTE) - PROBABILITIES OF THE KTR TIMBRE CLASSESXEN 22
C      INTRODUCED AS INPUT DATA. DEPENDING ON THE CLASS NUMBER I=KR AND XEN  23
C      ON THE POWER J=U OBTAINED FROM V3*EXPF(U)=DA                     XEN   24
C      EPSI - EPSILON FOR ACCURACY IN CALCULATING PN AND E(I,J),WHICH   XEN   25
C      IT IS ADVISABLE TO RETAIN.                                      XEN   26
C      (GN(I,J),I=1,KTR,J=1,KTS) - TABLE OF THE GIVEN LENGTH OF BREATH  XEN   27
C      FOR EACH INSTRUMENT. DEPENDING ON CLASS I AND INSTRUMENT J      XEN   28
C      GTNA - GREATEST NUMBER OF NOTES IN THE SEQUENCE OF DURATION A   XEN   29
C      GTNS - GREATEST NUMBER OF NOTES IN KW LOOPS                     XEN   30
C      (HAMIN(I,J),HAMAX(I,J),HBMIN(I,J),HBMAX(I,J),I=1,KTR,J=1,KTS)    XEN   31
C      TABLE OF INSTRUMENT COMPASS LIMITS. DEPENDING ON TIMBRE CLASS I XEN   32
C      AND INSTRUMENT J.   TEST INSTRUCTION 480 IN PART 6 DETERMINES   XEN   33
C      WHETHER THE HA OR THE HB TABLE IS FOLLOWED. THE NUMBER 7 IS     XEN   34
C      ARBITRARY.                                                      XEN   35
C      JW - ORDINAL NUMBER OF THE SEQUENCE COMPUTED.                   XEN   36
C      KNL - NUMBER OF LINES PER PAGE OF THE PRINTED RESULT.KNL=50     XEN   37
C      KR1 - NUMBER IN THE CLASS KR=1 USED FOR PERCUSSION OR INSTRUMENTS XEN 38
C      WITHOUT A DEFINITE PITCH.                                       XEN   39
C      KTE - POWER OF THE EXPONENTIAL COEFFICIENT E SUCH THAT          XEN   40
C      DA(MAX)=V3*(E**(KTE-1))                                         XEN   41
C      KTR - NUMBER OF TIMBRE CLASSES                                  XEN   42
C      KW - MAXIMUM NUMBER OF JW                                       XEN   43
C      KTEST1,TAV1,ETC - EXPRESSIONS USEFUL IN CALCULATING HOW LONG THE XEN  44
C      VARIOUS PARTS OF THE PROGRAM WILL RUN.                          XEN   45
C      KT1 - ZERO IF THE PROGRAM IS BEING RUN. NONZERO DURING DEBUGGING XEN  46
C      KT2 - NUMBER OF LOOPS, EQUAL TO 15 BY ARBITRARY DEFINITION.     XEN   47
C      (MODI(IX8),IX8=7,1)   AUXILIARY FUNCTION TO INTERPOLATE VALUES IN XEN 48
C      THE TETA(256) TABLE (SEE PART 7)                                XEN   49
C      NA - NUMBER OF SOUNDS CALCULATED FOR THE SEQUENCE A(NA=DA*A)    XEN   50
C      (NT(I),I=1,KTR) NUMBER OF INSTRUMENTS ALLOCATED TO EACH OF THE   XEN   51
C      KTR TIMBRE CLASSES.                                             XEN   52
C      (PN(I,J),I=1,KTR,J=1,KTS),(KTS=NT(I),I=1,KTR) TABLE OF PROBABILITYXEN 53
C      OF EACH INSTRUMENT OF THE CLASS I.                              XEN   54
C      (Q(I),I=1,KTR) PROBABILITIES OF THE KTR TIMBRE CLASSES, CONSIDEREDXEN 55
C      AS LINEAR FUNCTIONS OF THE DENSITY DA.                          XEN   56
C      (S(I),I=1,KTR) SUM OF THE SUCCESSIVE Q(I) PROBABILITIES. USED TO XEN  57
C      CHOOSE THE CLASS KR BY COMPARING IT TO A RANDOM NUMBER X1 (SEE   XEN   58
C      PART 3, LOOP 380 AND PART 5, LOOP 430).                        XEN   59
C      SINA - SUM OF THE COMPUTED NOTES IN THE JW CLOUDS NA. ALWAYS LESS XEN 60
C      THAN GTNS ( SEE TEST IN PART 10 ).                             XEN   61
C      SQPI - SQUARE ROOT OF PI ( 3.14159... )                        XEN   62
C      TA - SOUND ATTACK TIME ABCISSA.                                XEN   63
C      TETA(256) - TABLE OF THE 256 VALUES OF THE INTEGRAL OF THE NORMAL XEN 64
C      DISTRIBUTION CURVE WHICH IS USEFUL IN CALCULATING GLISSANDO SPEED XEN 65
```

```
C      AND SOUND EVENT DURATION.                                   XEN  66
C      VIGL - GLISSANDO SPEED (VITESSE GLISSANDO), WHICH CAN VARY AS, BE XEN  67
C      INDEPENDENT OF, OR VARY INVERSELY AS THE DENSITY OF THE SEQUENCE, XEN  68
C      THE ACTUAL MODE OF VARIATION EMPLOYED REMAINING THE SAME FOR THE  XEN  69
C      ENTIRE SEQUENCE (SEE PART 7).                               XEN  70
C      VITLIM - MAXIMUM LIMITING GLISSANDO SPEED (IN SEMITONES/SEC), XEN  71
C      SUBJECT TO MODIFICATION.                                    XEN  72
C      V3 - MINIMUM CLOUD DENSITY DA                               XEN  73
C      (Z1(I),Z2(I),I=1,8) TABLE COMPLEMENTARY TO THE TETA TABLE.  XEN  74
C                                                                  XEN  75
C                                                                  XEN  76
C      READ CONSTANTS AND TABLES                                   XEN  78
C                                                                  XEN  77
       DIMENSION Q(12),S(12),E(12,12),PN(12,50),SPN(12,50),NT(12), XEN  79
      *HAMIN(12,50),HAMAX(12,50),HBMIN(12,50),HBMAX(12,50),GN(12,50),H(12XEN  80
      *,50),TETA(256),VIGL(3),MODI(7),Z1(8),Z2(8),ALFA(3),AMAX(12) XEN  81
C                                                                  XEN  82
C                                                                  XEN  83
C                                                                  XEN  84
       I=1                                                         XEN  85
       DO 10 IX=1,7                                                XEN  86
       IX8=8-IX                                                    XEN  87
       MODI(IX8)=I                                                 XEN  88
   10  I=I+I                                                       XEN  89
C                                                                  XEN  90
       READ 20,(TETA(I),I=1,256)                                   XEN  91
   20  FORMAT(12F6.6)                                              XEN  92
       READ 30,(Z1(I),Z2(I),I=1,8)                                 XEN  93
   30  FORMAT(6(F3.2,F9.8)/F3.2,F9.8,E6.2,F9.8)                    XEN  94
       PRINT 40,TETA,Z1,Z2                                         XEN  95
   40  FORMAT(*1   THE TETA TABLE = *,/,21(12F10.6,/),4F10.6,/////, XEN  96
      ** THE Z1 TABLE = *,/,7F6.2,E12.3,///,* THE Z2 TABLE = *,/,8F14.8,/XEN  97
      *,1H1)                                                       XEN  98
       READ 50,DELTA,V3,A10,A20,A17,A30,A35,BF,SQPI,EPSI,VITLIM,ALEA, AXEN  99
      *LIM                                                         XEN 100
   50  FORMAT(F3.0,F3.3,5F3.1,F2.0,F8.7,F8.8,F4.2,F8.8,F5.2)       XEN 114
       READ 60,KT1,KT2,KW,KNL,KTR,KTE,KR1,GTNA,GTNS,(NT(I),I=1,KTR) XEN 115
   60  FORMAT(5I3,2I2,2F6.0,12I2)                                  XEN 126
       PRINT 70,DELTA,V3,A10,A20,A17,A30,A35,BF,SQPI,EPSI,VITLIM,ALEA, AXEN 127
      *LIM,KT1,KT2,KW,KNL,KTR,KTE,KR1,GTNA,GTNS,((I,NT(I)),I=1,KTR) XEN 128
   70  FORMAT(*1DELTA = *,F4.0,/,* V3 = *,F6.3,/,* A10 = *,F4.1,/, XEN 129
      ** A20 = *,F4.1,/,* A17 = *,F4.1,/,* A30 = *,F4.1,/,* A35 = *,F4.1,XEN 130
      */,* BF = *,F3.0,/,* SQPI =*,F11.8,/,* EPSI =*,F12.8,/,* VITLIM = *XEN 131
      *,F5.2,/,* ALEA =*,F12.8,/,* ALIM = *,F6.2,/,* KT1 = *,I3,/, XEN 132
      ** KT2 = *,I3,/,* KW = *,I3,/,* KNL = *,I3,/,* KTR = *,I3,/, XEN 133
      ** KTE = *,I2,/,* KR1 = *,I2,/,* GTNA = *,F7.0,/,* GTNS = *,F7.0, XEN 134
      */,12(* IN CLASS *,I2,*, THERE ARE *,I2,* INSTRUMENTS.*,/)) XEN 135
       READ 80,KTEST3,KTEST1,KTEST2                                XEN 136
   80  FORMAT(5I3)                                                 XEN 141
       PRINT 90,KTEST3,KTEST1,KTEST2                               XEN 142
   90  FORMAT(* KTEST3 = *,I3,/,* KTEST1 = *,I3,/,* KTEST2 = *,I3) XEN 143
C                                                                  XEN 144
       IF(KTEST3.NE.0) PRINT 830                                   XEN 145
       R=KTE-1                                                     XEN 146
       A10=A10*SQPI                                                XEN 147
       A20=A20*SQPI/R                                              XEN 148
       A30=A30*SQPI                                                XEN 149
C      IF ALEA IS NON-ZERO,THE RANDOM NUMBER IS GENERATED FROM THE TIME XEN 150
C      WHEN THE FOLLOWING INSTRUCTION IS EXECUTED. IF ALEA IS NON-ZERO XEN 151
C      EACH RUN OF THIS PROGRAM WILL PRODUCE DIFFERENT OUTPUT DATA. XEN 152
       IF(ALEA.NE.0.0) CALL RANFSET(TIMEF(1))                      XEN 153
```

```
      PRINT 830                                                    XEN   154
      DO 130 I=1,KTR                                               XEN   155
      Y=0.0                                                        XEN   156
      KTS=NT(I)                                                    XEN   157
      READ 100,(HAMIN(I,J),HAMAX(I,J),HBMIN(I,J),HBMAX(I,J),GN(I,J), XEN 158
     *PN(I,J),J=1,KTS)                                             XEN   159
  100 FORMAT(5(5F2.0,F3.3))                                        XEN   160
      PRINT 110,I,(J,HAMIN(I,J),HAMAX(I,J),HBMIN(I,J),HBMAX(I,J),GN(I,J) XEN 161
     *,PN(I,J),J=1,KTS)                                            XEN   162
  110 FORMAT(/////,* IN CLASS NUMBER *,I2,(/,* FOR INSTRUMENT NO. *,I2, XEN 163
     ** HAMIN = *,F3.0,*,HAMAX = *,F3.0,*,HBMIN = *,F3.0,*,HBMAX = *, XEN 164
     * F3.0,*,GN = *,F3.0,*, AND PN = *,F6.3))                     XEN   165
      DO 120 J=1,KTS                                               XEN   166
      Y=Y+PN(I,J)                                                  XEN   167
  120 SPN(I,J)=Y                                                   XEN   168
  130 IF (ABSF(Y-1.0).GE.EPSI) CALL EXIT                           XEN   169
C                                                                  XEN   170
      DO 150 I=1,KTR                                               XEN   171
      READ 140,(E(I,J),J=1,KTE)                                    XEN   172
  140 FORMAT(12F2.2)                                               XEN   173
  150 PRINT 160,I,(J,E(I,J),J=1,KTE)                               XEN   174
  160 FORMAT(//////,* CLASS NUMBER *,I2,/,(* IN DENSITY LEVEL *,I2, XEN   175
     ** HAS A PROBABILITY OF *,F6.2,/))                            XEN   176
      DO 180 J=1,KTE                                               XEN   177
      Y=0.0                                                        XEN   178
      DO 170 I=1,KTR                                               XEN   179
  170 Y=Y+E(I,J)                                                   XEN   180
  180 IF (ABSF(Y-1.0).GE.EPSI) CALL EXIT                           XEN   181
      DO 200 I=1,KTR                                               XEN   182
      AMAX(I)=1.0/E(I,1)                                           XEN   183
      DO 200 J=2,KTE                                               XEN   184
      AJ=J-1                                                       XEN   185
      AX=1.0/(E(I,J)*EXPF(AJ))                                     XEN   186
      IF (KT1.NE.0) PRINT 190,AX                                   XEN   187
  190 FORMAT(1H ,9E12.8)                                           XEN   188
  200 IF (AX.GT.AMAX(I)) AMAX(I)=AX                                XEN   189
      IF (KT1.NE.0) PRINT 210,AMAX                                 XEN   190
  210 FORMAT( 1H ,9E12.8)                                          XEN   191
C                                                                  XEN   192
      JW=1                                                         XEN   193
      SINA=0.0                                                     XEN   194
      IF (KTEST1.NE.0) TAV1=TIMEF(1)                               XEN   195
  220 NLINE=50                                                     XEN   196
C                                                                  XEN   197
C     PARTS 1 AND 2, DEFINE SEQUENCE A SECONDS AND CLOUD NA DURING A XEN  198
C                                                                  XEN   199
      KNA=0                                                        XEN   200
      K1=0                                                         XEN   201
  230 X1=RANF(-1)                                                  XEN   202
      A=-DELTA * LOGF(X1)                                          XEN   203
      IF(A.LE.ALIM) GO TO 250                                      XEN   204
      IF (K1.GE.KT2) GO TO 240                                     XEN   205
      K1=K1+1                                                      XEN   206
      GO TO 230                                                    XEN   207
  240 A=ALIM/2.0                                                   XEN   208
      X1=0.0                                                       XEN   209
  250 K2=0                                                         XEN   210
  260 X2=RANF(-1)                                                  XEN   211
      IF (JW.GT.1) GO TO 280                                       XEN   212
  270 UX=R*X2                                                      XEN   213
      GO TO 310                                                    XEN   214
```

```
 280  IF (RANF(-1).GE.0.5) GO TO 290                            XEN  215
      UX=UPR + R * (1.0-SQRTF(X2))                              XEN  216
      GO TO 300                                                 XEN  217
 290  UX=UPR - R * ( 1.0-SQRTF(X2))                             XEN  218
 300  IF ((UX.GE.0.0).AND.(UX.LE.R)) GO TO 310                  XEN  219
      IF (K2.GE.KT2) GO TO 270                                  XEN  220
      K2=K2+1                                                   XEN  221
      GO TO 260                                                 XEN  222
 310  U=UX                                                      XEN  223
      DA=V3 * EXPF(U)                                           XEN  224
      NA=XINTF(A * DA + 0.5) + 1                                XEN  225
      IF (GTNA.GT.FLOATF(NA)) GO TO 330                         XEN  226
      IF (KNA.GE.KT2) GO TO 320                                 XEN  227
      KNA=KNA+1                                                 XEN  228
      GO TO 230                                                 XEN  229
 320  A=DELTA                                                   XEN  230
      GO TO 260                                                 XEN  231
 330  UPR=U                                                     XEN  232
      IF (KT1.EQ.0)   GO TO 360                                 XEN  233
      PRINT 340,JW,KNA,K1,K2,X1,X2,A,DA,NA                      XEN  234
 340  FORMAT(1H1,4I8,3X,4E18.8,3X,I8)                           XEN  235
      NA=KT1                                                    XEN  236
      IF (KTEST3.NE.0) PRINT 350,JW,NA,A                        XEN  237
 350  FORMAT(1H0,2I9,F10.2)                                     XEN  238
C                                                               XEN  239
C     PART 3. DEFINE CONSTITUTION OF ORCHESTRA DURING SEQUENCE A XEN 240
C                                                               XEN  241
 360  SINA=SINA + FLOATF(NA)                                    XEN  242
      XLOGDA=U                                                  XEN  243
      XALOG=A20 *XLOGDA                                         XEN  244
      M=XINTF(XLOGDA)                                           XEN  245
      IF ((M+2).GT.KTE) M=KTE-2                                 XEN  246
      SR=0.0                                                    XEN  247
      M1=M+1                                                    XEN  248
      M2=M+2                                                    XEN  249
      DO 380 I=1,KTR                                            XEN  250
      ALFX=E(I,M1)                                              XEN  251
      BETA=E(I,M2)                                              XEN  252
      XM=M                                                      XEN  253
      QR=(XLOGDA-XM) * (BETA-ALFX) + ALFX                       XEN  254
      IF (KT1.NE.0) PRINT 370,XM,ALFX,BETA                      XEN  255
 370  FORMAT(1H ,3F20.8)                                        XEN  256
      Q(I)=QR                                                   XEN  257
      SR=SR+QR                                                  XEN  258
 380  S(I)=SR                                                   XEN  259
      IF (KT1.NE.0) PRINT 390,(Q(I),I=1,KTR),(S(I),I=1,KTR)     XEN  260
 390  FORMAT(1H ,12F9.4)                                        XEN  261
C                                                               XEN  262
C     PART 4.DEFINE INSTANT TA OF EACH POINT IN SEQUENCE A      XEN  263
C                                                               XEN  264
      IF (KTEST2.NE.0) TAV2=TIMEF(1)                            XEN  265
      N=1                                                       XEN  266
      T=0.0                                                     XEN  267
      TA=0.0                                                    XEN  268
      GO TO 410                                                 XEN  269
 400  N=N+1                                                     XEN  270
      X=RANF(-1)                                                XEN  271
      T=-LOGF(X)/DA                                             XEN  272
      TA=TA+T                                                   XEN  273
 410  IF (KT1.NE.0) PRINT 420,N,X,T,TA                          XEN  274
 420  FORMAT(//,I8,3E20.8)                                      XEN  275
```

```
C                                                                      XEN   276
C        PART 5.DEFINE CLASS AND INSTRUMENT NUMBER TO EACH POINT OF A  XEN   277
C                                                                      XEN   278
         X1=RANF(-1)                                                   XEN   279
         DO 430 I=1,KTR                                                XEN   280
 430  IF (X1.LE.S(I)) GO TO 440                                        XEN   281
         I=KTR                                                         XEN   282
 440  KTS=NT(I)                                                        XEN   283
         KR=I                                                          XEN   284
         X2=RANF(-1)                                                   XEN   285
         DO 450 J=1,KTS                                                XEN   286
         SPIEN=SPN(KR,J)                                               XEN   287
         INSTRM=J                                                      XEN   288
 450  IF (X2.LE.SPIEN) GO TO 460                                       XEN   289
         INSTRM=KTS                                                    XEN   290
 460  PIEN=PN(KR,INSTRM)                                               XEN   291
         IF (KT1.NE.0) PRINT 470,X1,S(KR),KR,X2,SPIEN,INSTRM           XEN   292
 470  FORMAT( 1H ,2E20.8,I6,2E20.8,I6 )                                XEN   293
C                                                                      XEN   294
C        PART 6.DEFINE PITCH HN FOR EACH POINT OF SEQUENCE A           XEN   295
C                                                                      XEN   296
         IF (KR.GT.1) GO TO 480                                        XEN   297
         IF (INSTRM.GE.KR1) GO TO 490                                  XEN   298
         HX=0.0                                                        XEN   299
         GO TO 560                                                     XEN   300
 480  IF (KR.LT.7) GO TO 490                                           XEN   301
         HSUP=HBMAX(KR,INSTRM)                                         XEN   302
         HINF=HBMIN(KR,INSTRM)                                         XEN   303
         GO TO 500                                                     XEN   304
 490  HSUP=HAMAX(KR,INSTRM)                                            XEN   305
         HINF=HAMIN(KR,INSTRM)                                         XEN   306
 500  HM=HSUP-HINF                                                     XEN   307
         HPR=H(KR,INSTRM)                                              XEN   308
         K=0                                                           XEN   309
         IF (HPR.LE.0.0) GO TO 520                                     XEN   310
 510  X=RANF(-1)                                                       XEN   311
         IF (N.GT.1) GO TO 530                                         XEN   312
 520  HX=HINF+HM*X RANF(-1)                                            XEN   313
         GO TO 560                                                     XEN   314
 530  IF (RANF(-1).GE.0.5) GO TO 540                                   XEN   315
         HX=HPR+HM * ( 1.0-SQRTF(X))                                   XEN   316
         GO TO 550                                                     XEN   317
 540  HX=HPR-HM * (1.0-SQRTF(X))                                       XEN   318
 550  IF((HX.GE.HINF).AND.(HX.LE.HSUP)) GO TO 560                      XEN   319
         IF (K.GE.KT2) GO TO 520                                       XEN   320
         K=K+1                                                         XEN   321
         GO TO 510                                                     XEN   322
 560  H(KR,INSTRM)=HX                                                  XEN   323
         IF (KT1.NE.0) PRINT 570,K,X,HX                                XEN   324
 570  FORMAT(1H ,I6,2E20.8)                                            XEN   325
C                                                                      XEN   326
C        PART 7.DEFINE SPEED VIGL TO EACH POINT OF A                   XEN   327
C                                                                      XEN   328
         IF (KR.EQ.5) GO TO 580                                        XEN   329
         VIGL(1)=0.0                                                   XEN   330
         VIGL(2)=0.0                                                   XEN   331
         VIGL(3)=0.0                                                   XEN   332
         X1=0.0                                                        XEN   333
         X2=0.0                                                        XEN   334
         XLAMBDA=0.0                                                   XEN   335
         GO TO 740                                                     XEN   336
```

```
 580  KX=1                                                         XEN  337
 590  X1=RANF(-1)                                                  XEN  338
      IF (X1-0.9997) 600,650,680                                   XEN  339
 600  I=128                                                        XEN  340
      DO 630 IX=1,7                                                XEN  341
      IF(TETA(I)-X1) 610,640,620                                   XEN  342
 610  I=I+MODI(IX)                                                 XEN  343
      GO TO 630                                                    XEN  344
 620  I=I-MODI(IX)                                                 XEN  345
 630  CONTINUE                                                     XEN  346
      IF(TETA(I)-X1) 670,640,660                                   XEN  347
 640  XLAMBDA=FLOATF(I-1)/100.0                                    XEN  348
      GO TO (720,760), KX                                          XEN  349
 650  XLAMBDA=2.55                                                 XEN  350
      GO TO (720,760),KX                                           XEN  351
 660  I=I-1                                                        XEN  352
 670  TX1=TETA(I)                                                  XEN  353
      XLAMBDA=(FLOATF(I-1)+(X1-TX1)/(TETA(I+1)-TX1))/100.0         XEN  354
      GO TO ( 720,760 ), KX                                        XEN  355
 680  DO 690 I=2,7                                                 XEN  356
      TX1=Z2(I)                                                    XEN  357
      IF(X1-TX1) 700,710,690                                       XEN  358
 690  CONTINUE                                                     XEN  359
      I=8                                                          XEN  360
      TX1=1.0                                                      XEN  361
 700  TX2=Z1(I)                                                    XEN  362
      XLAMBDA=TX2-((TX1-X1)/(TX1-Z2(I-1)))*(TX2-Z1(I-1))           XEN  363
      GO TO ( 720,760 ), KX                                        XEN  364
 710  XLAMBDA=Z1(I)                                                XEN  365
      GO TO( 720,760 ), KX                                         XEN  366
 720  ALFA(1)=A10+XALOG                                            XEN  367
      ALFA(3)=A30-XALOG                                            XEN  368
      X2=RANF(-1)                                                  XEN  369
      ALFA(2)=A17+A35*X2                                           XEN  370
      DO 730 I=1,3                                                 XEN  371
      VIGL(I)=INTF(ALFA(I)*XLAMBDA+0.5)                            XEN  372
      IF (VIGL(I).LT.0.0) VIGL(I)=-VIGL(I)                         XEN  373
      IF (VIGL(I).GT.VITLIM) VIGL(I)=VITLIM                        XEN  374
 730  IF (RANF(-1).LT.0.5) VIGL(I)=-VIGL(I)                        XEN  375
 740  IF(KT1.NE.0) PRINT 750,X1,X2,XLAMBDA,VIGL                    XEN  376
 750  FORMAT(1H ,6E19.8)                                           XEN  377
C                                                                  XEN  378
C         PART 8,DEFINE DURATION FOR EACH POINT OF A               XEN  379
C                                                                  XEN  380
      IF ((KR.EQ.7).OR.(KR.EQ.8)) GO TO 780                        XEN  381
      ZMAX=AMAX(KR)/(V3*PIEN)                                      XEN  382
      G=GN(KR,INSTRM)                                              XEN  383
      RO=G/LOGF(ZMAX)                                              XEN  384
      QPNDA=1.0/(Q(KR)*PIEN*DA)                                    XEN  385
      GE=ABSF(RO*LOGF(QPNDA))                                      XEN  386
      XMU=GE/2.0                                                   XEN  387
      SIGMA=GE/4.0                                                 XEN  388
      KX=2                                                         XEN  389
      GO TO 590                                                    XEN  390
 760  TAU=SIGMA*XLAMBDA*1.4142                                     XEN  391
      X2=RANF(-1)                                                  XEN  392
      IF (X2.GE.0.5) GO TO 770                                     XEN  393
      XDUR=XMU+TAU                                                 XEN  394
      GO TO 790                                                    XEN  395
 770  XDUR=XMU-TAU                                                 XEN  396
      IF (XDUR.GE.0.0) GO TO 790                                   XEN  397
```

```
      780 XDUR=0.0                                                        XEN 398
      790 IF(KT1.NE.0)PRINT 800,ZMAX,XMU,SIGMA,X1,XLAMBDA,X2,XDUR        XEN 399
      800 FORMAT(1H ,5E15.8,E11.4,E15.8)                                 XEN 400
C                                                                        XEN 401
C         PART 9.DEFINE INTENSITY FORM TO EACH POINT OF A               XEN 402
C                                                                        XEN 403
          IFORM=XINTF(RANF(-1)*BF+0.5)                                   XEN 404
          IF (KT1.EQ.0) GO TO 840                                       XEN 405
          IF (NLINE.LT.KNL) GO TO 810                                   XEN 406
          IF (NLINE.EQ.KNL) GO TO 820                                   XEN 407
          NLINE=1                                                        XEN 408
          GO TO 900                                                      XEN 409
      810 NLINE=NLINE+1                                                  XEN 410
          GO TO 900                                                      XEN 411
      820 PRINT 830                                                      XEN 412
      830 FORMAT(1H1)                                                    XEN 413
          NLINE=0                                                        XEN 414
          GO TO 900                                                      XEN 415
      840 IF (NLINE.GE.KNL) GO TO 850                                    XEN 416
          NLINE=NLINE+1                                                  XEN 417
          GO TO 880                                                      XEN 418
      850 PRINT 860,JW,A,NA,(Q(I),I=1,KTR)                               XEN 419
      860 FORMAT(*1   JW=*,I3,4X,*A=*,F8.2,4X,*NA=*,I6,4X,*Q(I)=*,12(F4.2,*/*XEN 420
         *),//)                                                          XEN 421
          PRINT 870                                                      XEN 422
      870 FORMAT(6X,*N*,8X,*START*,5X,*CLASS*,4X,*INSTRM*,4X,*PITCH*,6X, XEN 423
         **GLISS1*,4X,*GLISS2*,4X,*GLISS3*,8X,*DURATION*,5X,*DYNAM*)     XEN 424
          NLINE=1                                                        XEN 425
      880 PRINT 890,N,TA,KR,INSTRM,HX,(VIGL(I),I=1,3),XDUR,IFORM         XEN 426
      890 FORMAT(1H ,I7,F12.2,I9,I8,F11.1,F13.1,2F10.1,F14.2,I11)        XEN 427
C                                                                        XEN 428
C         PART 10.REPEAT SAME DEFINITIONS FOR ALL POINTS OF A           XEN 429
C                                                                        XEN 430
      900 IF (N.LT.NA) GO TO 400                                         XEN 431
C                                                                        XEN 432
C         PART 11. REPEAT SEQUENCES A                                   XEN 433
C                                                                        XEN 434
          IF (KTEST2.EQ.0) GO TO 910                                    XEN 435
          TAP2=TIMEF(1)-TAV2                                             XEN 436
          TAP2=TAP2/FLOATF(NA)                                           XEN 437
          PRINT 750,TAP2                                                 XEN 438
C                                                                        XEN 439
      910 IF (JW.GE.KW) GO TO 930                                        XEN 440
      920 JW=JW+1                                                        XEN 441
          IF (GTNS.GT.SINA) GO TO 220                                    XEN 442
      930 IF (KTEST1.EQ.0) CALL EXIT                                     XEN 443
      940 TAP1=TIMEF(-1)-TAV1                                            XEN 444
          TAP1=TAP1/FLOATF(KW)                                           XEN 445
          PRINT 750,TAP1                                                 XEN 446
C                                                                        XEN 447
          END                                                            XEN 448
C
C         DATA FOR ATREES (ST/10-3, 060962)
C
00000001130002260003390004510005640006760007890009010010130011250012 3600
134800145900156900168000179000190000200900211800222700233500244300255000
265700276300286900297400307900318300328600338900349100359300369400379400
389300399200409000418700428400438000447500456900466200475500484700493700
502700511700520500529200537900546500554900563300571600579800587900595900
603900611700619400627000634600642000649400656600663800670800677800684700
691400698100704700711200717500723800730000736100742100748000753800759500
```

765100770700776100781400786700791800796900801900806800811600816300820900
825400829900834200838500842700846800850800854800858600862400866100869800
873300876800880200883500886800890000893100896100899100902000904800907600
910300913000915500918100920500922900925200927500929700931900934000936100
938100940000941900943800945700947300949000950700952300953800955400956900
958300959700961100962400963700964900966100967300968400969500970600971600
972600973600974500975500976300977200978000978800979600980400981100981800
982500983200983800984400985000985600986100986700987200987700988200988600
989100989500989900990300990700991100991500991800992200992500992800993100
993400993700993900994200994400994700994900995100995300995500995700995900
996100996300996400996600996700996900997000997200997300997400997500997600
997700997900997960998050998140998230998320998400998480998550998620998680
998740998880998850998910998960999010999060999100999140999180999230999270
999300999340999370999940009994400999470999950099995309999560999580999600999630
999650999670999690999700
255099970000263099980000275099990000031309999900003460999999003770999999900
406099999999100E30100000000
040050100200177300355631772453901000000071000000000012000
000015050050012072000160002500012010102030902020101010202

010100001007001010000100900101000010120010100001011001010000100900
010100001012001010000100800101000010080010100001012001010000100800
010100001502001010000200200
1755000010999
3975000015999
297100002060017540000104000
348500001540015630000154001953000010200
397500001515029710000100901754000007090175500001009033363000010090
195300001007010130000102003485000015200156300001502000
000034670050000000154800500
000034670050000000154800500
000032681099990
000033631099990
000019531080000000101307200
000034871550000000157215500
25080408011309
08071602010110
03030420010110
02050325010112
03350315011505
02100302103907
02020203150207
02020202410207
03090317041609
03132003200509
02052801030409
45011202020106

JW= 1   A= 9.13   NA= 95
Q(I)=0.12/0.04/0.04/0.05/0.12/0.29/0.04/0.04/0.14/0.06/0.06/0.03/

N	START	CLASS	INSTRM	PITCH	GLISS1	GLISS2	GLISS3	DURATION	DYNAM
1	0.00	7	1	34.0	0.0	0.0	0.0	0.00	3
2	0.10	10	1	43.2	0.0	0.0	0.0	0.41	50
3	0.11	6	8	81.3	0.0	0.0	0.0	0.63	21
4	0.13	6	3	47.0	0.0	0.0	0.0	0.18	10
5	0.18	1	4	0.0	0.0	0.0	0.0	1.90	29
6	0.25	9	1	48.7	0.0	0.0	0.0	0.51	35
7	0.33	6	7	11.4	0.0	0.0	0.0	0.37	42
8	0.34	9	1	38.1	0.0	0.0	0.0	0.00	59
9	0.40	1	1	0.0	0.0	0.0	0.0	2.20	45
10	0.41	6	9	55.0	0.0	0.0	0.0	1.07	0
11	0.76	6	7	11.5	0.0	0.0	0.0	0.40	7
12	0.90	8	2	23.2	0.0	0.0	0.0	0.00	19
13	1.00	7	2	26.9	0.0	0.0	0.0	0.00	6
14	1.09	10	1	46.2	0.0	0.0	0.0	0.32	57
15	1.09	6	2	68.5	0.0	0.0	0.0	0.71	25
16	1.23	6	3	46.9	0.0	0.0	0.0	0.64	32
17	1.42	6	1	44.0	0.0	0.0	0.0	0.44	1
18	1.57	10	1	36.2	0.0	0.0	0.0	0.22	21
19	1.65	4	2	32.5	0.0	0.0	0.0	1.09	13
20	1.78	6	8	72.6	0.0	0.0	0.0	0.06	60
21	1.92	6	3	38.9	0.0	0.0	0.0	0.55	60
22	1.94	5	1	74.6	71.0	-25.0	-71.0	0.80	62
23	2.18	4	1	32.6	0.0	0.0	0.0	1.50	50
24	2.18	6	6	50.9	0.0	0.0	0.0	0.60	26
25	2.19	1	12	0.0	0.0	0.0	0.0	4.58	24
26	2.20	9	1	49.3	0.0	0.0	0.0	0.02	58
27	2.23	9	1	51.0	0.0	0.0	0.0	0.22	13
28	2.32	7	1	36.9	0.0	0.0	0.0	0.00	43
29	2.33	4	1	31.8	0.0	0.0	0.0	1.38	56
30	2.54	1	6	0.0	0.0	0.0	0.0	0.28	14
31	2.57	11	2	12.2	0.0	0.0	0.0	1.69	40
32	2.71	9	1	48.5	0.0	0.0	0.0	0.37	55
33	2.80	1	5	0.0	0.0	0.0	0.0	1.50	58
34	3.28	5	2	15.4	49.0	5.0	-31.0	0.52	21
35	3.33	1	7	0.0	0.0	0.0	0.0	1.38	8
36	3.38	5	2	47.3	-71.0	-17.0	46.0	1.05	4
37	3.55	10	1	37.6	0.0	0.0	0.0	0.14	24
38	3.56	1	9	0.0	0.0	0.0	0.0	1.30	0
39	3.60	9	1	64.3	0.0	0.0	0.0	0.19	13
40	3.64	12	2	52.2	0.0	0.0	0.0	3.72	9
41	3.65	6	5	59.0	0.0	0.0	0.0	0.83	28
42	3.71	5	3	38.8	25.0	2.0	-15.0	0.00	11
43	3.80	6	8	75.6	0.0	0.0	0.0	0.43	17
44	3.87	6	2	51.5	0.0	0.0	0.0	0.77	57
45	3.89	6	7	12.1	0.0	0.0	0.0	0.39	2
46	4.15	5	2	43.0	-71.0	24.0	71.0	1.16	2
47	4.15	5	1	80.3	36.0	4.0	22.0	0.85	50
48	4.25	9	1	59.9	0.0	0.0	0.0	0.10	10
49	4.31	12	2	40.1	0.0	0.0	0.0	2.49	33
50	4.33	1	10	0.0	0.0	0.0	0.0	0.46	34

Fig. V–4. Provisional Results of One Phase of the Analysis

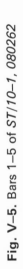

Fig. V-5. Bars 1–5 of *ST/10–1, 080262*

Chapter VI

Symbolic Music

Here we shall attack the thorny problem of the logic underlying musical composition. Logic, that queen of knowledge, monopolized by mathematics, wavers between her own name, borne through two millennia, and the name of algebra.

Let us leave the task of logically connecting the preceding chapters for the moment. We shall confine ourselves to following a path which may lead us to regions even more harmonious in the not too distant future.

A LOGICAL AND ALGEBRAIC SKETCH OF MUSICAL COMPOSITION

In this chapter we shall begin by imagining that we are suffering from a sudden amnesia. We shall thus be able to reascend to the fountain-head of the mental operations used in composition and attempt to extricate the general principles that are valid for all sorts of music. We shall not make a psycho-physiological study of perception, but shall simply try to understand more clearly the phenomenon of hearing and the thought-processes involved when listening to music. In this way we hope to forge a tool for the better comprehension of the works of the past and for the construction of new music. We shall therefore be obliged to collect, cut up, and solder scattered as well as organized entities and conceptions, while unraveling the thin thread of a logic, which will certainly present lacunae, but which will at least have the merit of existing.

CASE OF A SINGLE GENERIC ELEMENT

Let there be a sonic event which is not endless. It is seen as a whole, as an entity, and this overall perception is sufficient for the moment. Because of our amnesia, we decide that it is neuter—neither pleasant nor unpleasant.

Postulate. We shall systematically refuse a qualitative judgment on every sonic event. What will count will be the abstract relations within the event or between several events, and the logical operations which may be imposed on them. The emission of the sonic event is thus a kind of statement, inscription, or sonic symbol, which may be notated graphically by the letter *a*.

If it is emitted once it means nothing more than a single existence which appears and then disappears; we simply have *a*.

If it is emitted several times in succession, the events are compared and we conclude that they are *identical*, and no more. Identity and tautology are therefore implied by a repetition. But simultaneously another phenomenon, subjacent to the first, is created by reason of this very repetition: *modulation of time.* If the event were a Morse sound, the temporal abscissa would take a meaning external to the sound and independent of it. In addition to the deduction of tautology, then, repetition causes the appearance of a new phenomenon, which is inscribed in time and which modulates time.

To summarize: If no account is taken of the temporal element, then a single sonic event signifies only its statement. The sign, the symbol, the generic element *a* have been stated. A sonic event actually or mentally repeated signifies only an identity, a tautology:

$$a \lor a \lor a \lor a \cdots \lor a = a.$$

$\lor$ is an operator that means "put side by side without regard to time." The $=$ sign means that it is the same thing. This is all that can be done with a single sonic event.

CASE OF TWO OR MORE GENERIC ELEMENTS

Let there be two sonic events *a* and *b* such that *a* is not identical with *b*, and such that the two are distinct and easily recognizable, like the letters *a* and *b*, for example, which are only confused by a near-sighted person or when they are poorly written.

If no account is taken of the temporal element, then the two elements are considered as a pair. Consequently emitting first *a* then *b*, or first *b* then *a*, gives us no more information about these distinct events than when they are heard in isolation after long intervals of silence. And since no account is taken of the relation of similitude or of the time factor, we can write for $a \neq b$

$$a \vee b = b \vee a,$$

which means that a and b side by side do not create a new thing, having the same meaning as before. Therefore a commutative law exists.

In the case of three distinguishable events, a, b, c, a combination of two of these sonic symbols may be considered as forming another element, an entity in relation to the third:

$$(a \vee b) \vee c.$$

But since this associational operation produces nothing more we may write

$$(a \vee b) \vee c = a \vee (b \vee c).$$

This is an associative law.

The exclusion of the time factor leads therefore to two rules of composition outside-time—the commutative and the associative. (These two rules are extensible to the case of a single event.)

On the other hand, when the manifestations of the generic events a, b, c are considered in time, then commutativity may no longer be accepted. Thus

$$a \top b \neq b \top a,$$

$\top$ being the symbol of the law of composition which means "anterior to."

This asymmetry is the result of our traditional experience, of our customary one-to-one correspondence between events and time instants. It is raised when we consider time by itself without events, and the consequent metric time which admits *both* the commutative *and* the associative properties:

$$a \top b = b \top a \qquad \text{commutative law}$$
$$(a \top b) \top c = a \top (b \top c) \qquad \text{associative law.}$$

CONCEPT OF DISTANCE (INTERVAL)

The consideration of generic elements a, b, c, ... as entities does not permit much of an advance. To exploit and clarify what has just been said, we must penetrate the internal organization of the sonic symbols.

Every sonic event is perceived as a set of qualities that is modified during its life. On a primary level we perceive pitch, duration, timbre, attack, rugosity, etc. On another level we may distinguish complexities, degrees of order, variabilities, densities, homogeneities, fluctuations, thicknesses, etc. Our study will not attempt to elucidate these questions, which are not only difficult but at this moment secondary. They are also secondary because many of the qualities may be graduated, even if only broadly, and may be totally ordered. We shall therefore choose one quality and what will be said about it will be extensible to others.

Let us, then, consider a series of events discernible solely by pitch, such as is perceived by an observer who has lost his memory. Two elements, a, b, are not enough for him to create the notion of distance or interval. We must look for a third term, c, in order that the observer may, by successive comparisons and through his immediate sensations, form first, the concept of relative size (b compared to a and c), which is a primary expression of ranking; and then the notion of distance, of interval. This mental toil will end in the totally ordered classification not only of pitches, but also of melodic intervals. Given the set of pitch intervals

$$H = (h_a, h_b, h_c, \ldots)$$

and the binary relation S (greater than or equal to), we have

1. hSh for all $h \in H$, hence reflexivity;
2. $h_aSh_b \neq h_bSh_a$ except for $h_a = h_b$, hence antisymmetry;
3. h_aSh_b and h_bSh_c entail h_aSh_c, hence transitivity.

Thus the different aspects of the sensations produced by sonic events may eventually totally or partially constitute ordered sets according to the unit interval adopted. For example, if we adopted as the unit interval of pitch, not the relationship of the semitone ($\triangleq 1.059$) but a relationship of 1.00001, then the sets of pitches and intervals would be very vague and would not be totally ordered because the *differential sensitivity* of the human ear is inferior to this relationship. Generally for a sufficiently large unit distance, many of the qualities of sonic events can be totally ordered.

To conform with a first-degree acoustic experience, we shall suppose that the ultimate aspects of sonic events are frequency[1] (experienced as pitch), intensity, and duration, and that every sonic event may be constructed from these three when duly interwoven. In this case the number three is irreducible. For other assumptions on the microstructure of sonic events see the Preface and Chapter IX.

Structure of the Qualities of Sonic Events*

From a naive musical practice we have defined the concept of interval or distance. Now let us examine sets of intervals which are in fact isomorphic to the equivalence classes of the $N \times N$ product set of natural numbers.

1. Let there be a set H of pitch intervals (melodic). The law of internal composition states that to every couple $(h_a, h_b \in H)$ a third element may be made to correspond. This is the composite of h_a by h_b, which we shall notate $h_a + h_b = h_c$, such that $h_c \in H$. For example, let there be three sounds characterized by the pitches I, II, III, and let $h_{(I,II)}$, $h_{(II,III)}$ be the intervals in semitones separating the couples (I, II) and (II, III), respectively. The interval $h_{(I,III)}$ separating sound I and sound III will be equal to the sum of the semitones of the other two. We may therefore establish that the law of internal composition for conjuncted intervals is *addition*.

2. The law is associative:

$$h_a + (h_b + h_c) = (h_a + h_b) + h_c = h_a + h_b + h_c.$$

3. There exists a neutral element h_0 such that for every $h_a \in H$,

$$h_0 + h_a = h_a + h_0 = h_a.$$

For pitch the neutral element has a name, unison, or the zero interval; for intensity the zero interval is nameless; and for duration it is simultaneity.

4. For every h_a there exists a special element h'_a, called the inverse, such that

$$h'_a + h_a = h_a + h'_a = h_0 = 0.$$

Corresponding to an ascending melodic interval h_a, there may be a descending interval h'_a, which returns to the unison; to an increasing interval of intensity (expressed in positive decibels) may be added another diminishing interval (in negative *db*), such that it cancels the other's effect; corresponding to a positive time interval there may be a negative duration, such that the sum of the two is zero, or simultaneity.

5. The law is commutative:

$$h_a + h_b = h_b + h_a.$$

---

* Following Peano, we may state an axiomatics of pitch and construct the chromatic or whole-tone scale by means of three primary terms—origin, note, and the successor of...—and five primary propositions:

1. the origin is a note;
2. the successor of a note is a note;
3. notes having the same successor are identical;
4. the origin is not the successor of any note; and
5. if a property applies to the origin, and if when it applies to any note it also applies to its successor, then it applies to all notes (principal of induction).

See also Chap. VII, p. 194.

These five axioms have been established for pitch, outside-time. But the examples have extended them to the two other fundamental factors of sonic events, and we may state that the sets H (pitch intervals), G (intensity intervals), and U (durations) are furnished with an *Abelian additive group structure*.

To specify properly the difference and the relationship that exists between the temporal set T and the other sets examined outside-time, and in order not to confuse, for example, set U (durations characterizing a sonic event) with the time intervals chronologically separating sonic events belonging to set T, we shall summarize the successive stages of our comprehension.

SUMMARY

Let there be three events a, b, c emitted successively.
First stage: Three events are distinguished, and that is all.
Second stage: A "temporal succession" is distinguished, i.e., a correspondence between events and moments. There results from this

$$a \text{ before } b \neq b \text{ before } a \qquad \text{(non-commutativity)}.$$

Third stage: Three sonic events are distinguished which divide time into two sections within the events. These two sections may be compared and then expressed in multiples of a unit. Time becomes metric and the sections constitute generic elements of set T. They thus enjoy commutativity.

According to Piaget, the concept of time among children passes through these three phases (see Bibliography for Chapter VI).

Fourth stage: Three sonic events are distinguished; the time intervals are distinguished; and independence between the sonic events and the time intervals is recognized. An *algebra outside-time* is thus admitted for sonic events, and a secondary *temporal algebra* exists for temporal intervals; the two algebras are otherwise identical. (It is useless to repeat the arguments in order to show that the temporal intervals between the events constitute a set T, which is furnished with an Abelian additive group structure.) Finally, one-to-one correspondences are admitted between algebraic functions outside-time and temporal algebraic functions. They may constitute an algebra in-time.

In conclusion, most musical analysis and construction may be based on:
1. the study of an entity, the sonic event, which, according to our temporary assumption groups three characteristics, pitch, intensity, and duration, and which possesses a *structure outside-time*; 2. the study of another simpler entity,

time, which possesses a *temporal structure*; and 3. the correspondence between the structure outside-time and the temporal structure: the *structure in-time*.

Vector Space

Sets H (melodic intervals), G (intensity intervals), U (time intervals), and T (intervals of time separating the sonic events, and independent of them) are totally ordered. We also assume that they may be isomorphic under certain conditions with set R of the real numbers, and that an external law of composition for each of them may be established with set R. For every $a \in E$ (E is any one of the above sets) and for every element $A \in R$, there exists an element $b = Aa$ such that $b \in E$. For another approach to vector space, see the discussion of sets of intervals as a product of a group times a field, Chap. VIII, p. 210.

Let $\bar{X}$ be a sequence of three numbers x_1, x_2, x_3, corresponding to the elements of the sets H, G, U, respectively, and arranged in a certain order: $\bar{X} = (x_1, x_2, x_3)$. This sequence is a vector and x_1, x_2, x_3 are its *components*. The particular case of the vector in which all the components are zero is a zero vector, $\bar{O}$. It may also be called the origin of the coordinates, and by analogy with elementary geometry, the vector with the numbers (x_1, x_2, x_3) as components will be called point M of coordinates (x_1, x_2, x_3). Two points or vectors are said to be equal if they are defined by the same sequence: $x_i = y_i$.

The set of these sequences constitutes a vector space in three dimensions, E_3. There exist two laws of composition relative to E_3: 1. An *internal* law of composition, addition: If $\bar{X} = (x_1, x_2, x_3)$ and $\bar{Y} = (y_1, y_2, y_3)$, then

$$\bar{X} + \bar{Y} = (x_1 + y_1, x_2 + y_2, x_3 + y_3).$$

The following properties are verified: a. $\bar{X} + \bar{Y} = \bar{Y} + \bar{X}$ (commutative); b. $\bar{X} + (\bar{Y} + \bar{Z}) = (\bar{X} + \bar{Y}) + \bar{Z}$ (associative); and c. Given two vectors $\bar{X}$ and $\bar{Y}$, there exists a single vector $\bar{Z} = (z_1, z_2, z_3)$ such that $\bar{X} = \bar{Y} + \bar{Z}$. We have $z_i = x_i - y_i$; $\bar{Z}$ is called the difference of $\bar{X}$ and $\bar{Y}$ and is notated $\bar{Z} = \bar{X} - \bar{Y}$. In particular $\bar{X} + \bar{O} = \bar{O} + \bar{X} = \bar{X}$; and each vector $\bar{X}$ may be associated with the opposite vector $(-\bar{X})$, with components $(-x_1, -x_2, -x_3)$, such that $\bar{X} + (-\bar{X}) = \bar{O}$.

2. An external law of composition, multiplication by a scalar: If $p \in R$ and $\bar{X} \in E$, then

$$p\bar{X} = (px_1, px_2, px_3) \in E_3.$$

The following properties are verified for $(p, q) \in R$: a. $1 \cdot \bar{X} = \bar{X}$; b. $p(q\bar{X}) =$

$(pq)\bar{X}$ (associative); and $c.\ (p + q)\bar{X} = p\bar{X} + q\bar{X}$ and $p(\bar{X} + \bar{Y}) = p\bar{X} + p\bar{Y}$ (distributive).

BASIS AND REFERENT OF A VECTOR SPACE

If it is impossible to find a system of p numbers $a_1, a_2, a_3, \ldots, a_p$ which are not all zero, such that

$$a_1\bar{X}_1 + a_2\bar{X}_2 + \cdots + a_p\bar{X}_p = \bar{O},$$

and on the condition that the p vectors $\bar{X}_1, \bar{X}_2, \ldots, \bar{X}_p$ of the space E_n are not zero, then we shall say that these vectors are *linearly independent*.

Suppose a vector of E_n, of which the ith component is 1, and the others are 0. This vector $\bar{e}_i$ is the ith *unit vector* of E_n. There exist then 3 unit vectors of E_3, for example, $\bar{h}, \bar{g}, \bar{u}$, corresponding to the sets H, G, U, respectively; and these three vectors are linearly independent, for the relation

$$a_1\bar{h} + a_2\bar{g} + a_3\bar{u} = \bar{O}$$

entails $a_1 = a_2 = a_3 = 0$. Moreover, every vector $\bar{X} = (x_1,\ x_2,\ x_3)$ of E may be written

$$\bar{X} = x_1\bar{h} + x_2\bar{g} + x_3\bar{u}.$$

It immediately results from this that there may not exist in E_3 more than 3 linearly independent vectors. The set $\bar{h}, \bar{g}, \bar{u}$, constitutes a *basis* of E. By analogy with elementary geometry, we can say that $\overline{Oh}, \overline{Og}, \overline{Ou}$, are axes of coordinates, and that their set constitutes a *referent* of E_3. In such a space, all the referents have the same origin O.

Linear vectorial multiplicity. We say that a set V of vectors of E_n which is non-empty constitutes a *linear vectorial multiplicity* if it possesses the following properties:

1. If $\bar{X}$ is a vector of V, every vector $p\bar{X}$ belongs also to V whatever the scalar p may be.

2. If $\bar{X}$ and $\bar{Y}$ are two vectors of V, $\bar{X} + \bar{Y}$ also belongs to V. From this we deduce that: *a.* all linear vectorial multiplicity contains the vector $\bar{O}(0 \cdot \bar{X} = \bar{O})$; and *b.* every linear combination $a_1\bar{X}_1 + a_2\bar{X}_2 + \ldots + a_p\bar{X}_p$ of p vectors of V is a vector of V.

REMARKS

1. Every sonic event may be expressed as a vectorial multiplicity.

2. There exists only one base, $\bar{h}, \bar{g}, \bar{u}$. Every other quality of the sounds and every other more complex component should be analyzed as a linear combination of these three unit vectors. The dimension of V is therefore 3.

3. The scalars p, q, may not in practice take all values, for we would then move out of the audible area. But this restriction of a practical order does not invalidate the generality of these arguments and their applications.

For example, let O be the origin of a trihedral of reference with $\overline{Oh}$, $\overline{Og}$, $\overline{Ou}$, as referent, and a base $\bar{h}$, $\bar{g}$, $\bar{u}$, with the following units:

> for $\bar{h}$, 1 = semitone;
> for $\bar{g}$, 1 = 10 decibels;
> for $\bar{u}$, 1 = second.

The origin O will be chosen arbitrarily on the "absolute" scales established by tradition, in the manner of zero on the thermometer. Thus:

> for $\bar{h}$, O will be at C_3;   (A_3 = 440 Hz)
> for $\bar{g}$, O will be at 50 db;
> for $\bar{u}$, O will be at 10 sec;

and the vectors

$$X_1 = 5\bar{h} - 3\bar{g} + 5\bar{u}$$
$$X_2 = 7\bar{h} + 1\bar{g} - 1\bar{u}$$

may be written in traditional notation for 1 sec $\triangleq$ ♪.

$$pp \sim (50 - 30 = 20 \text{ dB})$$

$$f \sim (50 + 10 = 60 \text{ dB})$$

In the same way

$$X_1 + X_2 = (5 + 7)\bar{h} + (1 - 3)\bar{g} + (5 - 1)\bar{u} = 12\bar{h} - 2\bar{g} + 4\bar{u}.$$

$$mp \sim (50 - 20 = 30 \text{ dB})$$

We may similarly pursue the verification of all the preceding propositions.

We have established, thanks to vectorial algebra, a working language which may permit both analyses of the works of the past and new constructions by setting up interacting functions of the components (combinations of the sets H, G, U). Algebraic research in conjunction with experimental research by computers coupled to analogue converters might give us information on the linear relations of a vectorial multiplicity so as to obtain the timbres of existing instruments or of other kinds of sonic events.

The following is an analysis of a fragment of *Sonata*, Op. 57 (Appassionata), by Beethoven (see Fig. VI–1). We do not take the timbre into account since the piano is considered to have only one timbre, homogeneous over the register of this fragment.

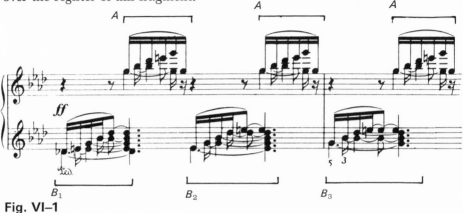

Fig. VI–1

Assume as unit vectors: $\bar{h}$, for which $1 \triangleq$ semitone; $\bar{g}$, for which $1 \triangleq 10 \, db$; and $\bar{u}$, for which $1 \triangleq$ ♪. Assume for the origins

 on the $\bar{h}$ axis,

$ff = 60 \, db$ (invariable) on the $\bar{g}$ axis, and
5♪ on the $\bar{u}$ axis.

ALGEBRA OUTSIDE-TIME (OPERATIONS AND RELATIONS IN SET A)

The vector $\bar{X}_0 = 18\bar{h} + 0\bar{g} + 5\bar{u}$ corresponds to G.
The vector $\bar{X}_1 = (18 + 3)\bar{h} + 0\bar{g} + 4\bar{u}$ corresponds to $B\flat$.
The vector $\bar{X}_2 = (18 + 6)\bar{h} + 0\bar{g} + 3\bar{u}$ corresponds to $D\flat$.
The vector $\bar{X}_3 = (18 + 9)\bar{h} + 0\bar{g} + 2\bar{u}$ corresponds to E.
The vector $\bar{X}_4 = (18 + 12)\bar{h} + 0\bar{g} + 1\bar{u}$ corresponds to G.
The vector $\bar{X}_5 = (18 + 0)\bar{h} + 0\bar{g} + 1\bar{u}$ corresponds to G.

(See Fig. VI–2.)

Let us also admit the free vector $\bar{v} = 3\bar{h} + 0\bar{g} - 1\bar{u}$; then the vectors $\bar{X}_i$ (for $i = 0, 1, 2, 3, 4$) are of the form $\bar{X}_i = \bar{X}_0 + \bar{v}i$.

We notice that set A consists of two vector families, $\bar{X}_i$ and $i\bar{v}$, combined by means of addition.

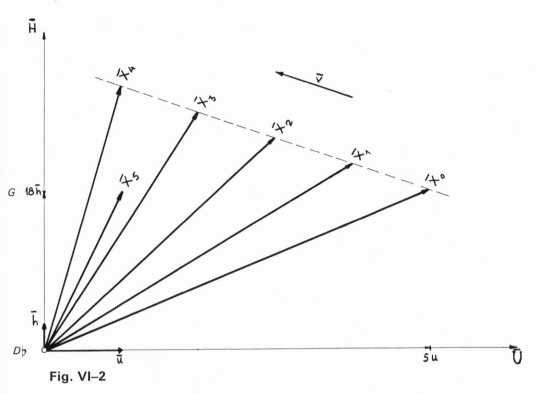

Fig. VI–2

A second law of composition exists in the set ($i = 0, 1, 2, 3, 4$); it is an arithmetic progression.

Finally, the scalar i leads to an antisymmetric variation of the components $\bar{h}$ and $\bar{u}$ of $\bar{X}_i$, the second $\bar{g}$ remaining invariant.

TEMPORAL ALGEBRA (IN SET T)

The sonic statement of the vectors $\bar{X}_i$ of set A is successive:

$$\bar{X}_0 \; \top \; \bar{X}_1 \; \top \; \bar{X}_2 \; \top \; \cdots$$

$\top$ being the operator "before."

This boils down to saying that the origin O of the base of $A \triangleq E_3 \triangleq V$ is displaced on the axis of time, a shifting that has nothing to do with the change of the base, which is in fact an operation within space E_3 of base $\bar{h}, \bar{g}, \bar{u}$. Thus in the case of a simultaneity (a chord) of the attacks of the six vectors described for set A, the displacement would be zero.

In Fig. VI–3 the segments designated on the axis of time by the origins O of $\bar{X}_i$ are equal and obey the function $\Delta t_i = \Delta t_j$, which is an internal law

of composition in set T; or consider an origin O' on the axis of time and a
segment unit equal to Δt; then $t_i = a + i\Delta t$, for $i = 1, 2, 3, 4, 5$.

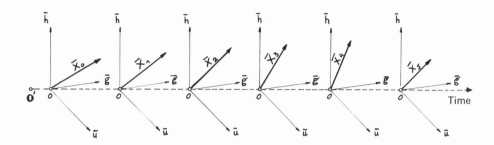

Fig. VI–3

ALGEBRA IN-TIME (RELATIONS BETWEEN SPACE E_3 AND SET T)

We may say that the vectors $\bar{X}_i$ of A have components H, G, U, which
may be expressed as a function of a parameter t_i. Here $t_i = i\Delta t$; the values
are lexicographically ordered and defined by the increasing order $i = 1, 2,$
3, 4, 5. This constitutes an association of each of the components with the
ordered set T. It is therefore an algebration of sonic events that is independent of time (algebra outside-time), as well as an algebration of sonic events
as a function of time (algebra in-time).

In general we admit that a vector $\bar{X}$ is a function of the parameter of
time t if its components are also a function of t. This is written

$$\bar{X}(t) = H(t)\bar{h} + G(t)\bar{g} + U(t)\bar{u}.$$

When these functions are continuous they have differentials. What is
the meaning of the variations of $\bar{X}$ as a function of time t? Suppose

$$\frac{d\bar{X}}{dt} = \frac{dH}{dt}\bar{h} + \frac{dG}{dt}\bar{g} + \frac{dU}{dt}\bar{u}.$$

If we neglect the variation of the component G, we will have the following
conditions: For $dH/dt = 0$, $H = c_h$, and $dU/dt = 0$, $U = c_u$, H and U will
be independent of the variation of t; and for c_h and $c_u \neq 0$, the sonic event
will be of invariable pitch and duration. If c_h and $c_u = 0$, there is no sound
(silence). (See Fig. VI–4.)

For $dH/dt = 0$, $H = c_h$, and $dU/dt = c_u$, $U = c_u t + k$, if c_h and
$c_u \neq 0$, we have an infinity of vectors at the unison. If $c_u = 0$, then we have
a single vector of constant pitch c_h and duration $U = k$. (See Fig. VI–5).

For $dH/dt = 0$, $H = c_h$, and $dU/dt = f(t)$, $U = F(t)$, we have an infinite family of vectors at the unison.

For $dH/dt = c_h$, $H = c_h t + k$, and $dU/dt = 0$, $U = c_u$, if $c_u < \varepsilon$, $\lim \varepsilon = 0$, we have a constant glissando of a single sound. If $c_u > 0$, then we have a chord composed of an infinity of vectors of duration c_u (thick constant glissando). (See Fig. VI–6.)

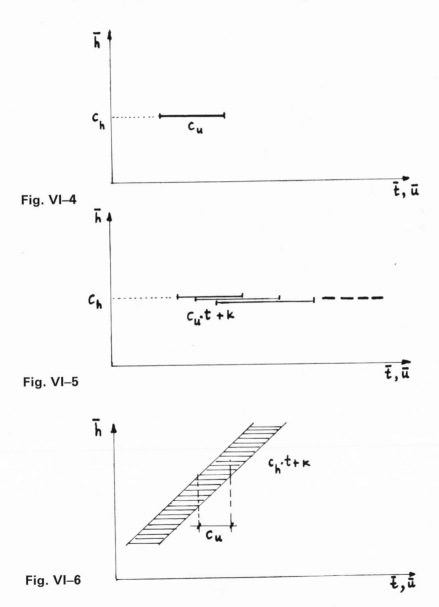

Fig. VI–4

Fig. VI–5

Fig. VI–6

For $dH/dt = c_h$, $H = c_h t + k$, and $dU/dt = c_u$, $U = c_u t + r$, we have a chord of an infinity of vectors of variable durations and pitches. (See Fig. VI–7.)

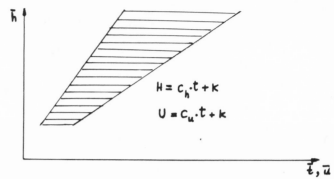

Fig. VI–7

For $dH/dt = c_h$, $H = c_h t + k$, and $dU/dt = f(t)$, $U = F(t)$, we have a chord of an infinity of vectors. (See Fig. VI–8.)

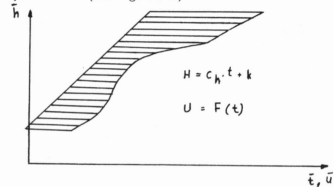

Fig. VI–8

For $dH/dt = f(t)$, $H = F(t)$, and $dU/dt = 0$, $U = c_u$, if $c_u < \varepsilon$, lim $\varepsilon = 0$, we have a thin variable glissando. If $c_u > 0$, then we have a chord of an infinity of vectors of duration c_u (thick variable glissando). (See Fig. VI–9.)

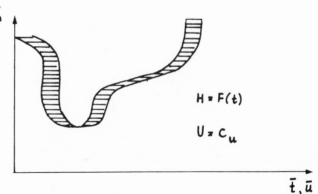

Fig. VI–9

For $dH/dt = f(t)$, $H = F(t)$, and $dU/dt = s(t)$, $U = S(t)$, we have a chord of an infinity of vectors. (See Fig. VI–10.)

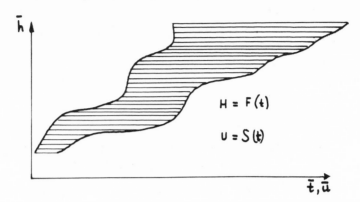

Fig. VI–10

In the example drawn from Beethoven, set A of the vectors X_i is not a continuous function of t. The correspondence may be written

$$\begin{array}{ccccccc} X_0 & X_1 & X_2 & X_3 & X_4 & X_5 \\ t_0 & t_1 & t_2 & t_3 & t_4 & t_5 \end{array}$$

Because of this correspondence the vectors are not commutable.

Set B is analogous to set A. The fundamental difference lies in the change of base in space $\dot{E}_3$ relative to the base of A. But we shall not pursue the analysis.

Remark

If our musical space has two dimensions, e.g., pitch-time, pitch-intensity, pressure-time, etc., it is interesting to introduce complex variables. Let x be the time and y the pitch, plotted on the i axis. Then $z = x + yi$ is a sound of pitch y with the attack at the instant x. Let there be a plane uv with the following equalities: $u = u(x, y)$, $v = v(x, y)$, and $w = u + vi$. They define a mapping which establishes a correspondence between points in the uv and xy planes. In general any w is a transformation of z.

The four forms of a melodic line (or of a twelve-tone row) can be represented by the following complex mappings:

$w = z$, with $u = x$ and $v = y$, which corresponds to identity (original form)
$w = |z|^2/z$, with $u = x$ and $v = -y$, which corresponds to inversion
$w = |z|^2/-z$ with $u = -x$ and $v = y$, which corresponds to retrogradation
$w = -z$, with $u = -x$ and $v = -y$, which corresponds to inverted retrogradation.

These transformations form the Klein group.

Other transformations, as yet unknown, even to present-day musicians, could be envisaged. They could be applied to any product of two sets of sound characteristics. For example, $w = (Az^2 + Bz + c)/(Dz^2 + Ez + F)$, which can be considered as a combination of two bilinear transformations separated by a transformation of the type $\rho = \sigma^2$. Furthermore, for a musical space of more than two dimensions we can introduce hypercomplex systems such as the system of quaternions.

EXTENSION OF THE THREE ALGEBRAS TO SETS OF SONIC EVENTS (an application)

We have noted in the above three kinds of algebras:

1. The algebra of the components of a sonic event, with its vector language, independent of the procession of time, therefore an *algebra outside-time*.

2. A *temporal algebra*, which the sonic events create on the axis of metric time, and which is independent of the vector space.

3. An *algebra in-time*, issuing from the correspondences and functional relations between the elements of the set of vectors $\bar{X}$ and of the set of metric time, T, independent of the set of $\bar{X}$.

All that has been said about sonic events themselves, their components, and about time can be generalized for sets of sonic events $\bar{X}$ and for sets T.

In this chapter we have assumed that the reader is familiar with the concept of the set, and in particular with the concept of the class as it is interpreted in Boolean algebra. We shall adopt this specific algebra, which is isomorphic with the theory of sets.

To simplify the exposition, we shall first take a concrete example by considering the *referential* or *universal set R*, consisting of all the sounds of a piano. We shall consider only the pitches; timbres, attacks, intensities, and durations will be utilized in order to clarify the exposition of the logical operations and relations which we shall impose on the set of pitches.

Suppose, then, a set A of keys that have a characteristic property. This will be set A, a subset of set R, which consists of all the keys of the piano. This subset is chosen a priori and the characteristic property is the particular choice of a certain number of keys.

For the amnesic observer this class may be presented by playing the keys one after the other, with a period of silence in between. He will deduce from this that he has heard a collection of sounds, or a listing of elements.

Another class, B, consisting of a certain number of keys, is chosen in the same way. It is stated after class A by causing the elements of B to sound.

The observer hearing the two classes, A and B, will note the temporal fact: A before B; $A \top B$, ($\top$ = before). Next he begins to notice relationships between the elements of the two classes. If certain elements or keys are common to both classes the classes *intersect*. If none are common, they are *disjoint*. If all the elements of B are common to one part of A he deduces that B is a class *included* in A. If all the elements of B are found in A, and all the elements of A are found in B, he deduces that the two classes are indistinguishable, that they are *equal*.

Let us choose A and B in such a way that they have some elements in common. Let the observer hear first A, then B, then the common part. He will deduce that: 1. there was a choice of keys, A; 2. there was a second choice of keys, B; and 3. the part common to A and B was considered. The operation of *intersection* (conjunction) has therefore been used:

$$A \cdot B \quad \text{or} \quad B \cdot A.$$

This operation has therefore engendered a new class, which was symbolized by the sonic enumeration of the part common to A and B.

If the observer, having heard A and B, hears a mixture of all the elements of A and B, he will deduce that a new class is being considered, and that a logical summation has been performed on the first two classes. This operation is the *union* (disjunction) and is written

$$A + B \quad \text{or} \quad B + A.$$

If class A has been symbolized or played to him and he is made to hear all the sounds of R except those of A, he will deduce that the complement of A with respect to R has been chosen. This is a new operation, *negation*, which is written $\bar{A}$.

Hitherto we have shown by an imaginary experiment that we can define and *state classes of sonic events* (while taking precautions for clarity in the symbolization); and effect three operations of fundamental importance: intersection, union, and negation.

On the other hand, an observer must undertake an intellectual task in order to deduce from this both classes and operations. On our plane of immediate comprehension, we replaced graphic signs by sonic events. We consider these sonic events as symbols of abstract entities furnished with abstract logical relations on which we may effect at least the fundamental operations of the logic of classes. We have not allowed special symbols for the statement of the classes; only the sonic enumeration of the generic elements was allowed (though in certain cases, if the classes are already known and if there is no ambiguity, shortcuts may be taken in the statement to admit a sort of mnemotechnical or even psychophysiological stenosymbolization).

We have not allowed special sonic symbols for the three operations which are expressed graphically by $\cdot$, $+$, $-$; only the classes resulting from these operations are expressed, and the operations are consequently deduced mentally by the observer. In the same way the observer must deduce the relation of equality of the two classes, and the relation of implication based on the concept of inclusion. The empty class, however, may be symbolized by a duly presented silence. In sum, then, we can only state classes, not the operations. The following is a list of correspondences between the sonic symbolization and the graphical symbolization as we have just defined it:

Graphic symbols	Sonic symbols
Classes A, B, C, ...	Sonic enumeration of the generic elements having the properties A, B, C, ... (with possible shortcuts)
Intersection $(\cdot)$	———
Union $(+)$	———
Negation $(-)$	———
Implication $(\to)$	———
Membership $(\in)$	———
$\bar{A}$	Sonic enumeration of the elements of R not included in A
$A \cdot B$	Sonic enumeration of the elements of $A \cdot B$
$A + B$	Sonic enumeration of the elements of $A + B$
$A \supset B$	———
$A = B$	———

This table shows that we can reason by pinning down our thoughts by means of sound. This is true even in the present case where, because of a concern for economy of means, and in order to remain close to that immediate intuition from which all sciences are built, we do not yet wish to propose sonic conventions symbolizing the operations $\cdot$, $+$, $-$, and the relations $=$, $\to$. Thus propositions of the form A, E, I, O may not be symbolized by sounds, nor may theorems. Syllogisms and demonstrations of theorems may only be inferred.

Besides these logical relations and operations outside-time, we have seen that we may obtain temporal classes (T classes) issuing from the sonic symbolization that defines distances or intervals on the axis of time. The role of time is again defined in a new way. It serves primarily as a crucible, mold, or space in which are inscribed the classes whose relations one must *decipher*. Time is in some ways equivalent to the area of a sheet of paper or a blackboard. It is only in a secondary sense that it may be considered as carrying generic elements (temporal distances) and relations or operations between these elements (temporal algebra).

Relations and correspondences may be established between these temporal classes and the outside-time classes, and we may recognize in-time operations and relations on the class level.

After these general considerations, we shall give an example of musical composition constructed with the aid of the algebra of classes. For this we *must* search out a necessity, a knot of interest.

Construction

Every Boolean expression or function $F(A, B, C)$, for example, of the three classes A, B, C can be expressed in the form called *disjunctive canonic*:

$$\sum_{i=1}^{8} \sigma_i k_i$$

where $\sigma_i = 0; 1$ and $k_i = A \cdot B \cdot C, A \cdot B \cdot \bar{C}, A \cdot \bar{B} \cdot C, A \cdot \bar{B} \cdot \bar{C}, \bar{A} \cdot B \cdot C, \bar{A} \cdot B \cdot \bar{C}, \bar{A} \cdot \bar{B} \cdot C, \bar{A} \cdot \bar{B} \cdot \bar{C}$.

A Boolean function with n variables can always be written in such a way as to bring in a maximum of operations $+$, $\cdot$, $-$, equal to $3n \cdot 2^{n-2} - 1$. For $n = 3$ this number is 17, and is found in the function

$$F = A \cdot B \cdot C + A \cdot \bar{B} \cdot \bar{C} + \bar{A} \cdot B \cdot \bar{C} + \bar{A} \cdot \bar{B} \cdot C. \tag{1}$$

For three classes, each of which intersects with the other two, function (1) can be represented by the Venn diagram in Fig. VI–11. The flow chart of the operations is shown in Fig. VI–12.

This same function F can be obtained with only ten operations:

$$F = (A \cdot B + \bar{A} \cdot \bar{B}) \cdot C + (\overline{A \cdot B + \bar{A} \cdot \bar{B}}) \cdot \bar{C}. \tag{2}$$

Its flow chart is given in Fig. VI–13.

If we compare the two expressions of F, each of which defines a different procedure in the composition of classes A, B, C, we notice a more elegant

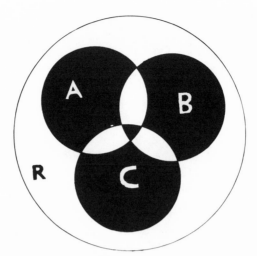

Fig. VI–11

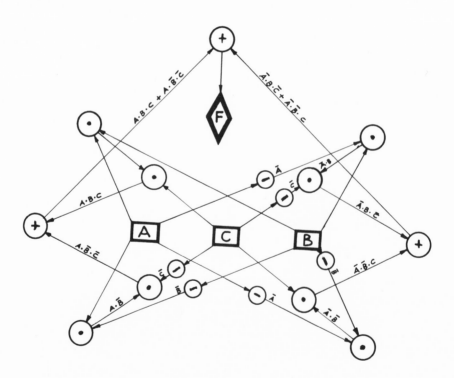

Fig. VI–12

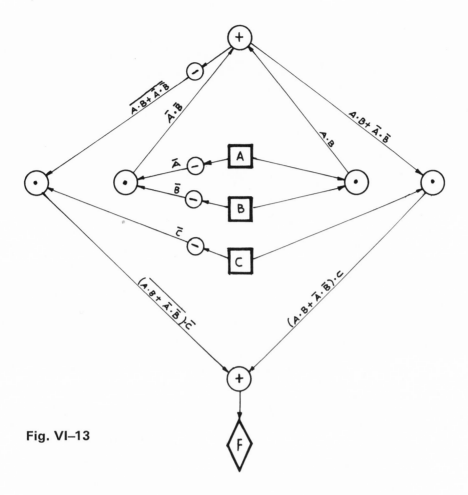

Fig. VI–13

symmetry in (1) than in (2). On the other hand (2) is more economical (ten operations as against seventeen). It is this comparison that was chosen for the realization of *Herma*, a work for piano. Fig. VI–14 shows the flow chart that directs the operations of (1) and (2) on two parallel planes, and Fig. VI–15 shows the precise plan of the construction of *Herma*.

The three classes *A*, *B*, *C* result in an appropriate set of keys of the piano. There exists a stochastic correspondence between the pitch components and the moments of occurrence in set *T*, which themselves follow a stochastic law. The intensities and densities (number of vectors/sec.), as well as the silences, help clarify the levels of the composition. This work was composed in 1960–61, and was first performed by the extraordinary Japanese pianist Yuji Takahashi in Tokyo in February 1962.

In conclusion we can say that our arguments are based on relatively simple generic elements. With much more complex generic elements we could still have described the same logical relations and operations. We would simply have changed the level. An algebra on several parallel levels is therefore possible with transverse operations and relations between the various levels.

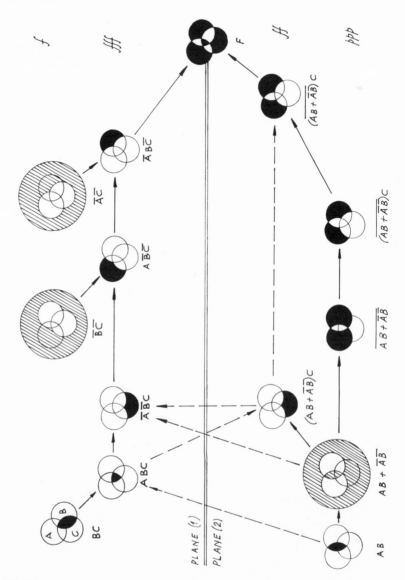

Fig. VI–14

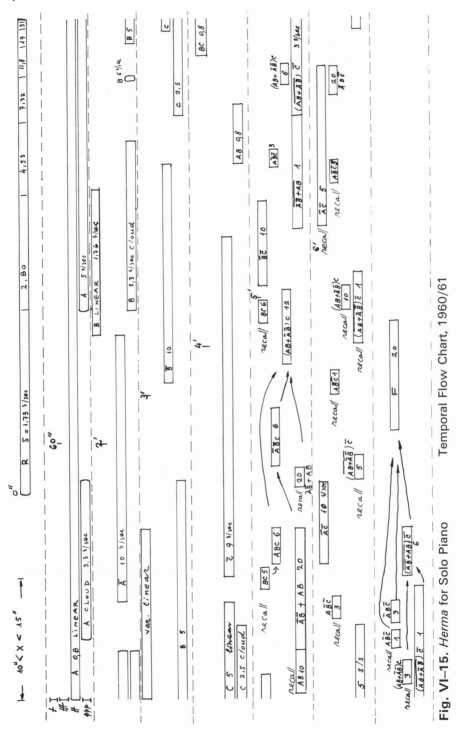

Fig. VI-15. *Herma* for Solo Piano   Temporal Flow Chart, 1960/61

Conclusions and Extensions
for Chapters I–VI

I have sketched the general framework of an artistic attitude which, for the first time, uses mathematics in three fundamental aspects: 1. as a philosophical summary of the entity and its evolution, e.g., Poisson's law; 2. as a qualitative foundation and mechanism of the Logos, e.g., symbolic logic, set theory, theory of chain events, game theory; and 3. as an instrument of mensuration which sharpens investigation, possible realizations, and perception, e.g., entropy calculus, matrix calculus, vector calculus.

To make music means to express human intelligence by sonic means. This is intelligence in its broadest sense, which includes not only the peregrinations of pure logic but also the "logic" of emotions and of intuition. The technics set forth here, although often rigorous in their internal structure, leave many openings through which the most complex and mysterious factors of the intelligence may penetrate. These technics carry on steadily between two age-old poles, which are unified by modern science and philosophy: determinism and fatality on the one hand, and free will and unconditioned choice on the other. Between the two poles actual everyday life goes on, partly fatalistic, partly modifiable, with the whole gamut of interpenetrations and interpretations.

In reality formalization and axiomatization constitute a procedural guide, better suited to modern thought. They permit, at the outset, the placing of sonic art on a more universal plane. Once more it can be considered on the same level as the stars, the numbers, and the riches of the human brain, as it was in the great periods of the ancient civilizations. The movements of sounds that cause movements in us in agreement with them "procure a common pleasure for those who do not know how to reason; and for those who do know, a reasoned joy through the imitation of the divine harmony which they realize in perishable movements" (Plato, *Timaeus*).

The theses advocated in this exposition are an initial sketch, but they have already been applied and extended. Imagine that all the hypotheses of generalized stochastic composition as described in Chapter II were to be applied to the phenomena of vision. Then, instead of acoustic grains, suppose quanta of light, i.e., photons. The components in the atomic, quantic hypothesis of sound—intensity, frequency, density, and lexicographic time—are then adapted to the quanta of light.

A single source of photons, a photon gun, could theoretically reproduce the acoustic screens described above through the emission of photons of a particular choice of frequencies, energies, and densities. In this way we could create a luminous flow analogous to that of music issuing from a sonic source. If we then join to this the coordinates of space, we could obtain a spatial music of light, a sort of space-light. It would only be necessary to activate photon guns in combination at all corners in a gloriously illuminated area of space. It is technically possible, but painters would have to emerge from the lethargy of their craft and forsake their brushes and their hands, unless a new type of visual artist were to lay hold of these new ideas, technics, and needs.

A new and rich work of visual art could arise, whose evolution would be ruled by huge computers (tools vital not only for the calculation of bombs or price indexes, but also for the artistic life of the future), a total audiovisual manifestation ruled in its compositional intelligence by machines serving other machines, which are, thanks to the *scientific arts*, directed by man.

Chapter VII

Towards a Metamusic

Today's technocrats and their followers treat music as a message which the composer (source) sends to a listener (receiver). In this way they believe that the solution to the problem of the nature of music and of the arts in general lies in formulae taken from information theory. Drawing up an account of bits or quanta of information transmitted and received would thus seem to provide them with "objective" and scientific criteria of aesthetic value. Yet apart from elementary statistical recipes this theory—which is valuable for technological communications—has proved incapable of giving the characteristics of aesthetic value even for a simple melody of J. S. Bach. Identifications of music with message, with communication, and with language are schematizations whose tendency is towards absurdities and desiccations. Certain African tom-toms cannot be included in this criticism, but they are an exception. Hazy music cannot be forced into too precise a theoretical mold. Perhaps, it will be possible later when present theories have been refined and new ones invented.

The followers of information theory or of cybernetics represent one extreme. At the other end there are the intuitionists, who may be broadly divided into two groups:

1. The "graphists," who exalt the graphic symbol above the sound of the music and make a kind of fetish of it. In this group it is the fashionable thing not to write notes, but to create any sort of design. The "music" is judged according to the beauty of the drawing. Related to this is the so-called aleatory music, which is an abuse of language, for the true term should be

English translation of Chapter VII by G. W. Hopkins.

180

the "improvised" music our grandfathers knew. This group is ignorant of the fact that graphical writing, whether it be symbolic, as in traditional notation, geometric, or numerical, should be no more than an image that is as *faithful* as possible to all the instructions the composer gives to the orchestra or to the machine.[1] This group is taking music outside itself.

2. Those who add a spectacle in the form of extra-musical scenic action to accompany the musical performance. Influenced by the "happenings" which express the confusion of certain artists, these composers take refuge in mimetics and disparate occurrences and thus betray their very limited confidence in pure music. In fact they concede certain defeat for their music in particular.

The two groups share a romantic attitude. They believe in immediate action and are not much concerned about its control by the mind. But since musical action, unless it is to risk falling into trivial improvisation, imprecision, and irresponsibility, imperiously demands reflection, these groups are in fact denying music and take it outside itself.

Linear Thought

I shall not say, like Aristotle, that the mean path is the best, for in music—as in politics—the middle means compromise. Rather lucidity and harshness of critical thought—in other words, action, reflection, and self-transformation by the sounds themselves—is the path to follow. Thus when scientific and mathematical thought serve music, or any human creative activity, it should amalgamate dialectically with intuition. Man is one, indivisible, and total. He thinks with his belly and feels with his mind. I would like to propose what, to my mind, covers the term "music":

1. It is a sort of comportment necessary for whoever thinks it and makes it.

2. It is an individual pleroma, a realization.

3. It is a fixing in sound of imagined virtualities (cosmological, philosophical, . . ., arguments).

4. It is normative, that is, unconsciously it is a model for being or for doing by sympathetic drive.

5. It is catalytic: its mere presence permits internal psychic or mental transformations in the same way as the crystal ball of the hypnotist.

6. It is the gratuitous play of a child.

7. It is a mystical (but atheistic) asceticism. Consequently expressions of sadness, joy, love, and dramatic situations are only very limited particular instances.

Musical syntax has undergone considerable upheaval and today it seems that innumerable possibilities coexist in a state of chaos. We have an abundance of theories, of (sometimes) individual styles, of more or less ancient "schools." But how does one make music? What can be communicated by oral teaching? (A burning question, if one is to reform musical education—a reform that is necessary in the entire world.)

It cannot be said that the informationists or the cyberneticians—much less the intuitionists—have posed the question of an ideological purge of the dross accumulated over the centuries as well as by present-day developments. In general they all remain ignorant of the substratum on which they found this theory or that action. Yet this substratum exists, and it will allow us to establish for the first time an axiomatic system, and to bring forth a formalization which will unify the ancient past, the present, and the future; moreover it will do so on a planetary scale, comprising the still separate universes of sound in Asia, Africa, etc.

In 1954[2] I denounced *linear thought* (polyphony), and demonstrated the contradictions of serial music. In its place I proposed a world of sound-masses, vast groups of sound-events, clouds, and galaxies governed by new characteristics such as density, degree of order, and rate of change, which required definitions and realizations using probability theory. Thus stochastic music was born. In fact this new, mass-conception with large numbers was more general than linear polyphony, for it could embrace it as a particular instance (by reducing the density of the clouds). General harmony? No, not yet.

Today these ideas and the realizations which accompany them have been around the world, and the exploration seems to be closed for all intents and purposes. However the tempered diatonic system—our musical terra firma on which all our music is founded—seems not to have been breached either by reflection or by music itself.[3] This is where the next stage will come. The exploration and transformations of this system will herald a new and immensely promising era. In order to understand its determinative importance we must look at its pre-Christian origins and at its subsequent development. Thus I shall point out the structure of the music of ancient Greece; and then that of Byzantine music, which has best preserved it while developing it, and has done so with greater fidelity than its sister, the occidental plainchant. After demonstrating their abstract logical construction in a modern way, I shall try to express in a simple but universal mathematical and logical language what was and what might be valid in time (transverse musicology) and in space (comparative musicology).

In order to do this I propose to make a distinction in musical architectures or categories between *outside-time*,[4] *in-time*, and *temporal*. A given pitch scale, for example, is an outside-time architecture, for no horizontal or vertical combination of its elements can alter it. The event in itself, that is, its actual occurrence, belongs to the temporal category. Finally, a melody or a chord on a given scale is produced by relating the outside-time category to the temporal category. Both are realizations in-time of outside-time constructions. I have dealt with this distinction already, but here I shall show how ancient and Byzantine music can be analyzed with the aid of these categories. This approach is very general since it permits both a universal axiomatization and a formalization of many of the aspects of the various kinds of music of our planet.

Structure of Ancient Music

Originally the Gregorian chant was founded on the structure of ancient music, *pace* Combarieu and the others who accused Hucbald of being behind the times. The rapid evolution of the music of Western Europe after the ninth century simplified and smoothed out the plainchant, and theory was left behind by practice. But shreds of the ancient theory can still be found in the secular music of the fifteenth and sixteenth centuries, witness the *Terminorum Musicae diffinitorium* of Johannis Tinctoris.[5] To look at antiquity scholars have been looking through the lens of the Gregorian chant and its modes, which have long ceased to be understood. We are only beginning to glimpse other directions in which the modes of the plainchant can be explained. Nowadays the specialists are saying that the modes are not in fact proto-scales, but that they are rather characterized by melodic formulae. To the best of my knowledge only Jacques Chailley[6] has introduced other concepts complementary to that of the scale, and he would seem to be correct. I believe we can go further and affirm that ancient music, at least up to the first centuries of Christianity, was not based at all on scales and modes related to the octave, but on tetrachords and *systems*.

Experts on ancient music (with the above exception) have ignored this fundamental reality, clouded as their minds have been by the tonal construction of post-medieval music. However, this is what the Greeks used in their music: a hierarchic structure whose complexity proceeded by successive "nesting," and by inclusions and intersections from the particular to the general; we can trace its main outline if we follow the writings of Aristoxenos:[7]

A. The *primary order* consists of the tone and its subdivisions. The whole

tone is defined as the amount by which the interval of a fifth (the pentachord, or dia pente) exceeds the interval of a fourth (the tetrachord, or dia
tessaron). The tone is divided into halves, called *semitones*; thirds, called
chromatic dieseis; and quarters, the extremely small *enharmonic dieseis*. No
interval smaller than the quarter-tone was used.

B. The *secondary order* consists of the tetrachord. It is bounded by the
interval of the *dia tessaron*, which is equal to two and a half tones, or thirty
twelfth-tones, which we shall call Aristoxenean segments. The two outer
notes always maintain the same interval, the fourth, while the two inner notes
are mobile. The positions of the inner notes determine the three genera of
the tetrachord (the intervals of the fifth and the octave play no part in it).
The position of the notes in the tetrachord are always counted from the
lowest note up:

1. The enharmonic genus contains two enharmonic dieseis, or
$3 + 3 + 24 = 30$ segments. If X equals the value of a tone, we can express
the enharmonic as $X^{1/4} \cdot X^{1/4} \cdot X^2 = X^{5/2}$.

2. The chromatic genus consists of three types: a. soft, containing two
chromatic dieseis, $4 + 4 + 22 = 30$, or $X^{1/3} \cdot X^{1/3} \cdot X^{(1/3 + 3/2)} = X^{5/2}$; b.
hemiolon (sesquialterus), containing two hemioloi dieseis, $4.5 + 4.5 + 21$
$= 30$ segments, or $X^{(3/2)(1/4)} \cdot X^{(3/2)(1/4)} \cdot X^{7/4} = X^{5/2}$; and c. "toniaion," consisting of two semitones and a trihemitone, $6 + 6 + 18 = 30$ segments,
or $X^{1/2} \cdot X^{1/2} \cdot X^{3/2} = X^{5/2}$.

3. The diatonic consists of: a. soft, containing a semitone, then three
enharmonic dieseis, then five enharmonic dieseis, $6 + 9 + 15 = 30$ seg-
ments, or $X^{1/2} \cdot X^{3/4} \cdot X^{5/4} = X^{5/2}$; b. syntonon, containing a semitone, a
whole tone, and another whole tone, $6 + 12 + 12 = 30$ segments, or
$X^{1/2} \cdot X \cdot X = X^{5/2}$.

C. The *tertiary order*, or the *system*, is essentially a combination of the
elements of the first two—tones and tetrachords either conjuncted or
separated by a tone. Thus we get the pentachord (outer interval the perfect
fifth) and the octochord (outer interval the octave, sometimes perfect). The
subdivisions of the system follow exactly those of the tetrachord. They are
also a function of connexity and of consonance.

D. The *quaternary order* consists of the tropes, the keys, or the modes,
which were probably just particularizations of the systems, derived by
means of cadential, melodic, dominant, registral, and other formulae, as in
Byzantine music, ragas, etc.

These orders account for the outside-time structure of Hellenic music.
After Aristoxenos all the ancient texts one can consult on this matter give

this same hierarchical procedure. Seemingly Aristoxenos was used as a model. But later, traditions parallel to Aristoxenos, defective interpretations, and sediments distorted this hierarchy, even in ancient times. Moreover, it seems that theoreticians like Aristides Quintilianos and Claudios Ptolemaeos had but little acquaintance with music.

This hierarchical "tree" was completed by transition algorithms—the metabolae—from one genus to another, from one system to another, or from one mode to another. This is a far cry from the simple modulations or transpositions of post-medieval tonal music.

Pentachords are subdivided into the same genera as the tetrachord they contain. They are derived from tetrachords, but nonetheless are used as primary concepts, on the same footing as the tetrachord, in order to define the interval of a tone. This vicious circle is accounted for by Aristoxenos' determination to remain faithful to musical experience (on which he insists), which alone defines the structure of tetrachords and of the entire harmonic edifice which results combinatorially from them. His whole axiomatics proceeds from there and his text is an example of a method to be followed. Yet the absolute (physical) value of the interval dia tessaron is left undefined, whereas the Pythagoreans defined it by the ratio 3/4 of the lengths of the strings. I believe this to be a sign of Aristoxenos' wisdom; the ratio 3/4 could in fact be a mean value.

Two Languages

Attention must be drawn to the fact that he makes use of the additive operation for the intervals, thus foreshadowing logarithms before their time; this contrasts with the practice of the Pythagoreans, who used the geometrical (exponential) language, which is multiplicative. Here, the method of Aristoxenos is fundamental since: 1. it constitutes one of the two ways in which musical theory has been expressed over the millennia; 2. by using addition it institutes a means of "calculation" that is more economical, simpler, and better suited to music; and 3. it lays the foundation of the tempered scale nearly twenty centuries before it was applied in Western Europe.

Over the centuries the two languages—arithmetic (operating by addition) and geometric (derived from the ratios of string lengths, and operating by multiplication)—have always intermingled and interpenetrated so as to create much useless confusion in the reckoning of intervals and consonances, and consequently in theories. In fact they are both expressions of group structure, having two non-identical operations; thus they have a formal equivalence.[8]

There is a hare-brained notion that has been sanctimoniously repeated by musicologists in recent times. "The Greeks," they say, "had descending scales instead of the ascending ones we have today." Yet there is no trace of this in either Aristoxenos or his successors, including Quintilianos[9] and Alypios, who give a new and fuller version of the steps of many of the tropes. On the contrary, the ancient writers always begin their theoretical explanations and nomenclature of the steps from the bottom. Another bit of foolishness is the supposed Aristoxenean scale, of which no trace is to be found in his text.[10]

Structure of Byzantine Music

Now we shall look at the structure of Byzantine music. It can contribute to an infinitely better understanding of ancient music, occidental plainchant, non-European musical traditions, and the dialectics of recent European music, with its wrong turns and dead-ends. It can also serve to foresee and construct the future from a view commanding the remote landscapes of the past as well as the electronic future. Thus new directions of research would acquire their full value. By contrast the deficiencies of serial music in certain domains and the damage it has done to musical evolution by its ignorant dogmatism will be indirectly exposed.

Byzantine music amalgamates the two means of calculation, the Pythagorean and the Aristoxenean, the multiplicative and the additive.[11] The fourth is expressed by the ratio 3/4 of the monochord, or by the 30 tempered segments (72 to the octave).[12] It contains three kinds of tones: major (9/8 or 12 segments), minor (10/9 or 10 segments), and minimal (16/15 or 8 segments). But smaller and larger intervals are constructed and the elementary units of the primary order are more complex than in Aristoxenos. Byzantine music gives a preponderant role to the *natural diatonic scale* (the supposed Aristoxenean scale) whose steps are in the following ratios to the first note: 1, 9/8, 5/4, 4/3, 27/16, 15/8, 2 (in segments 0, 12, 22, 30, 42, 54, 64, 72; or 0, 12, 23, 30, 42, 54, 65, 72). The degrees of this scale bear the alphabetical names A, B, Γ, Δ, E, Z, and H. Δ is the lowest note and corresponds roughly to G_2. This scale was propounded at least as far back as the first century by Didymos, and in the second century by Ptolemy, who permuted one term and recorded the shift of the tetrachord (tone-tone-semitone), which has remained unchanged ever since.[13] But apart from this dia pason (octave) attraction, the musical architecture is hierarchical and "nested" as in Aristoxenos, as follows:

A. The *primary order* is based on the three tones 9/8, 10/9, 16/15, a supermajor tone 7/6, the trihemitone 6/5, another major tone 15/14, the semitone or leima 256/243, the apotome of the minor tone 135/128, and finally the comma 81/80. This complexity results from the mixture of the two means of calculation.

B. The *secondary order* consists of the tetrachords, as defined in Aristoxenos, and similarly the pentachords and the octochords. The tetrachords are divided into three genera:

1. Diatonic, subdivided into: first scheme, $12 + 11 + 7 = 30$ segments, or $(9/8)(10/9)(16/15) = 4/3$, starting on Δ, H, etc; second scheme, $11 + 7 + 12 = 30$ segments, or $(10/9)(16/15)(9/8) = 4/3$, starting on E, A, etc; third scheme, $7 + 12 + 11 = 30$ segments, or $(16/15)(9/8)(10/9) = 4/3$, starting on Z, etc. Here we notice a developed combinatorial method that is not evident in Aristoxenos; only three of the six possible permutations of the three notes are used.

2. Chromatic, subdivided into:[14] a. soft chromatic, derived from the diatonic tetrachords of the first scheme, $7 + 16 + 7 = 30$ segments, or $(16/15)(7/6)(15/14) = 4/3$, starting on Δ, H, etc.; b. syntonon, or hard chromatic, derived from the diatonic tetrachords of the second scheme, $5 + 19 + 6 = 30$ segments, or $(256/243)(6/5)(135/128) = 4/3$, starting on E, A, etc.

3. Enharmonic, derived from the diatonic by alteration of the mobile notes and subdivided into: first scheme, $12 + 12 + 6 = 30$ segments, or $(9/8)(9/8)(256/243) = 4/3$, starting on Z, H, Γ, etc.; second scheme, $12 + 6 + 12 = 30$ segments, or $(9/8)(256/243)(9/8) = 4/3$, starting on Δ, H, A, etc.; third scheme, $6 + 12 + 12 = 30$ segments, or $(256/243)(9/8)(9/8) = 4/3$, starting on E, A, B, etc.

PARENTHESIS

We can see a phenomenon of absorption of the ancient enharmonic by the diatonic. This must have taken place during the first centuries of Christianity, as part of the Church fathers' struggle against paganism and certain of its manifestations in the arts. The diatonic had always been considered sober, severe, and noble, unlike the other types. In fact the chromatic genus, and especially the enharmonic, demanded a more advanced musical culture, as Aristoxenos and the other theoreticians had already pointed out, and such a culture was even scarcer among the masses of the Roman period. Consequently combinatorial speculations on the one hand and practical usage on the other must have caused the specific characteristics of the enharmonic to disappear in favor of the chromatic, a subdivision of which fell away in Byzantine music, and of the syntonon diatonic. This phenomenon of absorption is comparable to that of the scales (or modes) of the Renaissance by the major diatonic scale, which perpetuates the ancient syntonon diatonic.

However, this simplification is curious and it would be interesting to study the exact circumstances and causes. Apart from differences, or rather variants of ancient intervals, Byzantine typology is built strictly on the ancient. It builds up the next stage with tetrachords, using definitions which singularly shed light on the theory of the Aristoxenean systems; this was expounded in some detail by Ptolemy.[15]

THE SCALES

C. The *tertiary order* consists of the scales constructed with the help of systems having the same ancient rules of consonance, dissonance, and assonance (paraphonia). In Byzantine music the principle of iteration and juxtaposition of the system leads very clearly to scales, a development which is still fairly obscure in Aristoxenos and his successors, except for Ptolemy. Aristoxenos seems to have seen the system as a category and end in itself, and the concept of the scale did not emerge independently from the method which gave rise to it. In Byzantine music, on the other hand, the system was called a method of constructing scales. It is a sort of iterative operator, which starts from the lower category of tetrachords and their derivatives, the pentachord and the octochord, and builds up a chain of more complex organisms, in the same manner as chromosomes based on genes. From this point of view, *system-scale* coupling reached a stage of fulfillment that had been unknown in ancient times. The Byzantines defined the system as the simple or multiple repetition of two, several, or all the notes of a scale. "Scale" here means a succession of notes that is already organized, such as the tetrachord or its derivatives. Three systems are used in Byzantine music:

> the octachord or dia pason
> the pentachord or wheel (trochos)
> the tetrachord or triphony.

The system can unite elements by conjunct (synimenon) or disjunct (diazeugmenon) juxtaposition. The disjunct juxtaposition of two tetrachords one tone apart form the dia pason scale spanning a perfect octave. The conjunct juxtaposition of several of these perfect octave dia pason leads to the scales and modes with which we are familiar. The conjunct juxtaposition of several tetrachords (triphony) produces a scale in which the

octave is no longer a fixed sound in the tetrachord but one of its mobile
sounds. The same applies to the conjunct juxtaposition of several pentachords
(trochos).

The system can be applied to the three genera of tetrachords and to
each of their subdivisions, thus creating a very rich collection of scales.
Finally one may even mix the genera of tetrachords in the same scale (as in
the selidia of Ptolemy), which will result in a vast variety. Thus the scale
order is the product of a combinatorial method—indeed, of a gigantic
montage (harmony)—by iterative juxtapositions of organisms that are
already strongly differentiated, the tetrachords and their derivatives. The
scale as it is defined here is a richer and more universal conception than all
the impoverished conceptions of medieval and modern times. From this
point of view, it is not the tempered scale so much as the absorption by the
diatonic tetrachord (and its corresponding scale) of all the other combinations
or montages (harmonies) of the other tetrachords that represents a vast loss
of potential. (The diatonic scale is derived from a disjunct system of two
diatonic tetrachords separated by a whole tone, and is represented by the
white keys on the piano.) It is this potential, as much sensorial as abstract,
that we are seeking here to reinstate, albeit in a modern way, as will be
seen.

The following are examples of scales in segments of Byzantine tempering (or Aristoxenean, since the perfect fourth is equal to 30 segments):

Diatonic scales. Diatonic tetrachords: system by disjunct tetrachords,
12, 11, 7; 12; 11, 7, 12, starting on the lower Δ, 12, 11, 7; 12; 12, 11, 7,
starting on the lower *H* or *A*; system by tetrachord and pentachord, 7, 12,
11; 7, 12, 12, 11, starting on the lower *Z*; wheel system (trochos), 11, 7, 12,
12; 11, 7, 12, 12; 11, 7, 12, 12; etc.

Chromatic scales. Soft chromatic tetrachords: wheel system starting on
H, 7, 16, 7, 12; 7, 16, 7, 12; 7, 16, 7, 12; etc.

Enharmonic scales. Enharmonic tetrachords, second scheme: system by
disjunct tetrachords, starting on Δ, 12, 6, 12; 12; 12, 6, 12, corresponding
to the mode produced by all the white keys starting with *D*. The enharmonic
scales produced by the disjunct system form all the ecclesiastical scales or
modes of the West, and others, for example: chromatic tetrachord, first
scheme, by the triphonic system, starting on low *H*: 12, 12, 6; 12, 12, 6; 12,
12, 6; 12, 12, 6.

Mixed scales. Diatonic tetrachords, first scheme + soft chromatic;
disjunct system, starting on low *H*, 12, 11, 7; 12; 7, 16, 7. Hard chromatic
tetrachord + soft chromatic; disjunct system, starting on low *H*, 5, 19, 6;
12; 7, 16, 7; etc. All the montages are not used, and one can observe the

phenomenon of the absorption of imperfect octaves by the perfect octave by virtue of the basic rules of consonance. This is a limiting condition.

D. The *quaternary order* consists of the tropes or echoi (ichi). The echos is defined by:

the genera of tetrachords (or derivatives) constituting it

the system of juxtaposition

the attractions

the bases or fundamental notes

the dominant notes

the termini or cadences (katalixis)

the apichima or melodies introducing the mode

the ethos, which follows ancient definitions.

We shall not concern ourselves with the details of this quaternary order.

Thus we have succinctly expounded our analysis of the outside-time structure of Byzantine music.

THE METABOLAE

But this outside-time structure could not be satisfied with a compartmentalized hierarchy. It was necessary to have free circulation between the notes and their subdivisions, between the kinds of tetrachords, between the genera, between the systems, and between the echoi—hence the need for a sketch of the in-time structure, which we will now look at briefly. There exist operative signs which allow alterations, transpositions, modulations, and other transformations (metabolae). These signs are the phthorai and the chroai of notes, tetrachords, systems (or scales), and echoi.

Note metabolae

The metathesis: transition from a tetrachord of 30 segments (perfect fourth) to another tetrachord of 30 segments.

The parachordi: distortion of the interval corresponding to the 30 segments of a tetrachord into a larger interval and vice versa; or again, transition from one distorted tetrachord to another distorted tetrachord.

Genus Metabolae

Phthora characteristic of the genus, not changing note names

Changing note names

Using the parachordi

Using the chroai.

System metabolae

Transition from one system to another using the above metabolae.

Echos metabolae using special signs, the martyrikai phthorai or alterations of the mode initialization.

Because of the complexity of the metabolae, pedal notes (isokratima)
cannot be "trusted to the ignorant." Isokratima constitutes an art in itself,
for its function is to emphasize and pick out all the in-time fluctuations of the
outside-time structure that marks the music.

First Comments

It can easily be seen that the consummation of this outside-time structure is the most complex and most refined thing that could be invented by
monody. What could not be developed in polyphony has been brought to
such luxuriant fruition that to become familiar with it requires many years
of practical studies, such as those followed by the vocalists and instrumentalists of the high cultures of Asia. It seems, however, that none of the specialists in Byzantine music recognize the importance of this structure. It would
appear that interpreting ancient systems of notation has claimed their
attention to such an extent that they have ignored the living tradition of the
Byzantine Church and have put their names to incorrect assertions. Thus
it was only a few years ago that one of them[16] took the line of the Gregorian
specialists in attributing to the echoi characteristics other than those of the
oriental scales which had been taught them in the conformist schools. They
have finally discovered that the echoi contained certain characteristic melodic formulae, though of a sedimentary nature. But they have not been able
or willing to go further and abandon their soft refuge among the manuscripts.

Lack of understanding of ancient music,[17] of both Byzantine and Gregorian origin, is doubtless caused by the blindness resulting from the growth
of polyphony, a highly original invention of the barbarous and uncultivated
Occident following the schism of the churches. The passing of centuries and
the disappearance of the Byzantine state have sanctioned this neglect and
this severance. Thus the effort to feel a "harmonic" language that is much
more refined and complex than that of the syntonon diatonic and its scales
in octaves is perhaps beyond the usual ability of a Western music specialist,
even though the music of our own day may have been able to liberate him
partly from the overwhelming dominance of diatonic thinking. The only
exceptions are the specialists in the music of the Far East,[18] who have always
remained in close contact with musical practice and, dealing as they were
with living music, have been able to look for a harmony other than the tonal
harmony with twelve semitones. The height of error is to be found in the
transcriptions of Byzantine melodies[19] into Western notation using the
tempered system. Thus, thousands of transcribed melodies are completely

wrong! But the real criticism one must level at the Byzantinists is that in remaining aloof from the great musical tradition of the eastern church, they have ignored the existence of this abstract and sensual architecture, both complex and remarkably interlocking (harmonious), this developed remnant and genuine achievement of the Hellenic tradition. In this way they have retarded the progress of musicological research in the areas of:

> antiquity
> plainchant
> folk music of European lands, notably in the East[20]
> musical cultures of the civilizations of other continents
> better understanding of the musical evolution of Western Europe from
the middle ages up to the modern period
> the syntactical prospects for tomorrow's music, its enrichment, and its
survival.

Second Comments

I am motivated to present this architecture, which is linked to antiquity and doubtless to other cultures, because it is an elegant and lively witness to what I have tried to define as an outside-time category, algebra, or structure of music, as opposed to its other two categories, in-time and temporal. It has often been said (by Stravinsky, Messiaen, and others) that in music time is *everything*. Those who express this view forget the basic structures on which personal languages, such as "pre- or post-Webernian" serial music, rest, however simplified they may be. In order to understand the universal past and present, as well as prepare the future, it is necessary to distinguish structures, architectures, and sound organisms from their temporal manifestations. It is therefore necessary to take "snapshots," to make a series of veritable tomographies over time, to compare them and bring to light their relations and architectures, and vice versa. In addition, thanks to the metrical nature of time, one can furnish it too with an outside-time structure, leaving its true, unadorned nature, that of immediate reality, of instantaneous becoming, in the final analysis, to the temporal category alone.

In this way, time could be considered as a blank blackboard, on which symbols and relationships, architectures and abstract organisms are inscribed. The clash between organisms and architectures and instantaneous immediate reality gives rise to the primordial quality of the living consciousness.

The architectures of Greece and Byzantium are concerned with the pitches (the dominant character of the simple sound) of sound entities.

Here rhythms are also subjected to an organization, but a much simpler one. Therefore we shall not refer to it. Certainly these ancient and Byzantine models cannot serve as examples to be imitated or copied, but rather to exhibit a fundamental outside-time architecture which has been thwarted by the temporal architectures of modern (post-medieval) polyphonic music. These systems, including those of serial music, are still a somewhat confused magma of temporal and outside-time structures, for no one has yet thought of unravelling them. However we cannot do this here.

Progressive Degradation of Outside-Time Structures

The tonal organization that has resulted from venturing into polyphony and neglecting the ancients has leaned strongly, by virture of its very nature, on the temporal category, and defined the hierarchies of its harmonic functions as the in-time category. Outside-time is appreciably poorer, its "harmonics" being reduced to a single octave scale (C major on the two bases C and A), corresponding to the syntonon diatonic of the Pythagorean tradition or to the Byzantine enharmonic scales based on two disjunct tetrachords of the first scheme (for C) and on two disjunct tetrachords of the second and third scheme (for A). Two metabolae have been preserved: that of transposition (shifting of the scale) and that of modulation, which consists of transferring the base onto steps of the same scale. Another loss occurred with the adoption of the crude tempering of the semitone, the twelfth root of two. The consonances have been enriched by the interval of the third, which, until Debussy, had nearly ousted the traditional perfect fourths and fifths. The final stage of the evolution, atonalism, prepared by the theory and music of the romantics at the end of the nineteenth and the beginning of the twentieth centuries, practically abandoned all outside-time structure. This was endorsed by the dogmatic suppression of the Viennese school, who accepted only the ultimate total time ordering of the tempered chromatic scale. Of the four forms of the series, only the inversion of the intervals is related to an outside-time structure. Naturally the loss was felt, consciously or not, and symmetric relations between intervals were grafted onto the chromatic total in the choice of the notes of the series, but these always remained in the in-time category. Since then the situation has barely changed in the music of the post-Webernians. This degradation of the outside-time structures of music since late medieval times is perhaps the most characteristic fact about the evolution of Western European music, and it has led to an unparalleled excrescence of temporal and in-time structures. In this lies its originality and its contribution to the universal culture. But herein also lies its impoverishment, its loss of vitality, and also an apparent risk of reaching an impasse. For as it has thus far developed, European music is ill-suited to providing the world with a field of expression on a planetary scale, as a universality, and risks isolating and severing itself from historical necessities. We must open our eyes and try to build bridges towards other cultures, as well as towards the immediate future of musical thought, before we perish suffocating from electronic technology, either at the instrumental level or at the level of composition by computers.

Reintroduction of the Outside-Time Structure by Stochastics

By the introduction of the calculation of probability (stochastic music) the present small horizon of outside-time structures and asymmetries was completely explored and enclosed. But by the very fact of its introduction, stochastics gave an impetus to musical thought that carried it over this enclosure towards the clouds of sound events and towards the plasticity of large numbers articulated statistically. There was no longer any distinction between the vertical and the horizontal, and the indeterminism of in-time structures made a dignified entry into the musical edifice. And, to crown the Herakleitean dialectic, indeterminism, by means of particular stochastic functions, took on color and structure, giving rise to generous possibilities of organization. It was able to include in its scope determinism and, still somewhat vaguely, the outside-time structures of the past. The categories outside-time, in-time, and temporal, unequally amalgamated in the history of music, have suddenly taken on all their fundamental significance and for the first time can build a coherent and universal synthesis in the past, present, and future. This is, I insist, not only a possibility, but even a direction having priority. But as yet we have not managed to proceed beyond this stage. To do so we must add to our arsenal sharper tools, trenchant axiomatics and formalization.

SIEVE THEORY

It is necessary to give an axiomatization for the totally ordered structure (additive group structure = additive Aristoxenean structure) of the tempered chromatic scale.[21] The axiomatics of the tempered chromatic scale is based on Peano's axiomatics of numbers:

Preliminary terms. O = the stop at the origin; n = a stop; n' = a stop resulting from elementary displacement of n; D = the set of values of the particular sound characteristic (pitch, density, intensity, instant, speed, disorder . . .). The values are identical with the stops of the displacements.

First propositions (axioms).

1. Stop O is an element of D.

2. If stop n is an element of D then the new stop n' is an element of D.

3. If stops n and m are elements of D then the new stops n' and m' are identical if, and only if, stops n and m are identical.

4. If stop n is an element of D, it will be different from stop O at the origin.

5. If elements belonging to D have a special property P, such that stop O also has it, and if, for every element n of D having this property the element n' has it also, all the elements of D will have the property P.

We have just defined axiomatically a tempered chromatic scale not only of pitch, but also of all the sound properties or characteristics referred to above in D (density, intensity ...). Moreover, this abstract scale, as Bertrand Russell has rightly observed, à propos the axiomatics of numbers of Peano, has no unitary displacement that is either predetermined or related to an absolute size. Thus it may be constructed with tempered semitones, with Aristoxenean segments (twelfth-tones), with the commas of Didymos (81/80), with quarter-tones, with whole tones, thirds, fourths, fifths, octaves, etc. or with any other unit that is not a factor of a perfect octave.

Now let us define another equivalent scale based on this one but having a unitary displacement which is a multiple of the first. It can be expressed by the concept of *congruence modulo m*.

Definition. Two integers x and n are said to be *congruent modulo m* when m is a factor of $x - n$. It may be expressed as follows: $x \equiv n \pmod{m}$. Thus, two integers are congruent modulo m when and only when they differ by an exact (positive or negative) multiple of m; e.g., $4 \equiv 19 \pmod 5$, $3 \equiv 13 \pmod 8$, $14 \equiv 0 \pmod 7$.

Consequently, every integer is congruent modulo m with one and with only one value of n:

$$n = (0, 1, 2, \ldots, m - 2, m - 1).$$

Of each of these numbers it is said that it forms a *residual class modulo m*; they are, in fact, the smallest non-negative residues modulo m. $x \equiv n \pmod{m}$ is thus equivalent to $x = n + km$, where k is an integer.

$$k \in Z = \{0, \pm 1, \pm 2, \pm 3, \ldots\}.$$

For a given n and for any $k \in Z$, the numbers x will belong by definition to the residual class n modulo m. This class can be denoted m_n.

In order to grasp these ideas in terms of music, let us take the tempered semitone of our present-day scale as the unit of displacement. To this we shall again apply the above axiomatics, with say a value of 4 semitones (major third) as the elementary displacement.[22] We shall define a new chromatic scale. If the stop at the origin of the first scale is a $D\sharp$, the second scale will give us all the multiples of 4 semitones, in other words a "scale" of major thirds: $D\sharp, G, B, D'\sharp, G', B'$; these are the notes of the first scale whose order numbers are congruent with 0 modulo 4. They all belong to the residual class 0 modulo 4. The residual classes 1, 2, and 3 modulo 4 will use up all the notes of this chromatic total. These classes may be represented in the following manner:

$$\text{residual class 0 modulo } 4 : 4_0$$
$$\text{residual class 1 modulo } 4 : 4_1$$
$$\text{residual class 2 modulo } 4 : 4_2$$
$$\text{residual class 3 modulo } 4 : 4_3$$
$$\text{residual class 4 modulo } 4 : 4_0, \text{ etc.}$$

Since we are dealing with a sieving of the basic scale (elementary displacement by one semitone), each residual class forms a sieve allowing certain elements of the chromatic continuity to pass through. By extension the chromatic total will be represented as sieve 1_0. The scale of fourths will be given by sieve 5_n, in which $n = 0, 1, 2, 3, 4$. Every change of the index n will entail a transposition of this gamut. Thus the Debussian whole-tone scale, 2_n with $n = 0, 1$, has two transpositions:

$$2_0 \rightarrow C, D, E, F\sharp, G\sharp, A\sharp, C \cdots$$
$$2_1 \rightarrow C\sharp, D\sharp, F, G, A, B, C\sharp \cdots$$

Starting from these elementary sieves we can build more complex scales—all the scales we can imagine—with the help of the three operations of the Logic of Classes: union (disjunction) expressed as $\lor$, intersection (conjunction) expressed as $\land$, and complementation (negation) expressed as a bar inscribed over the modulo of the sieve. Thus

$$2_0 \lor 2_1 = \text{chromatic total (also expressible as } 1_0)$$
$$2_0 \land 2_1 = \text{no notes, or empty sieve, expressed as } \varnothing$$
$$\overline{2}_0 = 2_1 \text{ and } \overline{2}_1 = 2_0.$$

The major scale can be written as follows:

$$(\overline{3}_2 \land 4_0) \lor (\overline{3}_1 \land 4_1) \lor (3_2 \land 4_2) \lor (\overline{3}_0 \land 4_3).$$

By definition, this notation does not distinguish between all the modes on the white keys of the piano, for what we are defining here is the scale; modes are the architectures founded on these scales. Thus the white-key mode D, starting on D, will have the same notation as the C mode. But in order to distinguish the modes it would be possible to introduce non-commutativity in the logical expressions. On the other hand each of the 12 transpositions of this scale will be a combination of the cyclic permutations of the indices of sieves modulo 3 and 4. Thus the major scale transposed a semitone higher (shift to the right) will be written

$$(\overline{3}_0 \wedge 4_1) \vee (\overline{3}_2 \wedge 4_2) \vee (3_0 \wedge 4_3) \vee (\overline{3}_1 \wedge 4_0),$$

and in general

$$(\overline{3}_{n+2} \wedge 4_n) \vee (\overline{3}_{n+1} \wedge 4_{n+1}) \vee (3_{n+2} \wedge 4_{n+2}) \vee (\overline{3}_n \wedge 4_{n+3}),$$

where n can assume any value from 0 to 11, but reduced after the addition of the constant index of each of the sieves (moduli), modulo the corresponding sieve. The scale of D transposed onto C is written

$$(3_n \wedge 4_n) \vee (\overline{3}_{n+1} \wedge 4_{n+1}) \vee (\overline{3}_n \wedge 4_{n+2}) \vee (\overline{3}_{n+2} \wedge 4_{n+3}).$$

Musicology

Now let us change the basic unit (elementary displacement ELD) of the sieves and use the quarter-tone. The major scale will be written

$$(8_n \wedge \overline{3}_{n+1}) \vee (8_{n+2} \wedge \overline{3}_{n+2}) \vee (8_{n+4} \wedge 3_{n+1}) \vee (8_{n+6} \wedge \overline{3}_n),$$

with $n = 0, 1, 2, \ldots, 23$ (modulo 3 or 8). The same scale with still finer sieving (one octave = 72 Aristoxenean segments) will be written

$$(8_n \wedge (9_n \vee 9_{n+6})) \vee (8_{n+2} \wedge (9_{n+3} \vee 9_{n+6})) \vee (8_{n+4} \wedge 9_{n+3})$$
$$\vee (8_{n+6} \wedge (9_n \vee 9_{n+3})),$$

with $n = 0, 1, 2, \ldots, 71$ (modulo 8 or 9).

One of the mixed Byzantine scales, a disjunct system consisting of a chromatic tetrachord and a diatonic tetrachord, second scheme, separated by a major tone, is notated in Aristoxenean segments as 5, 19, 6; 12; 11, 7, 12, and will be transcribed logically as

$$(8_n \wedge (9_n \vee 9_{n+6})) \vee (9_{n+6} \wedge (8_{n+2} \vee 8_{n+4}))$$
$$\vee (8_{n+5} \wedge (9_{n+5} \vee 9_{n+8})) \vee (8_{n+6} \vee 9_{n+3}),$$

with $n = 0, 1, 2, \ldots, 71$ (modulo 8 or 9).

The Raga Bhairavi of the Andara-Sampurna type (pentatonic ascending, heptatonic descending),[23] expressed in terms of an Aristoxenean basic sieve (comprising an octave, periodicity 72), will be written as:
Pentatonic scale:

$$(8_n \wedge (9_n \vee 9_{n+3})) \vee (8_{n+2} \wedge (9_n \vee 9_{n+6})) \vee (8_{n+6} \wedge 9_{n+3})$$

Heptatonic scale:

$$(8_n \wedge (9_n \vee 9_{n+3})) \vee (8_{n+2} \wedge (9_n \vee 9_{n+6})) \vee (8_{n+4} \wedge (9_{n+4} \vee 9_{n+6}))$$
$$\vee (8_{n+6} \wedge (9_{n+3} \vee 9_{n+6}))$$

with $n = 0, 1, 2, \ldots, 71$ (modulo 8 or 9).

These two scales expressed in terms of a sieve having as its elementary displacement, ELD, the comma of Didymos, ELD $= 81/80$ (81/80 to the power $55.8 = 2$), thus having an octave periodicity of 56, will be written as:
Pentatonic scale:

$$(7_n \wedge (8_n \vee 8_{n+6})) \vee (7_{n+2} \wedge (8_{n+5} \vee 8_{n+7})) \vee (7_{n+5} \wedge 8_{n+1})$$

Heptatonic scale:

$$(7_n \wedge (8_n \vee 8_{n+6})) \vee (7_{n+2} \wedge (8_{n+5} \vee 8_{n+7})) \vee (7_{n+3} \wedge 8_{n+3})$$
$$\vee (7_{n+4} \wedge (8_{n+4} \vee 8_{n+6})) \vee (7_{n+5} \wedge 8_{n+1})$$

for $n = 0, 1, 2, \ldots, 55$ (modulo 7 or 8).

We have just seen how the sieve theory allows us to express any scale in terms of logical (hence mechanizable) functions, and thus unify our study of the structures of superior range with that of the total order. It can be useful in entirely new constructions. To this end let us imagine complex, non–octave-forming sieves.[24] Let us take as our sieve unit a tempered quarter-tone. An octave contains 24 quarter-tones. Thus we have to construct a compound sieve with a periodicity other than 24 or a multiple of 24, thus a periodicity non-congruent with $k \cdot 24$ modulo 24 (for $k = 0, 1, 2, \ldots$). An example would be any logical function of the sieve of moduli 11 and 7 (periodicity $11 \times 7 = 77 \neq k \cdot 24$), $(\overline{11_n \vee 11_{n+1}}) \wedge 7_{n+6}$. This establishes an asymmetric distribution of the steps of the chromatic quarter-tone scale. One can even use a compound sieve which throws periodicity outside the limits of the audible area; for example, any logical function of modules 17 and 18 ($f[17, 18]$), for $17 \times 18 = 306 > (11 \times 24)$.

Suprastructures

One can apply a stricter structure to a compound sieve or simply leave the choice of elements to a stochastic function. We shall obtain a statistical coloration of the chromatic total which has a higher level of complexity.

Using metabolae. We know that at every cyclic combination of the sieve indices (transpositions) and at every change in the module or moduli of the sieve (modulation) we obtain a metabola. As examples of metabolic transformations let us take the smallest residues that are prime to a positive number r. They will form an Abelian (commutative) group when the composition law for these residues is defined as multiplication with reduction to the least positive residue with regard to r. For a numerical example let $r = 18$; the residues $1, 5, 7, 11, 13, 17$ are primes to it, and their products after reduction modulo 18 will remain within this group (closure). The finite commutative group they form can be exemplified by the following fragment:

$$5 \times 7 = 35; 35 - 18 = 17;$$
$$11 \times 11 = 121; 121 - (6 \times 18) = 13; \text{ etc.}$$

Modules 1, 7, 13 form a cyclic sub-group of order 3. The following is a logical expression of the two sieves having modules 5 and 13:

$$L(5, 13) = (\overline{13_{n+4} \vee 13_{n+5} \vee 13_{n+7} \vee 13_{n+9}})$$
$$\wedge 5_{n+1} \vee (\overline{5_{n+2} \vee 5_{n+4}}) \wedge 13_{n+9} \vee 13_{n+6}.$$

One can imagine a transformation of modules in pairs, starting from the Abelian group defined above. Thus the cinematic diagram (in-time) will be

$$L(5, 13) \to L(11, 17) \to L(7, 11) \to L(5, 1) \to L(5, 5) \to \cdots \to L(5, 13)$$

so as to return to the initial term (closure).[25]

This sieve theory can be put into many kinds of architecture, so as to create included or successively intersecting classes, thus stages of increasing complexity; in other words, orientations towards increased determinisms in selection, and in topological textures of neighborhood.

Subsequently we can put into in-time practice this veritable histology of outside-time music by means of temporal functions, for instance by giving functions of change—of indices, moduli, or unitary displacement—in other words, encased logical functions parametric with time.

Sieve theory is very general and consequently is applicable to any other sound characteristics that may be provided with a totally ordered structure, such as intensity, instants, density, degrees of order, speed, etc. I have already said this elsewhere, as in the axiomatics of sieves. But this method can be applied equally to visual scales and to the optical arts of the future.

Moreover, in the immediate future we shall witness the exploration of this theory and its widespread use with the help of computers, for it is entirely mechanizable. Then, in a subsequent stage, there will be a study of partially ordered structures, such as are to be found in the classification of timbres, for example, by means of lattice or graph techniques.

Conclusion

I believe that music today could surpass itself by research into the outside-time category, which has been atrophied and dominated by the temporal category. Moreover this method can unify the expression of fundamental structures of all Asian, African, and European music. It has a considerable advantage: its mechanization—hence tests and models of all sorts can be fed into computers, which will effect great progress in the musical sciences.

In fact, what we are witnessing is an industrialization of music which has already started, whether we like it or not. It already floods our ears in many public places, shops, radio, TV, and airlines, the world over. It permits a consumption of music on a fantastic scale, never before approached. But this music is of the lowest kind, made from a collection of outdated clichés from the dregs of the musical mind. Now it is not a matter of stopping this invasion, which, after all, increases participation in music, even if only passively. It is rather a question of effecting a qualitative conversion of this music by exercising a radical but constructive critique of our ways of thinking and of making music. Only in this way, as I have tried to show in the present study, will the musician succeed in dominating and transforming this poison that is discharged into our ears, and only if he sets about it without further ado. But one must also envisage, and in the same way, a radical conversion of musical education, from primary studies onwards, throughout the entire world (all national councils for music take note). Non-decimal systems and the logic of classes are already taught in certain countries, so why not their application to a new musical theory, such as is sketched out here?

Chapter VIII

Towards a Philosophy of Music

PRELIMINARIES

We are going to attempt briefly: 1. an "unveiling of the historical tradition" of music,[1] and 2. to construct a music.

"Reasoning" about phenomena and their explanation was the greatest step accomplished by man in the course of his liberation and growth. This is why the Ionian pioneers—Thales, Anaximander, Anaximenes—must be considered as the starting point of our truest culture, that of "reason." When I say "reason," it is not in the sense of a logical sequence of arguments, syllogisms, or logico-technical mechanisms, but that very extraordinary quality of feeling an uneasiness, a curiosity, then of applying the question, ἔλεγχος. It is, in fact, impossible to imagine this advance, which, in Ionia, created cosmology from nothing, in spite of religions and powerful mystiques, which were early forms of "reasoning." For example, Orphism, which so influenced Pythagorism, taught that the human soul is a fallen god, that only *ek-stasis*, the departure from self, can reveal its true nature, and that with the aid of purifications (καθαρμοί) and sacraments (ὄργια) it can regain its lost position and escape the *Wheel of Birth* (τροχός γενέσεως, *bhavachakra*) that is to say, the fate of reincarnations as an animal or vegetable. I am citing this mystique because it seems to be a very old and widespread form of thought, which existed independently about the same time in the Hinduism of India.[2]

Above all, we must note that the opening taken by the Ionians has finally surpassed all mystiques and all religions, including Christianity.

English translation of Chapter VIII by John and Amber Challifour.

Never has the spirit of this philosophy been as universal as today: The U.S., China, U.S.S.R., and Europe, the present principal protagonists, restate it with a homogeneity and a uniformity that I would even dare to qualify as disturbing.

Having been established, the question (ἔλεγχος) embodied a Wheel of Birth *sui generis*, and the various pre-Socratic schools flourished by conditioning all further development of philosophy until our time. Two are in my opinion the high points of this period: the Pythagorean concept of numbers and the Parmenidean dialectics—both unique expressions of the same preoccupation.

As it went through its phases of adaptation, up to the fourth century B.C., the Pythagorean concept of numbers affirmed that things are numbers, or that all things are furnished with numbers, or that things are similar to numbers. This thesis developed (and this in particular interests the musician) from the study of musical intervals in order to obtain the orphic catharsis, for according to Aristoxenos, the Pythagoreans used music to cleanse the soul as they used medicine to cleanse the body. This method is found in other *orgia*, like that of Korybantes, as confirmed by Plato in the *Laws*. In every way, Pythagorism has permeated all occidental thought, first of all, Greek, then Byzantine, which transmitted it to Western Europe and to the Arabs.

All musical theorists, from Aristoxenos to Hucbald, Zarlino, and Rameau, have returned to the same theses colored by expressions of the moment. But the most incredible is that all intellectual activity, including the arts, is actually immersed in the world of numbers (I am omitting the few backward-looking or obscurantist movements). We are not far from the day when genetics, thanks to the geometric and combinatorial structure of DNA, will be able to metamorphise the Wheel of Birth at will, as we wish it, and as preconceived by Pythagoras. It will not be the *ek-stasis* (Orphic, Hindu, or Taoist) that will have arrived at one of the supreme goals of all time, that of controlling the quality of reincarnations (hereditary rebirths παλιγγενεσία) but the very force of the "theory," of the question, which is the essence of human action, and whose most striking expression is Pythagorism. We are all Pythagoreans.[3]

On the other hand, Parmenides was able to go to the heart of the question of change by denying it, in contrast to Herakleitos. He discovered the principle of the excluded middle and logical tautology, and this created such a dazzlement that he used them as a means of cutting out, in the evanescent change of senses, the notion of Being, of that which is, one, motionless, filling the universe, without birth and indestructible; the not-Being, not existing, circumscribed, and spherical (which Melissos had not understood).

> [F]or it will be forever impossible to prove that things that are not are; but restrain your thought from this route of inquiry. . . . Only one way remains for us to speak of, namely, *that it is*; on this route there are many signs indicating that it is uncreated and indestructible, for it is complete, undisturbed, and without end; it never was, nor will it be, for now it is all at once complete, one, continuous; for what kind of birth are you seeking for it? How and from where could it grow? I will neither let you say nor think that it came from what is not; for it is unutterable and unthinkable that a thing is not. And what need would have led it to be created sooner or later if it came from nothing? Therefore it must be, absolutely, or not at all.
>
> —Fragments 7 and 8 of *Poem*, by Parmenides[4]

Besides the abrupt and compact style of the thought, the method of the question is absolute. It leads to denial of the sensible world, which is only made of contradictory appearances that "two-faced" mortals accept as valid without turning a hair, and to stating that the only truth is the notion of reality itself. But this notion, substantiated with the help of abstract logical rules, needs no other concept than that of its opposite, the not-Being, the nothing that is immediately rendered impossible to formulate and to conceive.

This concision and this axiomatics, which surpasses the deities and cosmogonies fundamental to the first elements,[5] had a tremendous influence on Parmenides' contemporaries. This was the first absolute and complete materialism. Immediate repercussions were, in the main, the continuity of Anaxagoras and the atomic discontinuity of Leukippos. Thus, all intellectual action until our time has been profoundly imbued with this strict axiomatics. The principle of the conservation of energy in physics is remarkable. Energy is that which fills the universe in electromagnetic, kinetic, or material form by virtue of the equivalence matter—energy. It has become *that which is* "par excellence." Conservation implies that it does not vary by a single photon in the entire universe and that it has been thus throughout eternity. On the other hand, by the same reasoning, the logical truth is tautological: All that which is affirmed is a truth to which no alternative is conceivable (Wittgenstein). Modern knowledge accepts the void, but is it truly a non-Being? Or simply the designation of an unclarified complement?

After the failures of the nineteenth century, scientific thought became rather skeptical and pragmatic. It is this fact that has allowed it to adapt and develop to the utmost. "All happens as if . . ." implies this doubt, which is positive and optimistic. We place a provisional confidence in new theories, but we abandon them readily for more efficacious ones provided that the procedures of action have a suitable explanation which agrees with the whole. In fact, this attitude represents a retreat, a sort of fatalism. This is why today's Pythagorism is relative (exactly like the Parmenidean axiomatics) in all areas, including the arts.

Throughout the centuries, the arts have undergone transformations that paralleled two essential creations of human thought: the hierarchical principle and the principle of numbers. In fact, these principles have dominated music, particularly since the Renaissance, down to present-day procedures of composition. In school we emphasize unity and recommend the unity of themes and of their development; but the serial system imposes another hierarchy, with its own tautological unity embodied in the tone row and in the principle of perpetual variation, which is founded on this tautology . . .—in short, all these axiomatic principles that mark our lives agree perfectly with the inquiry of Being introduced twenty-five centuries ago by Parmenides.

It is not my intention to show that everything has already been discovered and that we are only plagiarists. This would be obvious nonsense. There is never repetition, but a sort of tautological identity throughout the vicissitudes of Being that might have mounted the Wheel of Birth. It would seem that some areas are less mutable than others, and that some regions of the world change very slowly indeed.

The *Poem* of Parmenides implicitly admits that necessity, need, causality, and justice identify with logic; since Being is born from this logic, pure chance is as impossible as not-Being. This is particularly clear in the phrase, "And what need would have led it to be born sooner or later, if it came from nothing?" This contradiction has dominated thought throughout the millennia. Here we approach another aspect of the dialectics, perhaps the most important in the practical plan of action—determinism. If logic indeed implies the absence of chance, then one can know all and even construct everything with logic. The problem of choice, of decision, and of the future, is resolved.

We know, moreover, that if an element of chance enters a deterministic construction all is undone. This is why religions and philosophies everywhere have always driven chance back to the limits of the universe. And what they utilized of chance in divination practices was absolutely not considered as such but as a mysterious web of signs, sent by the divinities (who were often contradictory but who knew well what they wanted), and which could be read by elect soothsayers. This web of signs can take many forms—the Chinese system of I-Ching, auguries predicting the future from the flight of birds and the entrails of sacrificed animals, even telling fortunes from tea leaves. This inability to admit pure chance has even persisted in modern mathematical probability theory, which has succeeded in incorporating it into some deterministic logical laws, so that *pure chance* and *pure determinism* are only two facets of one entity, as I shall soon demonstrate with an example.

To my knowledge, there is only one "unveiling" of pure chance in all of the history of thought, and it was Epicurus who dared to do it. Epicurus struggled against the deterministic networks of the atomists, Platonists, Aristoteleans, and Stoics, who finally arrived at the negation of free will and believed that man is subject to nature's will. For if all is logically ordered in the universe as well as in our bodies, which are products of it, then our will is subject to this logic and our freedom is nil. The Stoics admitted, for example, that no matter how small, every action on earth had a repercussion on the most distant star in the universe; today we would say that the network of connections is compact, sensitive, and without loss of information.

This period is unjustly slighted, for it was in this time that all kinds of sophisms were debated, beginning with the logical calculus of the Megarians, and it was the time in which the Stoics created the logic called modal, which was distinct from the Aristotelian logic of classes. Moreover, Stoicism, by its moral thesis, its fullness, and its scope, is without doubt basic to the formation of Christianity, to which it has yielded its place, thanks to the substitution of punishment in the person of Christ and to the myth of eternal reward at the Last Judgment—regal solace for mortals.

In order to give an axiomatic and cosmogonical foundation to the proposition of man's free will, Epicurus started with the atomic hypothesis and admitted that "in the straight line fall that transports the atoms across the void, ... at an undetermined moment the atoms deviate ever so little from the vertical ... but the deviation is so slight, the least possible, that we could not conceive of even seemingly oblique movements."[6] This is the theory of *ekklisis* (Lat. clinamen) set forth by Lucretius. A senseless principle is introduced into the grand deterministic atomic structure. Epicurus thus based the structure of the universe on determinism (the inexorable and parallel fall of atome) and, at the same time, on indeterminism (*ekklisis*). It is striking to compare his theory with the kinetic theory of gases first proposed by Daniel Bernoulli. It is founded on the corpuscular nature of matter and, at the same time, on determinism and indeterminism. No one but Epicurus had ever thought of utilizing chance as a principle or as a type of behavior.

It was not until 1654 that a doctrine on the use and understanding of chance appeared. Pascal, and especially Fermat, formulated it by studying "games of chance"—dice, cards, etc. Fermat stated the two primary rules of probabilities using multiplication and addition. In 1713 *Ars Conjectandi* by Jacques Bernoulli was published.[7] In this fundamental work Bernoulli enunciated a universal law, that of Large Numbers. Here it is as stated by E. Borel: "Let p be the probability of the favorable outcome and q the probability of the unfavorable outcome, and let ε be a small positive number. The probability that the difference between the observed ratio of favorable events to unfavorable events and the theoretical ratio p/q is larger in absolute value than ε will approach zero when the number of trials n becomes infinitely large."[8] Consider the example of the game of heads and tails. If the coin is perfectly symmetric, that is to say, absolutely true, we know that the probability p of heads (favorable outcome) and the probability q of tails (unfavorable outcome) are each equal to $1/2$, and the ratio p/q to 1. If we toss the coin n times, we will get heads P times and tails Q times, and the ratio P/Q will generally be different from 1. The Law of Large Numbers states that the more we play, that is to say the larger the number n becomes, the closer the ratio P/Q will approach 1.

Thus, Epicurus, *who admits the necessity of birth at an undetermined moment*, in exact contradiction to all thought, even modern, remains an isolated case;* for the aleatory, and truly stochastic event, is the result of an accepted ignorance, as H. Poincaré has perfectly defined it. If probability theory admits an uncertainty about the outcome of each toss, it encompasses this uncertainty in two ways. The first is hypothetical: ignorance of the trajectory produces the uncertainty; the other is deterministic: the Law of Large Numbers removes the uncertainty with the help of time (or of space). However, by examining the coin tossing closely, we will see how the symmetry is strictly bound to the unpredictability. If the coin is perfectly symmetrical, that is, perfectly homogeneous and with its mass uniformly distributed, then the uncertainty[9] at each toss will be a maximum and the probability for each side will be $1/2$. If we now alter the coin by redistributing the matter unsymmetrically, or by replacing a little aluminum with platinum, which has a specific weight eight times that of aluminum, the coin will tend to land with the heavier side down. The uncertainty will decrease and the probabilities for the two faces will be unequal. When the substitution of material is pushed to the limit, for example, if the aluminum is replaced with a slip of paper and the other side is entirely of platinum, then the uncertainty will approach zero, that is, towards the certainty that

* Except perhaps for Heisenberg.

the coin will land with the lighter side up. Here we have shown the inverse relation between uncertainty and symmetry. This remark seems to be a tautology, but it is nothing more than the mathematical definition of probability: *probability* is the ratio of the number of favorable outcomes to the number of possible outcomes when all outcomes are regarded as equally *likely*. Today, the axiomatic definition of probability does not remove this difficulty, it circumvents it.

MUSICAL STRUCTURES *EX NIHILO*

Thus we are, at this point in the exposition, still immersed in the lines of force introduced twenty-five centuries ago and which continue to regulate the basis of human activity with the greatest efficacy, or so it seems. It is the source of those problems about which we, in the darkness of our ignorance, concern ourselves: determinism or chance,[10] unity of style or eclecticism, calculated or not, intuition or constructivism, a priori or not, a metaphysics of music or music simply as a means of entertainment.

Actually, these are the questions that we should ask ourselves: 1. What consequence does the awareness of the Pythagorean-Parmenidean field have for musical composition? 2. In what ways? To which the answers are: 1. Reflection on *that which is* leads us directly to the reconstruction, as much as possible *ex nihilo*, of the ideas basic to musical composition, and above all to the rejection of every idea that does not undergo the inquiry (ἔλεγχος, δίζησις). 2. This reconstruction will be prompted by modern axiomatic methods.

Starting from certain premises we should be able to construct the most general musical edifice in which the utterances of Bach, Beethoven, or Schönberg, for example, would be unique realizations of a gigantic virtuality, rendered possible by this axiomatic removal and reconstruction.

It is necessary to divide musical construction into two parts (see Chapters VI and VII): 1. that which pertains to time, a mapping of entities or structures onto the ordered structure of time; and 2. that which is independent of temporal becomingness. There are, therefore, two categories: *in-time* and *outside-time*. Included in the category outside-time are the durations and constructions (relations and operations) that refer to elements (points, distances, functions) that belong to and that can be expressed on the time axis. The temporal is then reserved to the instantaneous creation.

In Chapter VII I made a survey of the structure of monophonic music, with its rich outside-time combinatory capability, based on the original texts of Aristoxenos of Tarentum and the manuals of actual Byzantine music. This structure illustrates in a remarkable way that which I understand by the category outside-time.

Polyphony has driven this category back into the subconscious of musicians of the European occident, but has not completely removed it; that would have been impossible. For about three centuries after Monteverdi, in-time architectures, expressed chiefly by the tonal (or modal) functions, dominated everywhere in central and occidental Europe. However, it is in France that the rebirth of outside-time preoccupations occurred, with Debussy and his invention of the whole-tone scale. Contact with three of the more conservative traditions of the Orientals was the cause of it: the plainchant, which had vanished, but which had been rediscovered by the abbots at Solesmes; one of the Byzantine traditions, experienced through Moussorgsky; and the Far East.

This rebirth continues magnificently through Messiaen, with his "modes of limited transpositions" and "non-retrogradable rhythms," but it never imposes itself as a general necessity and never goes beyond the framework of the scales. However Messiaen himself abandoned this vein, yielding to the pressure of serial music.

In order to put things in their proper historical perspective, it is necessary to prevail upon more powerful tools such as mathematics and logic and go to the bottom of things, to the structure of musical thought and composition. This is what I have tried to do in Chapters VI and VII and what I am going to develop in the analysis of *Nomos alpha*.

Here, however, I wish to emphasize the fact that it was Debussy and Messiaen[11] in France who reintroduced the category outside-time in the face of the general evolution that resulted in its own atrophy, to the advantage of structures in-time.[12] In effect, atonality does away with scales and accepts the outside-time neutrality of the half-tone scale.[13] (This situation, furthermore, has scarcely changed for fifty years.) The introduction of in-time order by Schönberg made up for this impoverishment. Later, with the stochastic processes that I introduced into musical composition, the hypertrophy of the category in-time became overwhelming and arrived at a dead end. It is in this cul-de-sac that music, abusively called aleatory, improvised, or graphic, is still stirring today.

Questions of choice in the category outside-time are disregarded by musicians as though they were unable to hear, and especially unable to think. In fact, they drift along unconscious, carried away by the agitations of superficial musical fashions which they undergo heedlessly. In depth,

however, the outside-time structures do exist and it is the privilege of man
not only to sustain them, but to construct them and to go beyond them.

Sustain them? Certainly; there are basic evidences of this order which
will permit us to inscribe our names in the Pythagorean-Parmenidean field
and to lay the platform from which our ideas will build bridges of understanding and insight into the past (we are after all products of millions of
years of the past), into the future (we are equally products of the future),
and into other sonic civilizations, so badly explained by the present-day
musicologies, for want of the original tools that we so graciously set up for
them.

Two axiomatics will open new doors, as we shall see in the analysis of
Nomos alpha. We shall start from a naive position concerning the perception
of sounds, naive in Europe as well as in Africa, Asia, or America. The
inhabitants of all these countries learned tens or hundreds of thousands of
years ago to distinguish (if the sounds were neither too long nor too short)
such characteristics as pitch, instants, loudness, roughness, rate of change,
color, timbre. They are even able to speak of the first three characteristics
in terms of intervals.

The first axiomatics leads us to the construction of all possible scales.
We will speak of pitch since it is more familiar, but the following arguments
will relate to all characteristics which are of the same nature (instants,
loudness, roughness, density, degree of disorder, rate of change).

We will start from the obvious assumption that within certain limits
men are able to recognize whether two modifications or displacements of
pitch are identical. For example, going from C to D is the same as going
from F to G. We will call this modification elementary displacement, ELD.
(It can be a comma, a half tone, an octave, etc.) It permits us to define any
Equally Tempered Chromatic Gamut as an ETCHG sieve.[14] By modifying the
displacement step ELD, we engender a new ETCHG sieve with the same
axiomatics. With this material we can go no farther. Here we introduce the
three logical operations (Aristotelean logic as seen by Boole) of *conjunction*
("and," intersection, notated $\wedge$), *disjunction* ("or," union, notated $\vee$), and
negation ("no," complement, notated $-$), and use them to create classes of
pitch (various ETCHG sieves).

The following is the logical expression with the conventions as indicated
in Chapter VII:

The major scale (ELD $= \frac{1}{4}$ tone):

$$(8_n \wedge \overline{3}_{n+1}) \vee (8_{n+2} \wedge 3_{n+2}) \vee (8_{n+4} \wedge 3_{n+1}) \vee (8_{n+6} \wedge \overline{3}_n)$$

where $n = 0, 1, 2, \ldots, 23$, modulo 3 or 8.

(It is possible to modify the step ELD by a "rational metabola." Thus the logical function of the major scale with an ELD equal to a quarter-tone can be based on an ELD = 1/3 tone or on any other portion of a tone. These two sieves, in turn, could be combined with the three logical operations to provide more complex scales. Finally, "irrational metabolae" of ELD may be introduced, which can only be applied in non-instrumental music. Accordingly, the ELD can be taken from the field of real numbers).

The scales of limited transpositions, nos. 4 and 7 of Olivier Messiaen[15] (ELD = 1/2 tone):

$$\overline{3}_n \wedge (4_{n+1} \vee 4_{n+3}) \vee \overline{3}_{n+1} \wedge (4_n \vee 4_{n+2})$$
$$4_{n+1} \vee 4_{n+3} \vee \overline{3}_{n+1} \wedge (4_n \vee 4_{n+2})$$

where $n = 0, 1, \ldots$, modulo 3 or 4.

The second axiomatics leads us to vector spaces and graphic and numerical representations.[16]

Two conjunct intervals a and b can be combined by a musical operation to produce a new interval c. This operation is called addition. To either an ascending or a descending interval we may add a second conjunct interval such that the result will be a unison; this second interval is the symmetric interval of the first. Unison is a neutral interval; that is, when it is added to any other interval, it does not modify it. We may also create intervals by association without changing the result. Finally, in composing intervals we can invert the orders of the intervals without changing the result. We have just shown that the naive experience of musicians since antiquity (cf. Aristoxenos) all over the earth attributes the structure of a commutative group to intervals.

Now we are able to combine this group with a field structure. At least two fields are possible: the set of real numbers, R, and the isomorphic set of points on a straight line. It is moreover possible to combine the Abelian group of intervals with the field C of complex numbers or with a field of characteristic P. By definition the combination of the group of intervals with a field forms a vector space in the following manner: As we have just said, interval group G possesses an internal law of composition, addition. Let a and b be two elements of the group. Thus we have:

1. $a + b = c, c \in G$
2. $a + b + c = (a + b) + c = a + (b + c)$ associativity
3. $a + o = o + a,$ with $o \in G$ the neutral element (unison)
4. $a + a' = o,$ with $a' = -a =$ the symmetric interval of a
5. $a + b = b + a$ commutativity

We notate the external composition of elements in G with those in the field C by a dot $\cdot$. If $\lambda, \mu \in C$ (where $C =$ the field of real numbers) then we have the following properties:

6. $\lambda \cdot a, \mu \cdot a \in G$
7. $1 \cdot a = a \cdot 1 = a$ (1 is the neutral element in C with respect to multiplication)
8. $\lambda \cdot (\mu a) = (\lambda \cdot \mu) \cdot a$ \hfill associativity of λ, μ
9. $\left.\begin{array}{l} (\lambda + \mu) \cdot a = \lambda \cdot a + \mu \cdot a \\ \lambda \cdot (a + b) = \lambda \cdot a + \lambda \cdot b \end{array}\right\}$ \hfill distributivity

MUSICAL NOTATIONS AND ENCODINGS

The vector space structure of intervals of certain sound characteristics permits us to treat their elements mathematically and to express them by the set of numbers, which is indispensable for dialogue with computers, or by the set of points on a straight line, graphic expression often being very convenient.

The two preceding axiomatics may be applied to all sound characteristics that possess the same structure. For example, at the moment it would not make sense to speak of a scale of timbre which might be universally accepted as the scales of pitch, instants, and intensity are. On the other hand, time, intensity, density (number of events per unit of time), the quantity of order or disorder (measured by entropy), etc., could be put into one-to-one correspondence with the set of real numbers R and the set of points on a straight line. (See Fig. VIII–1.)

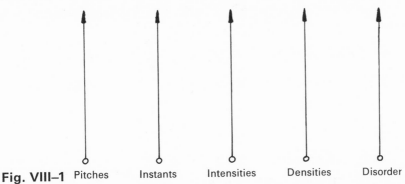

Fig. VIII–1 Pitches   Instants   Intensities   Densities   Disorder

Moreover, the phenomenon of sound is a correspondence of sound characteristics and therefore a correspondence of these axes. The simplest correspondence may be shown by Cartesian coordinates; for example, the two axes in Fig. VIII–2. The unique point (H, T) corresponds to the sound that has a pitch H at the instant T.

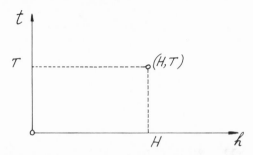

Fig. VIII–2

I must insist here on some facts that trouble many people and that are used by others as false guides. We are all acquainted with the traditional notation, perfected by thousands of years of effort, and which goes back to Ancient Greece. Here we have just represented sounds by two new methods: algebraically by a collection of numbers, and geometrically (or graphically by sketches).

These three types of notation are nothing more than three codes, and indeed there is no more reason to be dismayed by a page of figures than by a full musical score, just as there is no reason to be totemically amazed by a nicely elaborated graph. Each code has its advantages and disadvantages, and the code of classical musical notation is very refined and precise, a synthesis of the other two. It is absurd to think of giving an instrumentalist who knows only notes a diagram to decipher (I am neglecting here certain forms of regression—pseudomystics and mystifiers) or pages covered with numerical notation delivered directly by a computer (unless a special coder is added to it, which would translate the binary results into musical notation). But theoretically all music can be transcribed into these three codes at the same time. The graph and table in Fig. VIII–3 are an example of this correspondence: We must not lose sight of the fact that these three codes are only visual symbols of an auditory reality, itself considered as a symbol.

Graphical Encoding for Macrostructures

At this point of this exposition, the unveiling of history as well as the axiomatic reconstruction have been realized in part, and it would be useless to continue. However, before concluding, I would like to give an example of the advantage of a diagram in studying cases of great complexity.

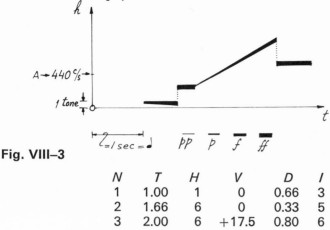

Fig. VIII–3

N	T	H	V	D	I
1	1.00	1	0	0.66	3
2	1.66	6	0	0.33	5
3	2.00	6	+17.5	0.80	6
4	2.80	13	0	?	5

N = note number
H = pitch in half tones with $+10 \triangleq A \triangleq 440\ Hz$
V = slope of glissando (if it exists) in semitones/sec,
    positive if ascending, negative if descending
D = duration in seconds
I = number corresponding to a list of intensity
    forms

Let us imagine some forms constructed with straight lines, using string glissandi, for example.[17] Is it possible to distinguish some elementary forms? Several of these elementary ruled fields are shown in Fig. VIII–4. In fact, they can constitute elements incorporated into larger configurations. Moreover it would be interesting to define and use in sequence the intermediary steps (continuous or discontinuous) from one element to another, especially to pass from the first to the last element in a more or less violent way. If one observes these sonic fields well, one can distinguish the following general qualities, variations of which can combine with these basic general forms:

1. Registers (medium, shrill, etc.)
2. Overall density (large orchestra, small ensemble, etc.)
3. Overall intensity
4. Variation of timbre (*arco, sul ponticello, tremolo,* etc.)
5. Fluctuations (local variations of 1., 2., 3., 4. above)
6. General progress of the form (transformation into other elementary forms)
7. Degree of order. (Total disorder can only make sense if it is calculated according to the kinetic theory of gases. Graphic representation is the most convenient for this study.)

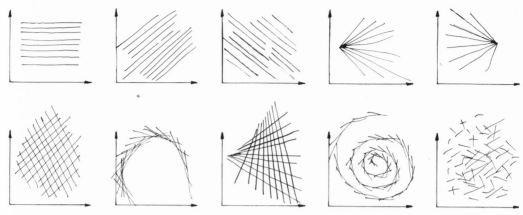

Fig. VIII–4

Let us now suppose the inverse, forms constructed by means of dis-continuity, by sound-points; for example, string pizzicati. Our previous remarks about continuity can be transferred to this case (see Fig. VIII–5). Points 1.–7. are identical, so very broad is the abstraction. Besides, a mixture of discontinuity and continuity gives us a new dimension.

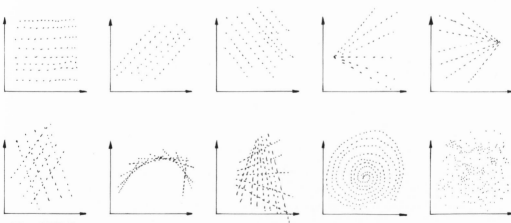

Fig. VIII–5

GENERAL CASE

Organization Outside-Time

Consider a set U and a comparison of U by U (a product $U \times U$) denoted $\psi(U, f)$. Then $\psi(U, f) \subset U \times U$ and for all pairs $(u, u_f) \in U \times U$ such that $u, u_f \in U$, either $(u, u_f) \in \psi(U, f)$, or $(u, u_f) \notin \psi(U, f)$. It is reflexive and $(u \sim u_f) \Rightarrow (u_f \sim u)$; $(u \sim u_f$ and $u_f \sim u') \Rightarrow u \sim u'$ for u, u', $u_f \in \psi(U, f)$.

Thus $\psi(U, f)$ is an equivalence class. In particular if U is isomorphic to the set Q of rational numbers, then $u \sim u_f$ if $|u - u_f| \leq \Delta u_f$ for arbitrary Δu_f.

Now we define $\psi(U, f)$ as the set of weak values of U, $\psi(U, m)$ as the set of average values, and $\psi(U, p)$ as the strong values. We then have

$$\psi = \psi(U, f) \cup \psi(U, m) \cup \psi(U, p) \subseteq U \times U$$

where ψ is the quotient set of U by ψ. The subsets of ψ may intersect or be disjoint, and may or may not form a partition of $U \times U$. Here

$$\psi(U, f) \dashv 3 \; \psi(U, m) \dashv 3 \; \psi(U, p)$$

are ordered by the relation $\dashv 3$ in such a way that the elements of $\psi(U, f)$ are smaller than those of $\psi(U, m)$ and those of $\psi(U, m)$ are smaller than those of $\psi(U, p)$. Then

$$\psi(U, f) \cap \psi(U, m) = \varnothing, \; \psi(U, m) \cap \psi(U, p) = \varnothing.$$

In each of these subsets we define four new equivalence relations and therefore four sub-classes:

$$\psi^i(U, f) \text{ with } u_f^i \sim (u_f^i)'$$

if and only if

$$|u_f^i - (u_f^i)'| \leq \Delta u_f^i \text{ with } u_f^i, (u_f^i)' \in \psi(U, f)$$

for $i = 1, 2, 3, 4$, with $\psi^i(U, f) \subset \psi(U, f)$ and $\psi^1(U, f) \dashv 3 \; \psi^2(U, f) \dashv 3 \; \psi^3(U, f) \dashv 3 \; \psi^4(U, f)$ ordered by the same relation $\dashv 3$. The same equivalence relations and sub-classes are defined for $\psi(U, m)$ and $\psi(U, p)$.

For simplification we write

$$u_i^f = \{u : \; u \in \psi^i(U, f)\},$$

and the same for u_j^m and u_k^p.

In the same way, equivalence sub-classes are created in two other sets, G and D. Here U represents the set of time values, G the set of intensity values, and D the set of density values with

$$U = \{u_i^f, u_j^m, u_k^p\}$$
$$G = \{g_i^f, g_j^m, g_k^p\}$$
$$D = \{d_i^f, d_j^m, d_k^p\}$$

for $i, j, k = 1, 2, 3, 4$.

Take part of the triple product $U \times G \times D$ composed of the points $(u_n^\tau, g_i^\rho, d_j^\sigma)$. Consider the *paths* $V1$: $\{u_i^p, g_i^m, d_i^f\}$, $V2$: $\{u_i^f, g_i^p, d_i^m\}, \ldots$, VS: $\{(u_1^p, u_2^f, u_3^m, u_4^p), (g_1^f, g_2^m, g_3^f, g_4^p), (d_1^m, d_2^f, d_3^p, d_4^m)\}$ for $i = 1, 2, 3, 4$. VS will be a subset of the triple product $U \times G \times D$ split into $4^3 = 64$ different points.

In each of these subsets choose a new subset K_j^λ defined by the n points K_j^λ ($j = 1, 2, \ldots, n$ and $\lambda = V1, V2, \ldots, VS$). These n points are considered as the n vertices of a regular polyhedron. Consider the transformations which leave the polyhedron unchanged, that is, its corresponding group.

To sum up, we have the following chain of inclusions:

ω	$\in$	$S^{K_s^\lambda}$	$\subset$	K_j^λ	$\subset$	λ	$\subset \psi \subseteq U \times G \times D.$
element		vertex of		set of		path λ	
of		the poly-		vertices		(subset of	
$U \times G \times D$		hedron K_j		of the		$U \times G \times D$)	
				polyhedron			

Consider the two other sets H (pitch) and X (sonic material, way of playing, etc.). Form the product $H \times X \times C$ in which C is the set of n forms or complexes or sound types C_i ($i = 1, 2, \ldots, n$); for example, a cloud of sound-points or a cloud of glissandi. Map the product $H \times X \times C$ onto the vertices of the polyhedron K_j^λ.

1. The complexes C_i traverse the fixed vertices and thus produce group transformations; we call this operation θ_0.

2. The complexes C_i are attached to corresponding vertices which remain fixed, but the $H \times X$ traverse the vertices, also producing group transformations; this operation is called θ_1.

3. The product $H \times X \times C$ traverses the vertices thus producing the group transformations of the polyhedron; we call this operation θ_μ because the product can change definition at each transformation of the polyhedron.

Organization In-Time

The last mapping will be inscribed in time in two possible ways in order to manifest the peculiarities of this polyhedral group or the symmetric group to which it is isomorphic: operation t_0—the vertices of the polyhedron are expressed successively (model of the symmetric group); operation t_1—the vertices are expressed simultaneously (n simultaneous voices).

Product $t_0 \times \theta_0$:

The vertices K_i^λ are expressed successively with:

1. only one sonic complex C_r, always the same one, for example, a cloud of sound-points only,

2. several sonic complexes, at most n, in one-to-one attachment with indices of vertices K_i^λ,

3. several sonic complexes whose successive appearances express the operations of the polyhedral group, the vertices i (defined by $U \times G \times D$) always appearing in the same order,

4. several sonic complexes always in the same order while the order of the vertices i reproduces the group transformations,

5. several sonic complexes transforming independently from the vertices of the polyhedron.

Product $t_0 \times \theta_1$:

The list which this product generates may be obtained from the preceding one by substituting $H \times X$ in place of c_i.

Product $t_0 \times \theta$:

This list may be readily established.

Case t_1 and θ_j is obtained from the preceding ones by analogy.

To these in-time operational products one ought to be able to add *in-space* operations when, for example, the sonic sources are distributed in space in significant manner, as in *Terrêtektorh* or *Nomos gamma*.

Organization Outside-Time

The three sets, D (densities), G (intensities), U (durations), are mapped onto three vector spaces or onto a single three-dimensional vector space. The following selection (subset) of equivalence classes, called path $V1$, is made: D (densities) strong, G (intensities) strong, U (durations) weak. Precise and ordered values have been given to these classes:

Set D	a	b	c	Set G		Set U	sec
	(Elements/sec)						
d_1	1.0	0.5	1	g_1	mf	u_1	2
d_2	1.5	1.08	2	g_2	f	u_2	3
d_3	2.0	2.32	3	g_3	ff	u_3	4
d_4	2.5	5.00	4	g_4	fff	u_4	5

A second selection (subset), called path $V2$, is formed in the following manner: D strong, G average, U strong, with ordered and precise values:

Set D	Elements/sec	Set G		Set U	sec
d_1	0.5	g_1	p	u_1	10
d_2	1	g_2	mp	u_2	17
d_3	2	g_3	mf	u_3	21
d_4	3	g_4	f	u_4	30

Eight "points" of the triple product $D \times G \times U$ are selected. For path $V1$:

$$K_1^r = d_1 g_1 u_1; \quad K_2^r = d_1 g_4 u_4; \quad K_3^r = d_4 g_4 a_4; \quad K_4^r = d_4 g_1 u_1;$$
$$K_5^r = d_2 g_2 u_2; \quad K_6^r = d_2 g_3 u_3; \quad K_7^r = d_3 g_3 u_3; \quad K_8^r = d_3 g_2 u_2.$$

r is the column (sub-class) of the table of set D. ($r = a, b, c$.)

For path $V2$:

$$K_1 = d_4 g_3 u_2; \quad K_2 = d_3 g_2 u_1; \quad K_3 = d_2 g_4 u_4; \quad K_4 = d_1 g_2 u_3;$$
$$K_5 = d_4 g_1 u_4; \quad K_6 = d_3 g_2 u_3; \quad K_7 = d_2 g_3 u_2; \quad K_8 = d_1 g_4 u_1.$$

I. These eight points are regarded as solidly connected to each other so as to form a cube (a mapping of these eight points onto the vertices of a cube). The group formed by substitutions among these eight points, isomorphic to the symmetric group P_4, is taken as the organizer principle. (See Fig. VIII–6.)

ANALYSIS OF *NOMOS ALPHA*

Organization In-Time

I. The symmetry transformations of a cube given by the elements K_i^r form the hexahedral group isomorphic to the symmetric group P_4. The rules for in-time setting are: 1. The vertices of the cube are sounded successively at each transformation thanks to a one-to-one correspondence. 2. The transformations are themselves successive (for a larger ensemble of instruments one could choose one of the possible simultaneities as in *Nomos gamma*). They follow various graphs (kinematic diagrams) inherent in the internal structure of this particular group. (See Figs. VIII–6, 7, 8.)

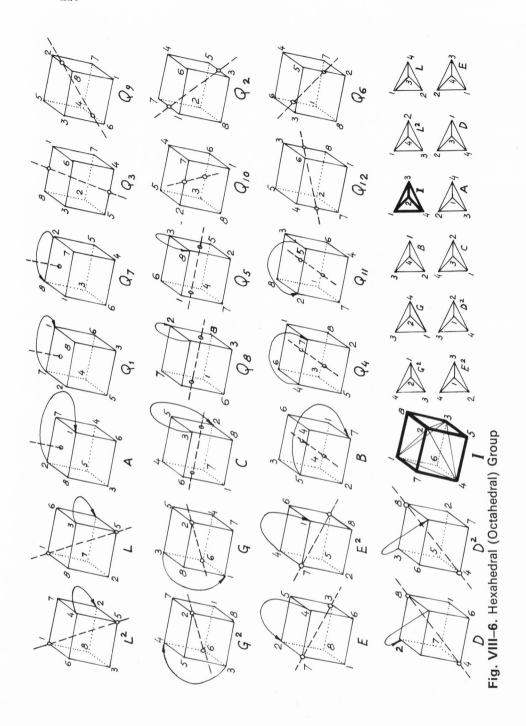

Fig. VIII–6. Hexahedral (Octahedral) Group

↓	I	A	B	C	D	D^2	E	E^2	G	G^2	L	L^2	Q_1	Q_2	Q_3	Q_4	Q_5	Q_6	Q_7	Q_8	Q_9	Q_{10}	Q_{11}	Q_{12}
I	I	A	B	C	D	D^2	E	E^2	G	G^2	L	L^2	Q_1	Q_2	Q_3	Q_4	Q_5	Q_6	Q_7	Q_8	Q_9	Q_{10}	Q_{11}	Q_{12}
A	A	I	C	B	G	L	G^2	L^2	D	E	D^2	E^2	Q_7	Q_4	Q_5	Q_2	Q_3	Q_{12}	Q_1	Q_{10}	Q_{11}	Q_8	Q_9	Q_6
B	B	C	I	A	L^2	E	D^2	G	E^2	L	G^2	D	Q_6	Q_9	Q_8	Q_{11}	Q_{10}	Q_1	Q_{12}	Q_3	Q_2	Q_5	Q_4	Q_7
C	C	B	A	I	E^2	G^2	L	D	L^2	D^2	E	G	Q_{12}	Q_{11}	Q_{10}	Q_9	Q_8	Q_7	Q_6	Q_5	Q_4	Q_3	Q_2	Q_1
D	D	L^2	E^2	G	D^2	I	C	L	E	A	B	G^2	Q_3	Q_6	Q_4	Q_1	Q_{11}	Q_{10}	Q_8	Q_9	Q_7	Q_2	Q_{12}	Q_5
D^2	D^2	G^2	L	E	I	D	G	B	C	L^2	E^2	A	Q_4	Q_{10}	Q_1	Q_3	Q_{12}	Q_2	Q_9	Q_7	Q_8	Q_6	Q_5	Q_{11}
E	E	L	G^2	D^2	B	L^2	E^2	I	A	D	G	C	Q_{11}	Q_5	Q_6	Q_8	Q_7	Q_9	Q_2	Q_{12}	Q_3	Q_1	Q_{10}	Q_4
E^2	E^2	G	D	L^2	G^2	C	I	E	L	B	A	D^2	Q_{10}	Q_7	Q_9	Q_{12}	Q_2	Q_3	Q_5	Q_4	Q_6	Q_{11}	Q_1	Q_8
G	G	E^2	L^2	D	L	A	B	D^2	G^2	I	C	E	Q_5	Q_2	Q_3	Q_7	Q_9	Q_8	Q_{10}	Q_{11}	Q_1	Q_4	Q_6	Q_3
G^2	G^2	D^2	E	L	C	E^2	L^2	A	I	G	D	B	Q_9	Q_3	Q_{12}	Q_{10}	Q_1	Q_4	Q_4	Q_6	Q_5	Q_7	Q_8	Q_2
L	L	E	D^2	G^2	A	G	D	C	B	E^2	L^2	I	Q_2	Q_8	Q_7	Q_5	Q_6	Q_4	Q_{11}	Q_1	Q_{10}	Q_{12}	Q_3	Q_9
L^2	L^2	D	G	E^2	E	B	A	G^2	D^2	C	I	L	Q_8	Q_1	Q_{11}	Q_6	Q_4	Q_5	Q_3	Q_2	Q_{12}	Q_9	Q_7	Q_{10}
Q_1	Q_1	Q_7	Q_{12}	Q_6	Q_9	Q_5	Q_8	Q_2	Q_{11}	Q_{10}	Q_3	Q_4	A	L^2	D^2	E^2	L	B	I	G^2	G	E	D	C
Q_2	Q_2	Q_{11}	Q_9	Q_4	Q_{10}	Q_6	Q_1	Q_8	Q_3	Q_{12}	Q_7	Q_5	E	I	G	C	L^2	D^2	L	E^2	B	D	A	G^2
Q_3	Q_3	Q_8	Q_5	Q_{10}	Q_7	Q_{11}	Q_9	Q_6	Q_{12}	Q_2	Q_4	Q_1	L^2	G^2	I	L	B	E^2	D	A	E	C	D^2	G
Q_4	Q_4	Q_9	Q_{11}	Q_2	Q_8	Q_{12}	Q_7	Q_{10}	Q_5	Q_6	Q_1	Q_3	G^2	A	D	B	E^2	L	D^2	L^2	C	G	I	E
Q_5	Q_5	Q_{10}	Q_3	Q_8	Q_1	Q_9	Q_{11}	Q_{12}	Q_6	Q_4	Q_2	Q_7	E^2	E	A	D^2	C	L^2	G	I	G^2	B	L	D
Q_6	Q_6	Q_{12}	Q_7	Q_1	Q_2	Q_{10}	Q_3	Q_9	Q_4	Q_5	Q_8	Q_{11}	C	D	E	G	G^2	I	B	L	E^2	D^2	L^2	A
Q_7	Q_7	Q_1	Q_6	Q_{12}	Q_{11}	Q_3	Q_{10}	Q_4	Q_9	Q_8	Q_5	Q_2	I	E^2	L	L^2	D^2	C	A	E	D	G^2	G	B
Q_8	Q_8	Q_3	Q_{10}	Q_5	Q_{12}	Q_4	Q_2	Q_1	Q_7	Q_9	Q_{11}	Q_6	D	L	B	G^2	I	G	L^2	C	D^2	A	E	E^2
Q_9	Q_9	Q_4	Q_2	Q_{11}	Q_5	Q_1	Q_6	Q_3	Q_8	Q_7	Q_{12}	Q_{10}	D^2	B	E^2	A	D	E	G^2	G	I	L^2	C	L
Q_{10}	Q_{10}	Q_5	Q_8	Q_3	Q_6	Q_2	Q_4	Q_7	Q_1	Q_{11}	Q_9	Q_{12}	G	D^2	C	E	A	D	E^2	B	L	I	G^2	L^2
Q_{11}	Q_{11}	Q_2	Q_4	Q_9	Q_3	Q_7	Q_{12}	Q_5	Q_{10}	Q_1	Q_6	Q_8	L	C	L^2	I	G	G^2	E	D	A	E^2	B	D^2
Q_{12}	Q_{12}	Q_6	Q_1	Q_7	Q_4	Q_8	Q_5	Q_{11}	Q_2	Q_3	Q_{10}	Q_9	B	G	G^2	D	E	A	C	D^2	L^2	L	E^2	I

Fig. VIII–7

Example : $DA = D$, then on D the transformation A (columns $\rightarrow$ rows) $= G$

Fig. VIII–6. Symmetric Group P_4 : (1, 2, 3, 4)

I	12345678	G	32417685	Q_5	68572413
A	21436587	G^2	42138657	Q_6	65782134
B	34127856	L	13425786	Q_7	87564312
C	43218765	L^2	14235867	Q_8	75863142
D	23146758	Q_1	78653421	Q_9	58761432
D^2	31247568	Q_2	76583214	Q_{10}	57681324
E	24316875	Q_3	86754231	Q_{11}	85674123
E^2	41328576	Q_4	67852341	Q_{12}	56871243

The numbers in roman type
also correspond to Group $P_4 = 4!$

Organization Outside-Time

II. Eight elements from the macroscopic sound complexes are mapped onto the letters C_i in three ways, α, β, γ:

α β γ

C_1 C_1 C_1 = ataxic cloud of sound-points

C_7 C_2 C_5 = relatively ordered ascending or descending cloud of sound-points

C_3 C_3 C_6 = relatively ordered cloud of sound-points, neither ascending nor descending

C_5 C_5 C_2 = ataxic field of sliding sounds

C_6 C_6 C_3 = relatively ordered ascending or descending field of sliding sounds

C_2 C_7 C_4 = relatively ordered field of sliding sounds, neither ascending nor descending

C_8 C_8 C_8 = atom represented on a cello by interferences of a quasi-unison

C_4 C_4 C_7 = ionized atom represented on a cello by interferences, accompanied by pizzicati

III. These letters are mapped one-to-one onto the eight vertices of a second cube. Thus a second hexahedral group is taken as the organizer principle.

Organization In-Time

II. The mapping of the eight forms onto the letters C_i change cyclically in the order α, β, γ, α, ... after each three substitutions of the cube.

III. The same is true for the cube of the letters C_i.

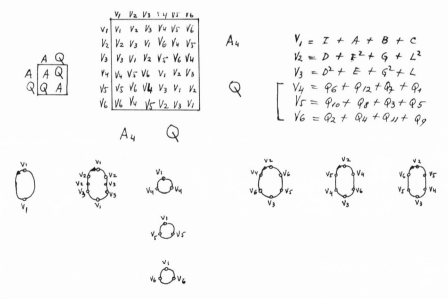

Fig. VIII–8

Organization Outside-Time

IV. Take the products $K_i^r \times C_j$ and $K_l \times C_m$. Then take the product set $H \times X$. Set H is the vector space of pitch, while set X is the set of ways of playing the C_i. This product is given by a table of double entries:

Extremely High													
Medium High													
Medium Low													
Extremely Low													

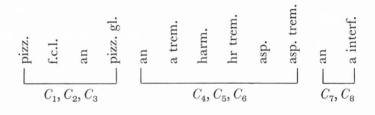

pizz.	f.c.l.	an	pizz. gl.	an	a trem.	harm.	hr trem.	asp.	asp. trem.	an	a interf.
C_1, C_2, C_3				C_4, C_5, C_6						C_7, C_8	

pizz. = pizzicati
f.c.l. = struck with the wood of the
      bow
an = normal arco
pizz. gl. = pizzicato-glissando
a trem. = normal arco with tremolo
harm. = harmonic sound

hr trem. = harmonic sound with
      tremolo
asp = arco sul ponticello
asp trem. = arco sul ponticello
      tremolo
a interf. = arco with interferences

Various methods of playing are attributed to the forms $C_1, \ldots, C_8$, as indicated in the table. The first and fourth rows, extremely high and extremely low pitches, are reserved for path $V2$. A sub-space of H' is attributed to path $V1$. It consists of the second and third rows of the preceding table, each divided into two. These four parts are defined in terms of the playing range of the corresponding column.

V. The mapping of C_1 onto the product set $H \times X$ is relatively independent and will be determined by a kinematic diagram of operations at the moment of the in-time setting.

Organization In-Time

IV. The products $K_i^r \times C_j$ and $K_l \times C_m$ are the result of the product of two graphs of closed transformations of the cube in itself. The mapping of the graphs is one-to-one and sounded successively; for example:

$$\left| \begin{array}{c} C_i \\ \downarrow K_j \end{array} \right. \longrightarrow \left| \begin{array}{c} \text{graph } (\overrightarrow{D\ Q_2}) \\ \downarrow \text{graph } (\overrightarrow{D\ Q_3}) \end{array} \right.$$

(See Figs. VIII–9, 10.)

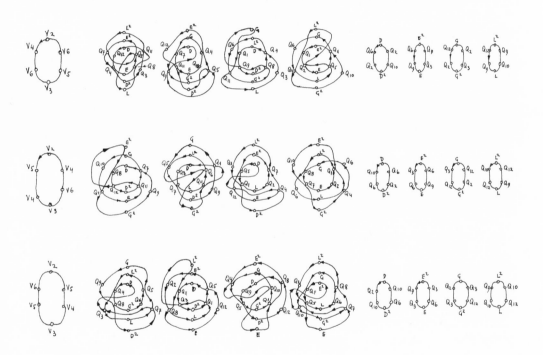

Fig. VIII–9

V. Each C_i is mapped onto one of the cells of $H \times X$ according to two principles: maximum expansion (minimum repetition), and maximum contrast or maximum resemblance. (See Fig. VIII–11.)

	α	β	γ	
d_1:	1.0	0.5	1	
d_2:	1.5	1.08	2	events/sec
d_3:	2.0	2.32	3	
d_4:	2.5	5.00	4	

PATH V1

$(\sigma_i = C_i)$

$i(\sigma)$ D	σ_2	σ_3	σ_1	σ_4	σ_6	σ_7	σ_5	σ_8
$i(k)$ D	k_2	k_3	k_1	k_4	k_6	k_7	k_5	k_8
$\Lambda\,(11,13)$ β								
$L\,(11,13)$	2.25	2.25	1.0	10.0	3.72	7.98	2.83	6.08
	♯♯♯	♯♯♯	mf	mf	♯♯	♯	f	f

$i(\sigma)$ Q_{12}	σ_5	σ_6	σ_8	σ_7	σ_1	σ_2	σ_4	σ_3
$i(k)$ Q_3	k_8	k_6	k_7	k_5	k_4	k_2	k_3	k_1
	6.08	3.72	7.98	2.83	10.0	2.25	2.25	1.00
	f	♯♯	♯♯	f	mf	♯♯♯	♯♯♯	mf

$i(\sigma)$ Q_4	σ_6	σ_7	σ_8	σ_5	σ_2	σ_3	σ_4	σ_1
$i(k)$ Q_7	k_8	k_7	k_5	k_6	k_4	k_3	k_1	k_2
	6.08	7.98	2.83	3.72	10.00	2.25	1.00	2.25
	f	♯♯	f	♯♯	mf	♯♯♯	mf	♯♯♯

$i(\sigma)$ E	σ_2	σ_4	σ_3	σ_1	σ_6	σ_8	σ_7	σ_5
$i(k)$ L	k_1	k_3	k_4	k_2	k_5	k_7	k_8	k_6
$\Lambda\,(13,11)$ γ								
$L\,(13,11)$	2	14	8	4.5	5.24	10.32	7.86	6.88
	mf	♯♯♯	mf	♯♯♯	f	♯♯	f	♯♯

$i(\sigma)$ Q_8	σ_7	σ_5	σ_8	σ_6	σ_3	σ_1	σ_4	σ_2
$i(k)$ Q_{11}	k_8	k_5	k_6	k_7	k_4	k_1	k_2	k_3
	7.86	5.24	6.88	10.32	8	2	4.5	14
	f	f	♯♯	♯♯	mf	mf	♯♯♯	♯♯♯

$i(\sigma)$ Q_2	σ_7	σ_6	σ_5	σ_8	σ_3	σ_2	σ_1	σ_4
$i(k)$ Q_6	k_6	k_5	k_7	k_8	k_2	k_1	k_3	k_4
	6.88	5.24	10.32	7.86	4.5	2	14	8
	♯♯	f	♯♯	f	♯♯♯	mf	♯♯♯	mf

Fig. VIII–10

For Path V1

$$K_1^\alpha = 1. \; mf \cdot 2 \qquad\quad = 2 \cdot mf \qquad\quad K_1^\beta = 0.5 \cdot mf \cdot 2 \qquad = 1.0 \cdot mf \qquad K_1^\delta = 1.0 \cdot mf \cdot 2.0 \qquad = 2.0 \cdot mf$$
$$K_2^\alpha = 1. \; \sharp\!\!\!\sharp \cdot 4 \cdot 5 \qquad = 4.5 \cdot \sharp\!\!\!\sharp \qquad K_2^\beta = 0.5 \cdot \sharp\!\!\!\sharp \cdot 4 \cdot 5 \qquad = 2.25 \cdot \sharp\!\!\!\sharp \qquad K_2^\delta = 1.0 \cdot \sharp\!\!\!\sharp \cdot 4 \cdot 5 \qquad = 4.5 \cdot \sharp\!\!\!\sharp$$
$$K_3^\alpha = 2.5 \cdot \sharp\!\!\!\sharp \cdot 4 \cdot 5 = 11.25 \sharp\!\!\!\sharp \qquad K_3^\beta = 5.0 \cdot \sharp\!\!\!\sharp \cdot 4 \cdot 5 \qquad = 22.5 \cdot \sharp\!\!\!\sharp \qquad K_3^\delta = 4.0 \cdot \sharp\!\!\!\sharp \cdot 4 \cdot 5 \qquad = 18.0 \cdot \sharp\!\!\!\sharp$$
$$K_4^\alpha = 2.5 \cdot mf \cdot 2 \qquad = 5 \cdot mf \qquad K_4^\beta = 5.0 \cdot mf \cdot 2 \qquad = 10.0 \, mf \qquad K_4^\delta = 4.0 \cdot mf \cdot 20 \qquad = 8.0 \cdot mf$$
$$K_5^\alpha = 1.5 \cdot f \cdot 2 \cdot 62' = 3.93 \, f \qquad K_5^\beta = 1.08 \cdot f \cdot 2 \cdot 62 \qquad = 2.83 \cdot f \qquad K_5^\delta = 2.0 \cdot f \cdot 2.62 \qquad = 5.24 \cdot f$$
$$K_6^\alpha = 1.5 \cdot \sharp\!\!\!\sharp \cdot 3 \cdot 44 = 5.15 \cdot \sharp\!\!\!\sharp \qquad K_6^\beta = 1.08 \cdot \sharp\!\!\!\sharp \cdot 3 \cdot 44 \qquad = 3.72 \cdot \sharp\!\!\!\sharp \qquad K_6^\delta = 2.0 \cdot \sharp\!\!\!\sharp \cdot 3 \cdot 44 \qquad = 6.88 \cdot \sharp\!\!\!\sharp$$
$$K_7^\alpha = 2.0 \cdot \sharp\!\!\!\sharp \cdot 3 \cdot 44 = 6.88 \cdot \sharp\!\!\!\sharp \qquad K_7^\beta = 2.32 \cdot \sharp\!\!\!\sharp \cdot 3 \cdot 44 \qquad = 7.98 \cdot \sharp\!\!\!\sharp \qquad K_7^\delta = 3.0 \cdot \sharp\!\!\!\sharp \cdot 3 \cdot 44 \qquad = 10.32 \cdot \sharp\!\!\!\sharp$$
$$K_8^\alpha = 2.0 \cdot f \cdot 2 \cdot 62 = 5 \cdot 24 \cdot f \qquad K_8^\beta = 2.32 \cdot f \cdot 2 \cdot 62 \qquad = 6.08 \cdot f \qquad K_8^\delta = 3.0 \cdot f \cdot 2 \cdot 62 \qquad = 7.86 \cdot f$$

$i\,(\sigma)\;E^2$	σ_4	σ_1	σ_3	σ_2	σ_8	σ_5	σ_7	σ_6
$i\,(k)\;L^2$	k_1	k_4	k_2	k_3	k_5	k_8	k_6	k_7
α								
$\wedge(11,5)$								
$L(11,5)$	2	5	4.5	11.25	3.93	5.24	5.15	6.88
	mf	mf	$\sharp\!\!\!\sharp$	$\sharp\!\!\!\sharp$	f	f	$\sharp\!\!\!\sharp$	$\sharp\!\!\!\sharp$

$i\,(\sigma)\;L^2$	σ_1	σ_4	σ_2	σ_3	σ_5	σ_8	σ_6	σ_7
$i\,(k)\;G$	k_3	k_2	k_4	k_1	k_7	k_6	k_8	k_5
γ								
$\wedge(7,5)$								
$L(7,5)$	14	4.5	8	2	10.32	6.88	7.86	5.24
	$\sharp\!\!\!\sharp$	$\sharp\!\!\!\sharp$	mf	mf	$\sharp\!\!\!\sharp$	$\sharp\!\!\!\sharp$	f	f

$i\,(\sigma)\;Q_7$	σ_8	σ_7	σ_5	σ_6	σ_4	σ_3	σ_1	σ_2
$i\,(k)\;Q_5$	k_6	k_8	k_5	k_7	k_2	k_4	k_1	k_3
	5.15	5.24	3.93	6.88	4.5	5	2	11.25
	$\sharp\!\!\!\sharp$	f	f	$\sharp\!\!\!\sharp$	$\sharp\!\!\!\sharp$	mf	mf	$\sharp\!\!\!\sharp$

$i\,(\sigma)\;Q_7$	σ_8	σ_7	σ_5	σ_6	σ_4	σ_3	σ_1	σ_2
$i\,(k)\;Q_5$	k_6	k_8	k_5	k_7	k_2	k_4	k_1	k_3
	6.88	7.86	5.24	10.32	4.5	8	2	14
	$\sharp\!\!\!\sharp$	f	f	$\sharp\!\!\!\sharp$	$\sharp\!\!\!\sharp$	mf	mf	$\sharp\!\!\!\sharp$

$i\,(\sigma)\;Q_4$	σ_6	σ_7	σ_8	σ_5	σ_2	σ_3	σ_4	σ_1
$i\,(k)\;Q_7$	k_8	k_7	k_5	k_6	k_4	k_3	k_1	k_2
	5.24	6.88	3.93	5.15	5	11.25	2	4.5
	f	$\sharp\!\!\!\sharp$	f	$\sharp\!\!\!\sharp$	mf	$\sharp\!\!\!\sharp$	mf	$\sharp\!\!\!\sharp$

$i\,(\sigma)\;Q_2$	σ_7	σ_6	σ_5	σ_8	σ_3	σ_2	σ_1	σ_4
$i\,(k)\;Q_6$	k_6	k_5	k_7	k_8	k_2	k_1	k_3	k_4
	6.88	5.24	10.32	7.86	4.5	2	14	8
	$\sharp\!\!\!\sharp$	f	$\sharp\!\!\!\sharp$	f	$\sharp\!\!\!\sharp$	mf	$\sharp\!\!\!\sharp$	mf

$i\,(\sigma)\;D^2$	σ_3	σ_1	σ_2	σ_4	σ_7	σ_5	σ_6	σ_8
$i\,(k)\;D^2$	k_3	k_1	k_2	k_4	k_7	k_5	k_6	k_8
β								
$\wedge(5,7)$								
$L(5,7)$	22.5	1	12.25	10	7.98	2.83	3.72	6.08
	$\sharp\!\!\!\sharp$	mf	$\sharp\!\!\!\sharp$	mf	$\sharp\!\!\!\sharp$	f	$\sharp\!\!\!\sharp$	f

$i\,(\sigma)\;L^2$	σ_1	σ_3	σ_4	σ_2	σ_5	σ_7	σ_8	σ_6
$i\,(k)\;G$	k_4	k_2	k_1	k_3	k_8	k_6	k_5	k_7
α								
$\wedge(5,11)$								
$L(5,11)$	5	4.5	2	11.25	5.24	5.15	3.93	6.88
	mf	$\sharp\!\!\!\sharp$	mf	$\sharp\!\!\!\sharp$	f	$\sharp\!\!\!\sharp$	f	$\sharp\!\!\!\sharp$

$i\,(\sigma)\;Q_3$	σ_8	σ_6	σ_7	σ_5	σ_4	σ_2	σ_3	σ_1
$i\,(k)\;Q_9$	k_5	k_8	k_7	k_6	k_1	k_4	k_3	k_2
	2.83	6.08	7.98	3.72	1	10	22.5	2.25
	f	f	$\sharp\!\!\!\sharp$	$\sharp\!\!\!\sharp$	mf	mf	$\sharp\!\!\!\sharp$	$\sharp\!\!\!\sharp$

$i\,(\sigma)\;Q_8$	σ_7	σ_5	σ_8	σ_6	σ_3	σ_1	σ_4	σ_2
$i\,(k)\;Q_{11}$	k_8	k_5	k_6	k_7	k_4	k_1	k_2	k_3
	5.24	3.93	5.15	6.88	5	2	4.5	11.25
	f	f	$\sharp\!\!\!\sharp$	$\sharp\!\!\!\sharp$	mf	mf	$\sharp\!\!\!\sharp$	$\sharp\!\!\!\sharp$

$i\,(\sigma)\;Q_{11}$	σ_8	σ_5	σ_6	σ_7	σ_4	σ_1	σ_2	σ_3
$i\,(k)\;Q_1$	k_7	k_8	k_6	k_5	k_3	k_4	k_2	k_1
	7.98	6.08	3.72	2.83	22.5	10	2.25	1
	$\sharp\!\!\!\sharp$	f	$\sharp\!\!\!\sharp$	f	$\sharp\!\!\!\sharp$	mf	$\sharp\!\!\!\sharp$	mf

$i\,(\sigma)\;Q_{11}$	σ_8	σ_5	σ_6	σ_7	σ_4	σ_1	σ_2	σ_3
$i\,(k)\;Q_1$	k_7	k_8	k_6	k_5	k_3	k_1	k_2	k_1
	6.88	5.24	5.15	3.93	11.25	5	4.5	2
	$\sharp\!\!\!\sharp$	f	$\sharp\!\!\!\sharp$	f	$\sharp\!\!\!\sharp$	mf	$\sharp\!\!\!\sharp$	mf

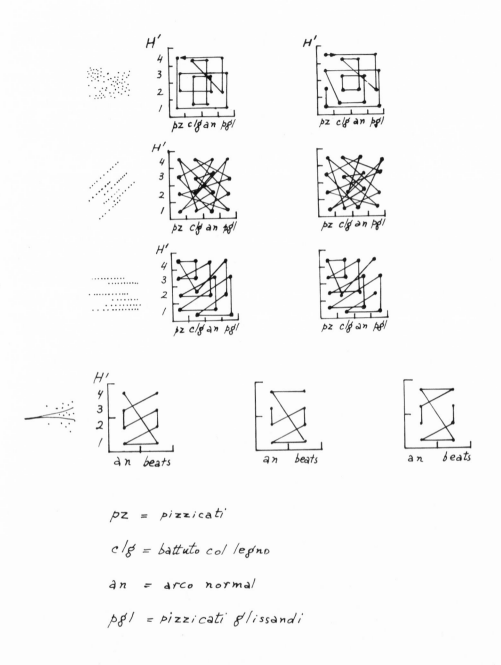

pz = pizzicati

c/g = battuto col legno

an = arco normal

pgl = pizzicati glissandi

Fig. VIII–11. Products $H' \times X$ in the Set of the C_i

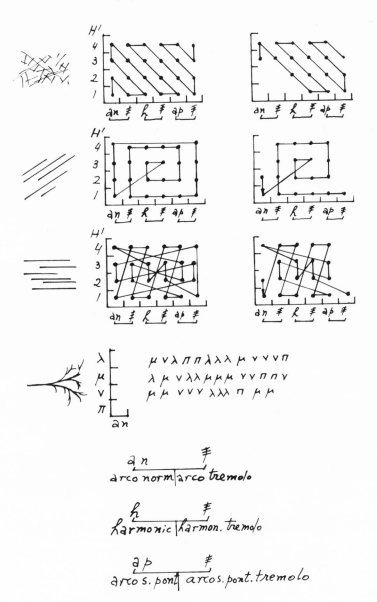

Organization Outside-Time

VI. The products $K_i^? \times C_i \times H' \times X$ and $K_j \times C_l \times H^{\text{extremes}} \times X$ are formed.

VII. The set of logical functions (a) is used in this piece. Its moduli are taken from the subset formed by the prime residual classes modulo 18, with multiplication, and reduction modulo 18.

$$L(m, n) = \overline{(n_i \vee n_j \vee n_k \vee n_l)} \wedge m_p \vee \overline{(m_q \vee m_r)} \wedge n_s \vee (n_t \vee n_u \vee n_w) \quad \text{(a)}$$

Its elements are developed:

1. From a departure function:

$$L(11, 13) = \overline{(13_3 \vee 13_5 \vee 13_7 \vee 13_9)} \wedge 11_2 \vee \overline{(11_4 \vee 11_8)}$$
$$\wedge \, 13_9 \vee (13_0 \vee 13_1 \vee 13_6)$$

2. From a "metabola" of moduli which is identical here to the graph coupling the elements of the preceding subset. This metabola gives the following functions: $L(11, 13)$, $L(17, 5)$, $L(13, 11)$, $L(17, 7)$, $L(11, 5)$, $L(1, 5)$, $L(5, 7)$, $L(17, 11)$, $L(7, 5)$, $L(17, 13)$, $L(5, 11)$, $L(1, 11)$. (See Fig. VIII–12, and Table of the Sieve Functions and Their Metabolae.)

3. From three substitution rules for indices (residual classes):

Rule a: $m_0 \rightarrow n_{0+1}$

Rule b: If all indices within a set of parentheses are equal, the next function $L(m, n)$ puts them in arithmetic progression modulo the corresponding sieve.

Rule c: Conversion of indices as a consequence of moduli metabolae (see Rule c. Table):

$$m_j \rightarrow n_x, \quad x = j(n/m); \quad \text{for example,} \quad 7_4 \rightarrow 11_x, \quad x = 4(11/7) \sim 6.$$

4. From a metabola of ELD (elementary displacement: one quarter-tone for path $V1$, three-quarters of a tone for path $V2$).

The two types of metabolae which generate the elements of set $L(m, n)$ can be used outside-time or inscribed in-time. In the first case, they give us the totality of the elements; in the second case, these elements appear in a temporal order. Nevertheless a *structure* of temporal order is subjacent even in the first case.

5. From a special metabola that would simultaneously attribute different notes to the origins of the sieves constituting the function $L(m, n)$.

Organization In-Time

VI. The elements of the product $K_i^r \times C_j \times H' \times X$ of the path $V1$ are sounded successively, except for interpolation of elements of the product $K_i \times C_i \times H^{\text{extremes}} \times X$ from path $V2$, which are sounded intermittently.

VII. Each of the three substitutions of the two cubes K_i and C_j, the logical function $L(m, n)$ (see Fig. VIII–11), changes following its kinematic diagram, developed from the group: multiplication by pairs of residual classes and reduction modulo 18. (See Fig. VIII–10.)

Table of the Sieve Functions and Their Metabolae

$$L(11, 13) = (\overline{13_3 + 13_5 + 13_7 + 13_9})11_2 + (\overline{11_4 + 11_8})13_9$$
$$+ 13_0 + 13_1 + 13_6$$

$$L(17, 5) = (\overline{5_1 + 5_2 + 5_3 + 5_4})17_1 + (\overline{17_7 + 17_{13}})5_4 + 5_1 + 5_0 + 5_2$$

$$L(13, 11) = (\overline{11_2 + 11_4 + 11_7 + 11_9})13_0 + (\overline{13_5 + 13_{10}})11_9$$
$$+ 11_2 + 11_1 + 11_4$$

$$L(17, 7) = (\overline{7_1 + 7_3 + 7_5 + 7_6})17_1 + (\overline{17_6 + 17_{13}})7_6 + 7_1 + 7_0 + 7_3$$

$$L(11, 5) = (\overline{5_0 + 5_2 + 5_3 + 5_4})11_0 + (\overline{11_4 + 11_8})5_4 + 5_0 + 5_1 + 5_2$$

$$L(1, 5) = (\overline{5_1 + 5_2 + 5_3 + 5_4})1_1 + (\overline{1_1 + 1_1})5_4 + 5_1 + 5_2 + 5_3$$

$$L(5, 7) = (\overline{7_1 + 7_3 + 7_4 + 7_6})5_0 + (\overline{5_0 + 5_1})7_6 + 7_1 + 7_3 + 7_4$$

$$L(17, 11) = (\overline{11_2 + 11_5 + 11_6 + 11_9})11_1 + (\overline{17_1 + 17_3})11_9$$
$$+ 11_2 + 11_5 + 11_6$$

$$L(7, 5) = (\overline{5_1 + 5_2 + 5_3 + 5_4})7_0 + (\overline{7_0 + 7_1})5_4 + 5_1 + 5_2 + 5_3$$

$$L(17, 13) = (\overline{13_3 + 13_5 + 13_8 + 13_{10}})17_1 + (\overline{17_1 + 17_2})13_{10}$$
$$+ 13_3 + 13_5 + 13_8$$

$$L(5, 11) = (\overline{11_3 + 11_4 + 11_7 + 11_8})5_0 + (\overline{5_0 + 5_1})11_8 + 11_3 + 11_4 + 11_7$$

$$L(1, 11) = (\overline{11_3 + 11_4 + 11_7 + 11_8})1_1 + (\overline{1_1 + 1_0})11_8 + 11_3 + 11_4 + 11_7$$

Rule c. Table

$$\frac{n}{m}: \quad \frac{5}{5} = 1$$

$\frac{7}{5} = 1.4$	$\frac{7}{7} = 1$		
$\frac{11}{5} = 2.2$	$\frac{11}{7} = 1.57$	$\frac{11}{11} = 1$	
$\frac{13}{5} = 2.6$	$\frac{13}{7} = 1.85$	$\frac{13}{11} = 1.2$	$\frac{13}{13} = 1$
$\frac{17}{5} = 3.4$	$\frac{17}{7} = 2.43$	$\frac{17}{11} = 1.54$	$\frac{17}{13} = 1.3$

Group and sub-group of residual classes obtained by ordinary multiplication followed by reduction relative to the modulus 18

·	1	5	7	11	13	17
1	1	5	7	11	13	17
5	5	7	17	1	11	13
7	7	17	13	5	1	11
11	11	1	5	13	17	7
13	13	11	1	17	7	5
17	17	13	11	7	5	1

·	1	7	13
1	1	7	13
7	7	13	1
13	13	1	7

DETAILED ANALYSIS OF THE BEGINNING OF THE SCORE $(L(11, 13))^{18}$

Thanks to the metabola in 5. of the outside-time organization, the origins of the partial sieves $(\overline{13_3 \vee 13_5 \vee 13_7 \vee 13_9}) \wedge 11_2 \vee (\overline{11_4 \vee 11_8}) \wedge 13_9$ and $13_0 \vee 13_1 \vee 13_6$ correspond to $A_3\#$ and A_3 , respectively, for $A_3 = 440$ Hz. Hence the sieve $L(11, 13)$ will produce the following pitches: $\ldots C_2\natural, C_2\#, D_2, D_2\natural, F_2, F_2\#, G_2, G_2\#, A_2, B_2\natural, C_3, C_3\#, D_3\#, D_3\#, F_3\natural, F_3\#, G_3\#, A_3\natural, A_3\#, B_3, C_4\natural, D_4\natural, E_4, E_4\natural, G_4, A_4, A_4 \#, A_4\# , \ldots$

The order applied to the sonic complexes (S_n) and to the density, intensity, and duration combinations (K_n) are for transformation β:

$S_1 =$ $K_1 = 1$ *mf*

$S_2 =$ $K_2 = 2.25$ *fff*

$S_3 =$ $K_3 = 22.5$ *fff*

$S_4 =$ $K_4 = 10$ *mf*

$$S_5 = \text{(figure)} \qquad K_5 = 2.83 \quad f$$

$$S_6 = \text{(figure)} \qquad K_6 = 3.72 \quad f\!f$$

$$S_7 = \text{(figure)} \qquad K_7 = 7.98 \quad f\!f$$

$$S_8 = \text{(figure)} \qquad K_8 = 6.08 \quad f$$

(In this text C_n is replaced by S_n.)

First sequence (see Fig. VIII–13):

	1	2	3	4	5	6	7	8
	↓	↓	↓	↓	↓	↓	↓	↓
$D(S_n) =$	S_2	S_3	S_1	S_4	S_6	S_7	S_5	S_8
$D(K_n) =$	K_2	K_3	K_1	K_4	K_6	K_7	K_5	K_8
	2.25	22.5	1	10	3.72	7.98	2.83	6.08
	$f\!f\!f$	$f\!f\!f$	mf	mf	$f\!f$	$f\!f$	f	f

This part begins with a pizzicato glide on the note C, $f\!f\!f$ (the sliding starts ppp). The slope of the glide is zero at first and then very weak (1/4 tone per 2.5 seconds).

S_3 consists of $C\flat$ $C\#$ D struck col legno, $f\!f\!f$ (with p in the middle). In S_8 there is an introduction of beats obtained by raising $G\#\!\#$ towards A.

Second sequence, beginning at Q_{12}/Q_3:

	1	2	3	4	5	6	7	8
	↓	↓	↓	↓	↓	↓	↓	↓
$Q_{12}(S_n) =$	S_5	S_6	S_8	S_7	S_1	S_2	S_4	S_3
$Q_3(K_n) =$	K_8	K_6	K_7	K_5	K_4	K_2	K_3	K_1
	6.08	3.72	7.98	2.83	10	2.25	22.5	1.0
	f	$f\!f$	$f\!f$	f	mf	$f\!f\!f$	$f\!f\!f$	mf

Note, as in the preceding part, the previously calculated contraction of the values of duration.

S_1 is ataxic, lasting more than a second.

Third sequence, beginning at Q_4/Q_7:

	1	2	3	4	5	6	7	8
	↓	↓	↓	↓	↓	↓	↓	↓
$Q_4(S_n) =$	S_6	S_7	S_8	S_5	S_2	S_3	S_4	S_1
$Q_7(K_n) =$	K_8	K_7	K_5	K_6	K_4	K_3	K_1	K_2
	6.08	7.98	2.83	3.72	10	22.5	1.0	2.25
	f	$f\!f$	f	$f\!f$	mf	$f\!f\!f$	mf	$f\!f\!f$

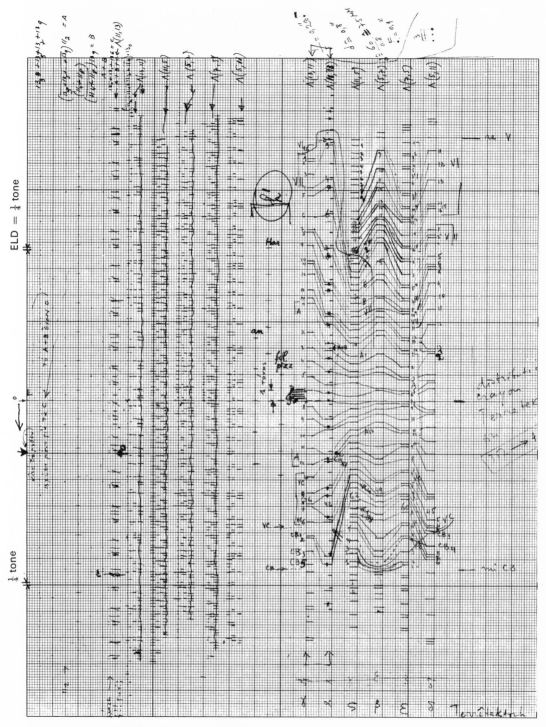

Fig. VIII–12. *Nomos alpha* Sieves

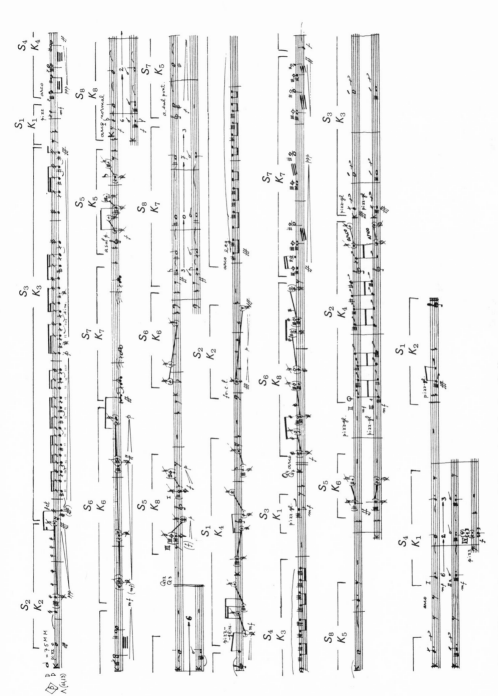

Fig. VIII–13. Opening Bars of *Nomos alpha* for Cello

In S_8 the slopes of the glissandi in opposite directions cancel each other. The enlargement in S_4 is produced by displacement of the lower line and the inducement of beats. The cloud is introduced by a pizzicato on the C string; the index finger of the left hand is placed on the string at the place where one would play the note in square brackets; then by plucking that part of the string between the nut and the index finger with the left thumb, the sound that results will be the note in parentheses.

NOMOS GAMMA—A GENERALIZATION OF NOMOS ALPHA

The finite combinatorial construction expressed by finite groups and performed on one cello in *Nomos alpha* is transposed to full orchestra in *Nomos gamma* (1967/68). The ninety-eight musicians are scattered in the audience; this scattering allows the amplification of *Nomos alpha*'s structure. *Terrêtektorh* (1965/66), which preceded *Nomos gamma*, innovated the scattering of the orchestra and proposed two fundamental changes:

a. The quasi-stochastic sprinkling of the orchestral musicians among the audience. The orchestra is in the audience and the audience is in the orchestra. The public should be free to move or to sit on camp-stools given out at the entrance to the hall. Each musician of the orchestra should be seated on an individual, but unresonant, daïs with his desk and instruments. The hall where the piece is to be performed should be cleared of every movable object that might cause aural or visual obstruction (seats, stage, etc.) A large ball-room having (if it were circular) a minimum diameter of 45 yards would serve in default of a new kind of architecture which will have to be devised for all types of present-day music, for neither amphitheatres, and still less normal theatres or concert-halls, are suitable.

The scattering of the musicians brings in a radically new kinetic conception of music which no modern electro-acoustical means could match.[19] For if it is not possible to imagine 90 magnetic tape tracks relaying to 90 loud speakers disseminated all over the auditorium, on the contrary it is quite possible to achieve this with a classical orchestra of 90 musicians. The musical composition will thereby be entirely enriched throughout the hall both in spatial dimension and in movement. The speeds and accelerations of the movement of the sounds will be realized, and new and powerful functions will be able to be made use of, such as logarithmic or Archimedean spirals, in-time and geometrically. Ordered or disordered sonorous masses, rolling one against the other like waves . . . etc., will be possible.

Terrêtektorh is thus a "Sonotron": an accelerator of sonorous particles, a disintegrator of sonorous masses, a synthesizer. It puts the sound and the music all around the listener and close up to him. It tears down the psychological and auditive curtain that separates him from the players when positioned far off on a pedestal, itself frequently enough placed inside a box. The orchestral musician rediscovers his responsibility as an artist, as an individual.

   b. The orchestral colour is moved towards the spectrum of dry sounds, full of noise, in order to broaden the sound-palette of the orchestra and to give maximum effect to the scattering mentioned above. For this effect, each of the 90 musicians has, besides his normal string or wind instrument, three percussion instruments, viz. Wood-block, Maracas, and Whip as well as small Siren-whistles, which are of three registers and give sounds resembling flames. So if necessary, a shower of hail or even a murmuring of pine-forests can encompass each listener, or in fact any other atmosphere or linear concept either static or in motion. Finally the listener, each one individually, will find himself either perched on top of a mountain in the middle of a storm which attacks him from all sides, or in a frail barque tossing on the open sea, or again in a universe dotted about with little stars of sound, moving in compact nebulae or isolated.[20]

Now the crux or thesis of *Nomos gamma* is a combinatorial organization of correspondences, finite and outside the time of the sets of sound characteristics. Various groups are exploited; their inner structure and their interdependency are put in relief musically: cyclic group of order 6, groups of the rectangle (Klein), the triangle, the square, the pentagon, the hexagon, the tetrahedron, and the hexahedron.

   The isomorphisms are established in many ways, that is, each one of the preceding groups is expressed by different sets and correspondences, thus obtaining structures set up on several interrelated levels. Various groups are interlocked, intermingled, and interwoven. Thus a vast sonic tapestry of non-temporal essence is formed (which incidentally includes the organization of time and durations). The space also contributes, and is organically treated, in the same manner as the more abstract sets of sound elements.

   A powerful *deterministic and finite machinery* is thus promulgated. Is it symmetrical to the *probabilistic and stochastic machineries* already proposed? The two poles, one of pure chance, the other of pure determinacy, are dialectically blended in man's mind (and perhaps in nature as well, as Epicurus or Heisenberg wished it). The mind of man should be able to travel back and forth constantly, with ease and elegance, through the fantastic wall, of disarray caused by irrationality, that separates determinacy from indeterminacy.

We will now consider some examples. It goes without saying that *Nomos gamma* is not entirely defined by group transformations. Arbitrary ranges of decisions are disseminated into the piece, as in all my works except for those originated by the stochastic program in Chap. V. However *Nomos gamma* represents a stage in the method of mechanization by computers for this category of problem.

Measures 1–16 (three oboes, then three clarinets)

OUTSIDE-TIME STRUCTURE

Set of pitches: $H = \{H_1, H_2, H_3, H_4, H_5\}$. Origins: $D_3, G\#_3, D_4, G\#_4, D_5$, respectively, with range ± 3 semitones.

Set of durations: $U = \{U_1, U_2, U_3, U_4\}$. Origins: ♩♪, o, ♩♩♪, o♩♩, respectively, with range $\pm$ one sixteenth-note and a half note ~ 1 sec.

Set of intensities: $G = \{G_1, G_2, G_3, G_4\}$. $G_1 = \{ppp, \overset{>}{ppp}, pp, \overset{>}{pp}, \overset{>}{pp}, p\}$, $G_2 = \{\overset{>}{p}, \overset{>}{p}, mp, \overset{>}{mp}, \overset{>}{mp}, mf, \overset{>}{mf}\}$, $G_3 = \{\overset{>}{mf}, f, \overset{>}{f}, \overset{>}{f}, sf, ff, \overset{>}{ff}\}$, $G_4 = \{\overset{>}{ff}, sff, fff, fff, \overset{>}{fff}, sfff, sfff\}$. Origins: $pp, \overset{>}{mp}, \overset{>}{f}, fff$, respectively.

Product sets: $K = H \times U \times G$. Each one of the points of the product set is defined by a sieve modulo n considered as an element of an additive group (e.g., $n = 3, \ldots, 3_0 \to 3_1 \to 3_1 \to 3_2 \to 3_0 \to 3_2 \to 3_2 \to 3_1 \to \cdots$) and by its unit, that is, the elementary displacement ELD:

$K_1 = H_4 \times G_2 \times U_1$			$K_2 = H_4 \times G_3 \times U_2$			$K_3 = H_4 \times G_1 \times U_1$		
Moduli:	2	2	2	2	2	2	2	2	2
ELD:	$\frac{1}{4}$ tone		$\frac{1}{8}$ sec	$\frac{1}{4}$ tone		$\frac{1}{5}$ sec	$\frac{1}{4}$ tone		$\frac{1}{6}$ sec
$K_4 = H_4 \times G_3 \times U_1$			$K_5 = H_4 \times G_2 \times U_2$			$K_6 = H_4 \times G_3 \times U_3$		
Moduli:	3	2	3	3	2	3	3	2	3
ELD:	$\frac{1}{4}$ tone		$\frac{1}{8}$ sec	$\frac{1}{4}$ tone		$\frac{1}{5}$ sec	$\frac{1}{4}$ tone		$\frac{1}{6}$ sec

In addition, K_2 and K_3 are deformed by translations and homothetic transformations of the H values.

Let us now consider the three points K_1, K_2, K_3 of the product $H \times G \times U$, and map them one-to-one onto three successive moments of time. We thus define the triangle group with the following elements:

$$\{I, A, A^2, B, \overrightarrow{BA}, BA^2\} \leftrightarrow \{123, 312, 231, 132, 213, 321\}$$

IN-TIME STRUCTURE

For each transformation of the triangle the vertices are stated by K_1, K_2, K_3, which are played successively by the oboes and the clarinets, according to the above permutation group and to the following circuit: BA, BA^2, A, B, BA^2, A^2.

Measures 16–22 (three oboes and three clarinets)

OUTSIDE-TIME STRUCTURE

Form the product $K_i \times C_i$: $K_1 \times C_1$, $K_2 \times C_2$, $K_3 \times C_3$, in which the C_i are the ways of playing. C_1 = smooth sound without vibrato, C_2 = flutter tongue, C_3 = quilisma (irregular oscillations of pitch).

Consider now two triangles whose respective vertices are the three oboes and the three clarinets. The $K_i \times C_i$ values are the names of the vertices. All the one-to-one mappings of the $K_i \times C_i$ names onto the three space positions of the three oboes or of the three clarinets form one triangle group.

IN-TIME STRUCTURE

To each group transformation the names $K_i \times C_i$ are stated simultaneously by the three oboes, which alternate with the three clarinets. The circuits are chosen to be I, BA, BA, I, A^2, B, BA, A, BA^2 and I, B, B.

Measures 404–42—A Sound Tapestry

The string orchestra (sixteen first violins, fourteen second violins, twelve violas, ten cellos, and eight double basses) is divided into two times three teams of eight instruments each: ϕ_1, ϕ_2, ϕ_3, ψ_1, ψ_2, ψ_3. The remaining twelve strings duplicate the ones sitting nearest them. In the text that follows the ϕ_i and ψ_j are considered equivalent in pairs ($\phi_i \sim \psi_i$). Therefore we shall only deal with the ϕ_i.

LEVEL I—OUTSIDE-TIME STRUCTURE

The eight positions of the instruments of each ϕ_i are purposely taken into consideration. Onto these positions (instruments) we map one-to-one eight ways of playing drawn from set X = {on the bridge tremolo, on the bridge tremolo and trill, sul ponticello smooth, sul ponticello tremolo, smooth natural harmonic notes, irregular dense strokes with the wood of the bow, normal arco with tremolo, pizzicato-glissando ascending or descending}. We have thus formed a cube: KVBOS 1.

Onto these same eight positions (instruments) of ϕ_i we map one-to-one eight dynamic forms of intensity taken from the following sets: g_λ =

{ppp crescendo, $\overset{>}{ppp}$ diminuendo, pp cresc, $\overset{>}{pp}$ dim, p cresc, $\overset{>}{p}$ dim, mp cresc, $\overset{>}{mp}$ dim}, g_μ = {mf cresc, $\overset{>}{mf}$ dim, f cresc, $\overset{>}{f}$ dim, ff cresc, ff dim, fff cresc, $\overset{>}{fff}$ dim}, g_ξ = {p dim, $\overset{>}{p}$ cresc, mp dim, $\overset{>}{mp}$ cresc, mf dim, $\overset{>}{mf}$ cresc, f dim, $\overset{>}{f}$ cresc}. We have thus defined a second cube: KVBOS 2.

LEVEL 1—IN-TIME STRUCTURE

Each one of these cubes is transformed into itself following the kinematic diagrams of the hexahedral group (cf. *Nomos alpha*, p. 225); for example, KVBOS 1 following D^2Q_{12} ... and KVBOS 2 following $Q_{11}Q_7$. ...

LEVEL 2—OUTSIDE-TIME STRUCTURE

The three partitions ϕ_1, ϕ_2, ϕ_3 are now considered as a triplet of points in space. We map onto them, one-to-one, three distinct pitch ranges H_α, H_β, H_γ in which the instrumentalists of the preceding cubes will play. We have thus formed a triangle TRIA 1.

Onto these same three points we map one-to-one three elements drawn from the product (durations × intensities), $U \times G$ = {2.5 sec g_λ, 0.5 sec g_μ, 1.5 sec g_ξ}. We have thus defined a second triangle TRIA 2.

LEVEL 2—IN-TIME STRUCTURE

When the two cubes play a Level 1 transformation, the two triangles simultaneously perform a transformation of the triangle group. If I, A, A^2, B, BA, BA^2 are the group elements, then *TRIA* 1 proceeds according to the kinematic diagram A, B, BA^2, A^2, BA, BA^2, and *TRIA* 2 proceeds simultaneously according to A, BA^2, BA, A^2, B, AB.

LEVEL 3—OUTSIDE-TIME STRUCTURE

Form the product $C_i \times M_j$ with three macroscopic types: C_1 = clouds of webs of pitch glissandi, C_2 = clouds of sound-points, and C_3 = clouds of sounds with quilisma. Three sieves with modulus $M = 3$ are taken: $3_0, 3_1, 3_2$. From this product we select five elements: $C_1 \times 3_0 = I$, $C_1 \times 3_1 = A$, $C_1 \times 3_2 = A^3$, $C_2 \times 3_0 = A^4$, $C_3 \times 3_1 = A^5$, which could belong to the cyclic group of order 6.

LEVEL 3—IN-TIME STRUCTURE

The nested transformation of Levels 1 and 2 are plunged into the product $C_i \times M_j$, which traverses successively $C_1 \times 3_2$, $C_2 \times 3_0$, $C_1 \times 3_1$, $C_3 \times 3_1$, $C_1 \times 3_0 \leftrightarrow A^3$, A^4, A, A^5, I, during the corresponding arbitrary durations of 20 sec, 7.5 sec, 12.5 sec, 12.5 sec, 7.5 sec.

LEVEL 4—OUTSIDE-TIME STRUCTURE

The partition of the string orchestra into teams ϕ_i, ψ_j is done in two modes: compact and dispersed. The compact mode is itself divided into two cases: Compact I and Compact II. For example,

in Compact I, $\phi_1 = \{VI_{13}, VII_1, VII_2, VII_{14}, A_7, VC_2, VC_6, CB_4\}$
in Compact II, $\phi_1 = \{VI_1, VI_7, VI_8, VI_9, VI_{10}, A_8, VC_3, CB_2\}$
in the dispersed mode, $\phi_1 = \{VI_2, VI_3, VI_6, VII_1, VII_6, VII_{11}, CB_3, CB_7\}$

($VI_i = i$th first violin, $VII_i = i$th second violin, $A_i = i$th viola, $VC_i = i$th cello, $CB_i = i$th double bass.) These partitions cannot occur simultaneously.

LEVEL 4—IN-TIME STRUCTURE

All the mechanisms that sprang from Levels 1, 2, 3 are in turn plunged into the various above definitions of the ϕ_i and ψ_j teams, and successively into Compact I during the 27.5 sec duration, into the dispersed mode during the 17.5 sec duration, into Compact II during 5 sec, into the dispersed mode during 5 sec, and into Compact I during 5 sec.

DESTINY'S INDICATORS

Thus the *inquiry* applied to music leads us to the innermost parts of our mind. Modern axiomatics disentangle once more, in a more precise manner now, the significant grooves that the past has etched on the rock of our being. These mental premises confirm and justify the billions of years of accumulation and destruction of signs. But awareness of their limitation, their closure, forces us to destroy them.

All of a sudden it is unthinkable that the human mind forges its conception of time and space in childhood and *never* alters it.[21] Thus the bottom of the cave would not reflect the beings who are behind us, but would be a filtering glass that would allow us to guess at what is at the very heart of the universe. It is this bottom that must be broken up.
Consequences: 1. It would be necessary to change the ordered structures of time and space, those of logic, . . . 2. Art, and sciences annexed to it, should realize this mutation.

Let us resolve the duality *mortal-eternal*: the future is in the past and vice-versa; the evanescence of the present is abolished, it is everywhere at the same time; the *here* is also two billion light-years away. . . .

The space ships that ambitious technology have produced may not carry us as far as liberation from our mental shackles could. This is the fantastic perspective that *art-science* opens to us in the Pythagorean-Parmenidean field.

Chapter IX

New Proposals in Microsound Structure

FOURIER SERIES–BASIC IMPORTANCE AND INADEQUACY

The physico-mathematical apparatus of acoustics [2, 23] is plunged into the theories of energy propagation in an elastic medium, in which harmonic analysis is the cornerstone.

The same apparatus finds in the units of electronic circuit design the practical medium where it is realized and checked.

The prodigious development of radio and TV transmissions has expanded the Fourier harmonic analysis to very broad and heterogeneous domains.

Other theories, quite far apart, e.g., servomechanisms and probability, find necessary backing in Fourier series.

In music ancient traditions of scales, as well as those of string and pipe resonances, also lead to circular functions and their linear combinations [24].

In consequence, any attempt to produce a sound artificially could not be conceived outside the framework of the above physico-mathematical and electronic apparatus, which relies on Fourier series.

Indeed the long route traversed by the *acousmatics* of the Pythagoreans seemed to have found its natural bed. Musical theoreticians did base their theories on Fourier, more or less directly, in order to support the argument about the *natural harmony* of tonality. Moreover, in defining tonality, the 20th-century deprecators of the new musical languages based their arguments on the theory of vibration of elastic bodies and media, that is, in the end, on Fourier analysis. But they were thus creating a paradox, for although they wanted to keep music in the intuitive and instinctive domain, in order to legitimatize the tonal universe they made use of physico-mathematical arguments!

The Impasse of Harmonic Analysis and Some Reasons

Two major difficulties compel us to think in another way:

1. The defeat by the thrust of the new languages of the theory according to which harmony, counterpoint, etc., must stem, just from the *basis* formed by circular functions. E.g., how can we justify such harmonic configurations of recent instrumental or electro-acoustic music as a cloud of gliding sounds? Thus, harmonic analysis has been short-circuited in spite of touching attempts like Hindemith's explanation of Schönberg's system [25]. Life and sound adventures jostle the traditional theses, which are nevertheless still being taught in the conservatories (rudimentally, of course). It is therefore natural to think that the disruptions in music in the last 60 years tend to prove once again that music and its "rules" are socio-cultural and historical *conditionings*, and hence modifiable. These conditions seem to be based roughly on *a.* the absolute limits of our senses and their deforming power (e.g., Fletcher contours); *b.* our canvass of mental structures, some of which were treated in the preceding chapters (ordering, groups, etc.); *c.* the means of sound production (orchestral instruments, electro-acoustic sound synthesis, storage and transformation analogue systems, digital sound synthesis with computers and digital to analogue converters). If we modify any one of these three points, our socio-cultural conditioning will also tend to change in spite of an obvious inertia inherent in a sort of "entropy" of the social facts.

2. The obvious failure, since the birth of oscillating circuits in electronics, to reconstitute any sound, even the simple sounds of some orchestral instruments! *a.* The Trautoniums, Theremins, and Martenots, all pre-World War II attempts, prove it. *b.* Since the war, all "electronic" music has also failed, in spite of the big hopes of the fifties, to pull electro-acoustic music out of its cradle of the so-called electronic pure sounds produced by frequency generators. Any electronic music based on such sounds only, is marked by their simplistic sonority, which resembles radio atmospherics or heterodyning. The serial system, which has been used so much by electronic music composers, could not by any means improve the result, since it itself is much too elementary. Only when the "pure" electronic sounds were framed by other "concrete" sounds, which were much richer and much more interesting (thanks to E. Varèse, Pierre Schaeffer, and Pierre Henry),

could electronic music become really powerful. *c.* The most recent attempts to use the flower of modern technology, computers coupled to converters, have shown that in spite of some relative successes [26], the sonorous results are even less interesting than those made ten years ago in the classic electro-acoustic studios by means of frequency generators, filters, modulators, and reverberation units.

In line with these critiques, what are the causes of these failures? In my opinion the following are some of them:

1. Meyer-Eppler's studies [1] have shown that the spectral analysis of even the simplest orchestral sounds (they will form a reference system for a long time to come) presents variations of spectral lines in frequency as well as in amplitude. But these tiny (second order) variations are among those that make the difference between a lifeless sound made up of a sum of harmonics produced by a frequency generator and a sound of the same sum of harmonics played on an orchestral instrument. These tiny variations, which take place in the permanent, stationary part of a sound, would certainly require new theories of approach, using another functional basis and a harmonic analysis on a higher level, e.g., stochastic processes, Markov chains, correlated or autocorrelated relations, or theses of pattern and form recognition. Even so, analysis theories of orchestral sounds [27] would result in very long and complex calculations, so that if we had to simulate such an orchestral sound from a computer and from harmonic analysis on a first level, we would need a tremendous amount of computer time, which is impossible for the moment.

2. It seems that the transient part of the sound is far more important than the permanent part in timbre recognition and in music in general [28]. Now, the more the music moves toward complex sonorities close to "noise," the more numerous and complicated the transients become, and the more their synthesis from trigonometric functions becomes a mountain of difficulties, even more unacceptable to a computer than the permanent states. It is as though we wanted to express a sinuous mountain silhouette by using portions of circles. In fact, it is thousands of times more complicated. The intelligent ear is infinitely demanding, and its voracity for information is far from having been satisfied. This problem of a considerable amount of calculation is comparable to the 19th-century classical mechanics problem that led to the kinetic gas theory.

3. There is no pattern and form recognition theory, dependent on harmonic analysis or not, that would enable us to translate curves synthesized by means of trigonometric functions in the perception of forms or

configurations. For instance, it is impossible for us to define equivalence classes of very diversified oscilloscope curves, which the ear throws into the same bag. Furthermore, the ear makes no distinction between things that actual acoustic theories differentiate (e.g., phase differences, differential sensitivity ability), and vice versa.

The Wrong Concept of Juxtaposing Finite Elements

Perhaps the ultimate reason for such difficulties lies in the improvised entanglement of notions of finity and infinity. For example, in sinusoidal oscillation there is a unit element, the variation included in 2π. Then this *finite* variation is repeated endlessly. Seen as an economy of means, this procedure can be one of the possible optimizations. We labor during a limited span of time (one period), then repeat the product indefinitely with almost no additional labor. Basically, therefore, we have a mechanism (e.g., the sine function) engendering a finite temporal object, which is repeated for as long as we wish. This long object is now considered as a new element, to which we juxtapose similar ones. The odds are that one can draw any variation of one variable (e.g., atmospheric pressure) as a function of time by means of a finite superposition (sum) of the preceding elements. In doing this we expect to obtain an irregular curve, with increasing irregularity as we approach "noises." On the oscilloscope such a curve would look quite complex. If we ask the eye to recognize particular forms or symmetries on this curve it would almost certainly be unable to make any judgment from samples lasting say 10 microseconds because it would have to follow them too fast or too slowly: too fast for the everyday limits of visual attention, and too slow for the TV limits, which plunge the instantaneous judgment into the level of global perception of forms and colors. On the other hand, for the same sample duration, the ear is made to recognize forms and patterns, and therefore senses the correlations between fragments of the pressure curve at various levels of understanding. We ignore the laws and rules of this ability of the ear in the more complex and general cases that we are interested in. However, in the case in which we superpose sine curves, we know that below a certain degree of complexity the ear disentangles the constituents, and that above it the sensation is transformed into timbre, color, power, movement, roughness, and degree of disorder; and this brings us into a tunnel of ignorance. To summarize, we expect that by judiciously piling up simple elements (pure sounds, sine functions) we will create any desired sounds (pressure curve), even those that come close to very strong irregularities—almost stochastic ones. This same statement holds even when the unit element of the iteration is taken from a function other than the sine. In general, and regardless of the specific function of the unit element, this procedure can be called *synthesis by finite juxtaposed elements*. In my opinion it is from here that the deep contradictions stem that should prevent us from using it.*

NEW PROPOSAL IN MICROCOMPOSITION BASED ON PROBABILITY DISTRIBUTIONS

We shall raise the contradiction, and by doing so we hope to open a new path in microsound synthesis research—one that without pretending to be able to simulate already known sounds, will nevertheless launch music, its psychophysiology, and acoustics in a direction that is quite interesting and unexpected.

Instead of starting from the unit element concept and its tireless iteration and from the increasing irregular superposition of such iterated unit elements, we can start from a disorder concept and then introduce means that would increase or reduce it. This is like saying that we take the inverse road: We do not wish to construct a complex sound edifice by using discontinuous unit elements (bricks = sine or other functions); we wish to construct sounds with continuous variations that are not made out of unit elements. This method would use stochastic variations of the sound pressure directly. We can imagine the pressure variations produced by a particle capriciously moving around equilibrium positions along the pressure ordinate in a non-deterministic way. Therefore we can imagine the use of any "random walk" or multiple combinations of them.

Method 1. Every probability function is a particular stochastic variation, which has its own personality (personal behavior of the particle). We shall then use *any* one of them. They can be discontinuous or continuous; e.g., Poisson, exponential (ce^{-cx}), normal, uniform, Cauchy $(t[\pi(t^2+x^2)]^{-1})$, arc sin $(\pi^{-1}[x(1-x)]^{-1/2})$, logistic $[(\alpha e^{-\alpha x-\beta})(1+e^{-\alpha x-\beta})^{-1}]$ distributions.

Method 2. Combinations of a random variable X with itself can be established. Example: If $f(x)$ is the probability function of X we can form $S_n = X_1 + X_2 + \cdots + X_n$ (by means of the n-fold convolution of $f(x)$ with itself) or $P_K = X_1 \cdot X_2 \cdots X_K$, or any linear, polynomial, . . ., function of the variable X.

---

* In spite of this criticism I would like to draw attention to the magnificent manipulatory language Music V of Max V. Mathews, which achieves the final step in this procedure and automates it [29]. This language certainly represents the realization of the dream of an electronic music composer in the fifties.

Method 3. The random variables (pressure, time) can be functions of other variables (elastic forces), even of random variables. Example: The pressure variable x is under the influence of a centrifugal or centripetal force $\phi(x, t)$. For instance, if the particle (pressure) is influenced by a force wx (w being a constant) and also obeys a Wiener-Lévy process, then its density will be

$$q_t(x, y) = (w^{1/2}/[\pi(1 - e^{-2wt})]^{-1/2}) \exp\left[-w(y - xe^{-wt})^2/(1 - e^{-2wt})\right],$$

where x and y are the values of the variable at the instants 0 and t, respectively. (This is also known as the Ornstein-Uhlenbeck process.)

Method 4. The random variable moves between two reflecting (elastic) barriers. Example: If we again have a Wiener-Lévy process with two reflecting barriers at $a > 0$ and zero, then the density of this random walk will be

$$q_t(x, y) = (2\pi t)^{-1/2} \sum_{k=0}^{\pm\infty} (\exp\left[-(y - x + 2ka)^2/2t\right] \\ + \exp\left[-(y + x + 2ka)^2/2t\right]),$$

where x and y are the values of the variables at the instants 0 and t, respectively, and $k = 0, \pm 1, \pm 2, \ldots$.

Method 5. The parameters of a probability function can be considered as variables of other probability functions (randomization, mixtures) [30]. Examples:

a. t is the parameter of a Poisson distribution $f(k) = (\alpha t)^k(k!)^{-1}e^{-\alpha t}$, and the random variable of the exponential density $g(t) = \beta e^{-\beta t}$. The combination is

$$f(k) * g(t) = w(k) = \int_{-\infty}^{\infty} (\alpha t)^k(k!)^{-1}e^{-\alpha t}\beta e^{-\beta t}\, dt = \beta(\alpha+\beta)^{-1}[\alpha(\alpha+\beta)^{-1}]^k,$$

which is a geometric distribution.

b. p and q are the probabilities of a random walk with jumps ± 1 (Bernoulli distribution). The time intervals between successive jumps are random variables with common density e^{-t} (Poisson distribution). Then the probability of the position n at instant t will be $f_n(t) = I_n(2t\sqrt{pq})e^{-t}(p/q)^{n/2}$, where

$$I_n(x) = \sum_{k=0}^{\infty} [k!\Gamma(k + n + 1)]^{-1}(x/2)^{2k+n}$$

is the modified Bessel function of the first kind of order n.

Method 6. Linear, polynomial, ..., combinations of probability functions f_i are considered as well as composite functions (mixtures of a family of distributions, transformations in Banach space, subordination, etc.).

a. If A and B are any pair of intervals on the line, and $Q(A, B) = $ prob $\{X \in A, Y \in B\}$ with $q(x, B) = $ prob $\{X = x, Y \in B\}$ (q, under appropriate regularity conditions being a probability distribution in B for a given x and a continuous function in x for a fixed B; that is, a conditional probability of the event $\{Y \in B\}$, given that $X = x$), and $\mu\{A\}$ is a probability distribution of $x \in A$, then $Q(A, B) = \int_A q(x, B)\mu\{dx\}$ represents a mixture of the family of distributions $q(X, B)$, which depends on the parameter x, with μ serving as the distribution of the randomized parameter [30].

b. Interlocking probability distributions (modulation). If $f_1, f_2, \ldots,$ f_n are the probability distributions of the random variables $X^1, X^2, \ldots,$ X^n, respectively, then we can form

$$S^i_{\sigma i} = X^i_1 + X^i_2 + \cdots + X^i_{\sigma i} \quad \text{and} \quad S^n\left(\sum_{i=1}^{n} S^i_{\sigma i}\right) = S^1_{\sigma 1} + S^2_{\sigma 2} + \cdots + S^n_{\sigma n}$$

or

$$P^k_{\gamma k} = X^k_1 \cdot X^k_2 \cdots X^k_{\gamma k} \quad \text{and} \quad P^n\left(\prod_{k=1}^{n} P^k_{\gamma k}\right) = P^1_{\gamma 1} \cdot P^2_{\gamma 2} \cdots P^n_{\gamma n},$$

or any combination (functional or stochastic) of these sums and products. Furthermore, the σi and γk could be generated by either independent determined functions, independent stochastic processes, or interrelated determined or indetermined processes. In some of these cases we would have the theory of renewal processes, if, for instance, the σi were considered waiting times Ti. From another point of view, some of these cases would also correspond to the time series analysis of statistics. In reality, the ear seems to realize such an analysis when in a given sound it recognizes the fundamental tone pitch together with timbre, fluctuation, or casual irregularities of that sound! In fact, time series analysis should have been invented by composers, if they had—.

c. Subordination [30]. Suppose $\{X(t)\}$, a Markovian process with continuous transition probabilities

$$Q_t(x, \Gamma) = \text{prob}\ \{X(T(t + s)) \in \Gamma | X(T(s)) = x\}$$

(stochastic kernel independent of s), and $\{T(t)\}$, a process with non-negative independent increments. Then $\{X(T(t))\}$ is a Markov process with transition probabilities

$$P_t(x, \Gamma) = \int_0^\infty Q_s(x, \Gamma) U_t\{ds\},$$

where U_t is the infinitely divisible distribution of $T(t)$. This P_t is said to be *subordinated* to $\{X(t)\}$, using the operational time $T(t)$ as the *directing* process.

Method 7. The probability functions can be filed into classes, that is, into parent curve configurations. These classes are then considered as elements of higher order sets. The classification is obtained through at least three kinds of criteria, which can be interrelated: *a.* analytical source of derived probability distribution; gamma, beta, . . ., and related densities, such as the density of χ^2 with n degrees of freedom (Pearson); Student's t density; Maxwell's density; *b.* other mathematical criteria, such as stability, infinite divisibility; and *c.* characteristic features of the curve designs: at level 0, where the values of the random variable are accepted as such; at level 1, where their values are accumulated, etc.

Macrocomposition

Method 8. Further manipulations with classes of distributions envisaged by Method 7 introduce us to the domain of macrocomposition. But we will not continue these speculations since many things that have been exposed in the preceding chapters could be used fruitfully in obvious ways. For example, sound molecules produced by the above methods could be injected into the ST(ochastic) program of Chap. V, the program forming the macrostructure. The same could be said about Chaps. II and III (Markovian processes at a macrolevel). As for Chaps. VI and VIII (symbolic music and group organization) establishing a complex microprogram is not as easy, but it is full of rich and unexpected possibilities.

All of the above new proposals are being investigated at the Centers for Mathematical and Automated Music (CMAM) at both the School of Music of Indiana University, Bloomington, Indiana, and the Nuclear Research Center of the Collège de France, in Paris. Digital to analogue converters with 16 bits resolution at a rate of $0.5 \cdot 10^5$ samples per second are available in both places.

Figs. IX, 1–8 were calculated and plotted at the Research Computing Center of Indiana University under the supervision of Cornelia Colyer. These graphs could correspond to a sound duration of 8 milliseconds, the ordinates being the sound pressures.

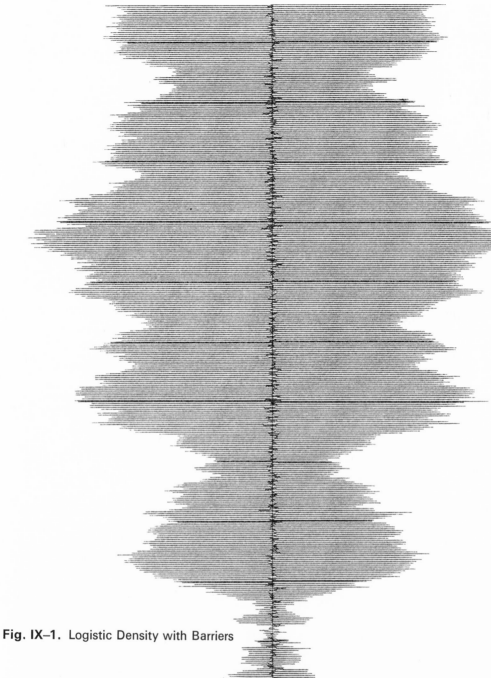

Fig. IX–1. Logistic Density with Barriers

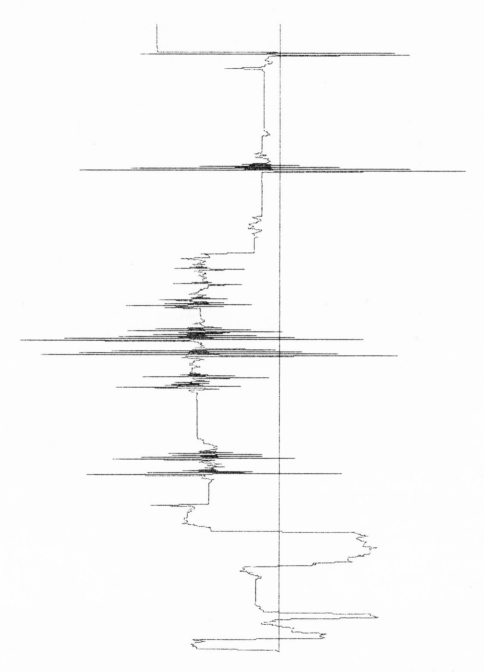

Fig. IX–2. Exponential × Cauchy Densities with Barriers and Randomized Time

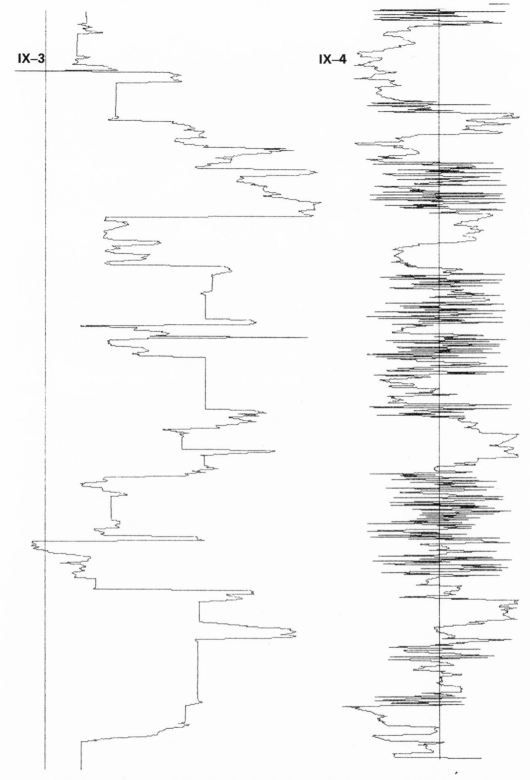

Fig. IX–3. Exponential × Cauchy Densities with Barriers and Randomized Time

Fig. IX–4. Exponential × Cauchy Densities with Barriers and Randomized Time

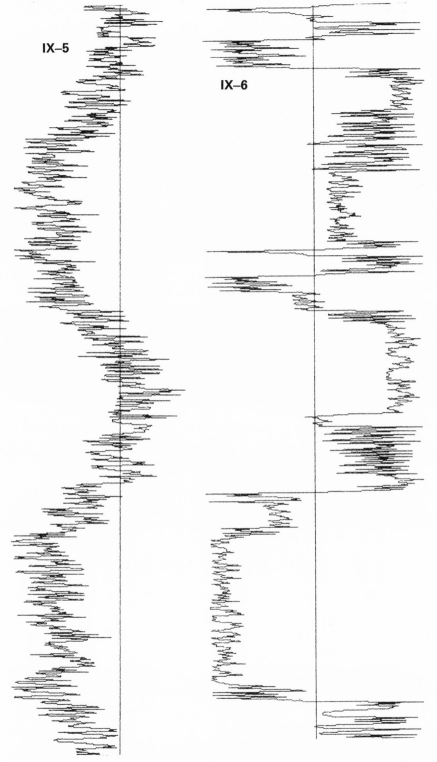

Fig. IX–5. Hyperbolic Cosine × Exponential Densities with Barriers and Determined Time

Fig. IX–6. Hyperbolic Cosine × Exponential Densities with Barriers and Randomized Time

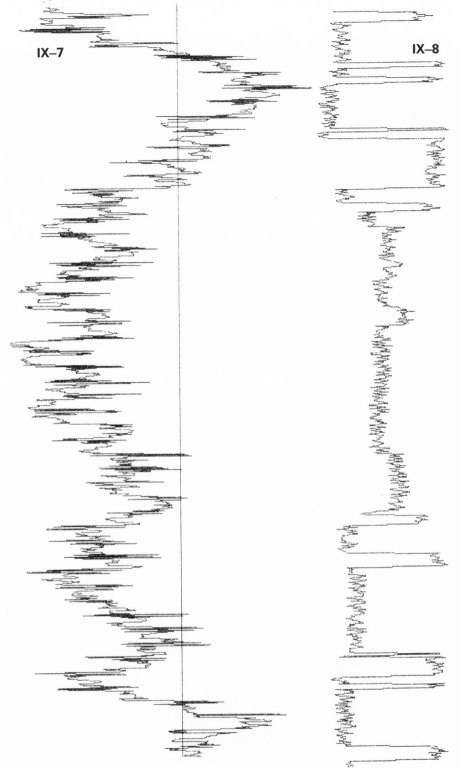

Fig. IX–7. Hyperbolic Cosine × Exponential × Cauchy Densities with Barriers and Determined Time

Fig. IX–8. Logistic × Exponential Densities with Barriers and Randomized Time

Appendix I
[7] [20]

TWO LAWS OF CONTINUOUS PROBABILITY

First Law

$$P_x = ce^{-cx}\, dx.$$

Let OA be a segment of a straight line of length l on which we place n points. Their linear density is $c = n/l$. Suppose that l and n increase indefinitely while c remains constant. Suppose also that these points are numbered $A_1, A_p, A_q, \ldots$ and are distributed from left to right beginning at the origin 0. Let

$$x_1 = A_1 A_p,\ x_2 = A_p A_q,\ x_3 = A_q A_r,\ \ldots,\ x_i = A_s A_t.$$

The probability that the ith segment will have a length x_i between x and $x + dx$ is

$$P_x = e^{-cx} c\, dx.$$

Now the probability p_n, that there will be n points on a segment x, is given by the recurrence formula

$$\frac{p_{n+1}}{p_n} = \frac{cx}{n+1}.$$

Therefore $p_1 = (cx/1)p_0$. But $p_0 = e^{-cx}$ and

$$e^{-cx} = 1 - \frac{cx}{1!} + \frac{(cx)^2}{2!} - \frac{(cx)^3}{3!} + \cdots.$$

If x is very small and if we denote it by dx, we have

$$p_0 = 1 - c\, dx + \frac{c^2(dx)^2}{2!} \cdots.$$

255

Since the powers of dx are infinitely small for high values, $p_0 = 1 - c\,dx$ and $p_1 = c\,dx\,p_0 = c\,dx$. Hence, the probability P_x is composed of the probability $p_0 = e^{-cx}$, that there will be no point on the segment x, and the probability $p_1 = c\,dx$, that there will be a point in dx.

APPROXIMATE CALCULATION OF THE SAME PROBABILITY
(FOR CALCULATION BY HAND)

Let there be d points to be placed on a straight line of length l. The linear density is $c = d/l$ points on length l. If the lengths are expressed in units v then $l = av$ $(a > 0)$ and $cv = d/a$ points in the unit of length v.

Then $x_i = iv$ $(i = 0, 1, 2, 3, \ldots)$, and the probability, the asymptotic limit of the relative frequency of the segment x_i, will be

$$P_{x_i} = e^{-civ}c\Delta x_i. \tag{1}$$

We shall now define the quantity Δx_i. The probability (1) is composed of the probability $p_0 = e^{-civ}$, that there will be no point on x_i, and the probability $p_1 = c\Delta x_i$, that there will be a point in Δx_i if $(c\Delta x_i)^2$ is small enough to be ignored. Set

$$0 < (c\Delta x_i)^2 < 10^{-n}.$$

where n is a sufficiently large natural number; this expression becomes

$$0 < \Delta x_i < c^{-1} \cdot 10^{-n/2}.$$

Substitute a constant z for Δx_i such that for every x_i

$$z \le \Delta x_i < c^{-1} \cdot 10^{-n/2}. \tag{2}$$

Then equation (1) is written

$$P_{x_i} = e^{-civ} \cdot cz \tag{3}$$

and must satisfy the condition

$$\sum_{i=0}^{i=\infty} e^{-civ} \cdot cz = 1,$$

or

$$z = 1/c \cdot \sum_{i=0}^{i=\infty} c^{-civ}.$$

But since $cv > 0$, $e^{-cv} < 1$, so that

$$\sum_{i=0}^{i=\infty} (e^{-cv})^i = 1/(1 - e^{-cv})$$

and finally

$$z = \frac{1 - e^{-cv}}{c}.$$

Now from (2)

$$\frac{1 - e^{-cv}}{c} < \frac{10^{-n/2}}{c}.$$

Therefore

$$0 < (1 - e^{-cv}) < 10^{-n/2},$$

then

$$(1 - 10^{-n/2}) < e^{-cv} < 1.$$

Thus, for $cv > 0$ we have $e^{-cv} < 1$, and for $cv < -\log(1 - 10^{-n/2})$ we have $e^{-cv} > (1 - 10^{-n/2})$. And since $0 < 10^{-n/2} < 1$ we have

$$-\log(1 - 10^{-n/2}) = 10^{-n/2} + \frac{10^{-(n/2)2}}{2} + \frac{10^{-(n/2)3}}{3} + \frac{10^{-(n/2)4}}{4} + \cdots$$

and

$$10^{-n/2} < -\log(1 - 10^{-n/2}).$$

In order that $e^{-cv} > 1 - 10^{-n/2}$ it is therefore sufficient that

$$cv \leq 10^{-n/2}. \tag{4}$$

Then we may take

$$\Delta x_i = z = \frac{1 - e^{-cv}}{c} \tag{5}$$

and substitute this value in formula (1), from which we can now set up probability tables. Here is an example:

Let $d = 10$ points as mean value to be spread on a straight line segment of length $l = 100$ cm. We have to define x_i and P_{x_i} as a function of i, given that $(c\Delta x_i)^2 = 10^{-4}$ is considered to be negligible.

From (4), $cv = 10^{-4/2} = 0.01$ points in v. Now $c = d/l = 10/100$ points/cm, therefore $c = 0.1$ points/cm, $v = 0.01/0.1 = 0.1$ cm, and $x_i = 0.1i$ cm $\triangleq i$ mm.

From (5),

$$\Delta x_i = \frac{1 - e^{-0.01}}{0.1} = (1 - 0.9905)10 = 0.0995 \triangleq 0.1 \text{ cm}.$$

From (1),

$$P_{x_i} = e^{-0.01i} \cdot 0.1 \cdot 0.1 = 0.01 \cdot (0.099005)^i.$$

For calculation by machine see Chapter V.

Second Law

$$f(j)\, dj = \frac{2}{a}\left(1 - \frac{j}{a}\right) dj.$$

Each variable (pitch, intensity, density, etc.) forms an interval (distance) with its predecessor. Each interval is identified with a segment x taken on the axis of the variable. Let there be two points A and B on this axis corresponding to the lower and upper limits of the variable. It is then a matter of drawing at random a segment within AB whose length is included between j and $j + dj$ for $0 \le j \le AB$. Then the probability of this event is:

$$P_j = f(j)\, dj = \frac{2}{a}\left(1 - \frac{j}{a}\right) dj \tag{1}$$

for $a = AB$.

APPROXIMATE DEFINITION OF THIS PROBABILITY FOR CALCULATION BY HAND

By taking dj as a constant and j as discontinuous we set $dj = c, j = iv$ with $v = a/m$ for $i = 0, 1, 2, 3, \ldots, m$. Equation (1) becomes

$$P_j = \frac{2}{a}\left(1 - \frac{iv}{a}\right) c. \tag{2}$$

But

$$\sum_{i=0}^{i=m} P_j = \frac{2c}{a}(m + 1) - \frac{2cv}{a^2}\sum_{i=0}^{i=m} i = \frac{2c(m + 1)}{a} - \frac{2cvm(m + 1)}{2a^2} = 1,$$

whence

$$dj = c = \frac{a}{m + 1}.$$

On the other hand P_j must be taken as a function of the decimal approximation required:

$$P_j = \frac{2}{m + 1}\left(1 - \frac{i}{m}\right) \le 10^{-n} \qquad (n = 0, 1, 2, 3, \ldots).$$

P_j is at a maximum when $i = 0$, whence $m \ge 2 \cdot 10^n - 1$; so for $m = 2 \cdot 10^n - 1$ we have $v = a/(2 \cdot 10^n - 1)$ and $dj = a/(2 \cdot 10^n)$, and (1) becomes

$$P_j = P_i = \frac{1}{10^n}\left(1 - \frac{i}{2 \cdot 10^n - 1}\right).$$

DEFINITION OF THE SAME PROBABILITY FOR COMPUTER CALCULATION

We know that the computer can only draw numbers y_0 at random (of equal probability) $0 \le y_0 \le 1$. Using the probability law of density $P_j = f(j)\, dj$, we have for some interval x_0

$$\text{prob. } (0 \le j \le x_0) = \int_0^{x_0} f(j)\, dj = \frac{2x_0}{a} - \frac{x_0^2}{a^2} = F(x_0),$$

where $F(x_0)$ is the distribution function of j. But $F(x_0) = \text{prob. } (0 \le y \le y_0) = y_0$. Therefore

$$\frac{2x_0}{a} - \frac{x_0^2}{a^2} = y_0 \quad \text{and} \quad x_0 = a[1 \pm \sqrt{(1 - y_0)}],$$

and by rejecting the positive root, since x_0 must remain smaller than a, we obtain

$$x_0 = a[1 - \sqrt{(1 - y_0)}]$$

for all $0 \le x_0 \le a$.

Appendix II
[14]

Let there be states $E_1, E_2, E_3, \ldots, E_r$ with $r < \infty$; and let one of these events necessarily occur at each trial. The probability that event E_k will take place when E_h has occurred at the previous trial is p_{hk};

$$\sum_k p_{hj} = 1, \quad \text{with } k = 1, 2, \ldots, r.$$

$P_{hk}^{(n)}$ is the probability that in n trials we will pass from state E_h to state E_k;

$$\sum_k P_{hk}^{(n)} = 1, \quad \text{with } k = 1, 2, \ldots, r.$$

If for $n \to \infty$ one of the $P_{hk}^{(n)}$ tends towards a limit P_{hk}, this limit is expressed by the sum of all the products $P_{hj}p_{jk}$, j being the index of one of the intermediate states E_j $(1 \le j \le r)$:

$$P_{hk} = P_{h1}p_{1k} + P_{h2}p_{2k} + \cdots + P_{hr}p_{rk}.$$

The sum of all the limits P_{hk} is equal to 1:

$$P_{h1} + P_{h2} + P_{h3} + \cdots + P_{hr} = 1.$$

We can form tables or matrices $D^{(n)}$ as follows:

$$D^{(n)} = \begin{vmatrix} P_{11}^{(n)}, & P_{21}^{(n)}, & \cdots, & P_{r1}^{(n)} \\ \vdots & & & \\ P_{1m}^{(n)}, & P_{2m}^{(n)}, & \cdots, & P_{rm}^{(n)} \\ \vdots & & & \\ P_{1r}^{(n)}, & P_{2r}^{(n)}, & \cdots, & P_{rr}^{(n)} \end{vmatrix}$$

Regular case. If at least one of the tables $D^{(n)}$ contains at least one line m of which all the elements are positive, then the $P_{hk}^{(n)}$ have limits P_{hk}, and among the P_{hk} there exists at least one, P_m, which has a non-zero limit independent of n and of h. This is the *regular case*.

Positive regular case. If at least one of the tables $D^{(n)}$ has all positive elements, then all the P_{hk} have non-zero limits P_k independent of the initial index h. This is the *positive regular case*.

The probabilities $P_k = X_k$ constitute the system of solutions of the $r + 1$ equations with r unknowns:

$$X_1 = X_1 p_{11} + X_2 p_{21} + \cdots + X_r p_{r1}$$
$$X_2 = X_1 p_{12} + X_2 p_{22} + \cdots + X_r p_{r2}$$
$$X_3 = X_1 p_{13} + X_2 p_{23} + \cdots + X_r p_{r3}$$
$$\vdots$$
$$X_m = X_1 p_{1m} + X_2 p_{2m} + \cdots + X_r p_{rm}$$
$$\vdots$$
$$X_r = X_1 p_{1r} + X_2 p_{2r} + \cdots + X_r p_{rr}$$
$$1 = X_1 + X_2 + \cdots + X_r$$

But these equations are not independent, for the sum of the first r equations yields an identity. After the substitution of the last equation for one of the first r equations, there remains a system of r equations with r unknowns. Now there is a demonstration showing that in the regular case the system has only one solution, also that $D^{(n)} = D^n$ (nth power of D).

Selected Bibliography

1. Meyer-Epler, W. *Grundlagen und Anwendungen der Informations Theorie.* Berlin: Springer-Verlag, 1959.

2. Stevens, S. S., and Davis, H. *Hearing.* New York: John Wiley and Sons, 1948.

3. Winckel, F. *Music: Sound and Sensation.* New York: Dover Publications, 1967.

4. Schaeffer, P. *A la recherche d'une musique concrète.* Paris: Editions du Seuil, 1952.

5. Moles, A. *Information Theory and Esthetic Perception.* Urbana: University of Illinois Press, 1966.

6. Xenakis, I. "Les Trois Paraboles," *Nutida Musik,* no. 4. Stockholm: Sveriges Radio, 1958–59.

7. Borel, E. *Principes et formules classiques du calcul des probabilités.* Paris: Gauthier-Villars, 1947.

8. Xenakis, I. "La crise de la musique sérielle," and "Wahrscheinlichkeitstheorie und Musik," *Gravesaner Blätter,* nos. 1, 6. Mainz: Ars Viva Verlag, 1955, 1956.

9. Vessereau, A. *Méthodes statistiques en biologie et en agronomie.* Paris: J. B. Baillière et Fils, 1948.

10. Mather, K. *Statistical Analysis in Biology.* London: Methuen, 1951.

11. Lévy, P. *Calcul des probabilités.* Paris: Gauthier-Villars et Cie, 1925.

12. Borel, E. *Eléments de la théorie des probabilités.* Paris: Albin Michel, 1950.

13. Xenakis, I. "In Search of a Stochastic Music," *Gravesaner Blätter,* no. 11/12. Mainz: Ars Viva Verlag, 1957.

14. Fréchet, M. *Méthode des fonctions arbitraires. Théorie des événements en chaîne dans le cas d'un nombre fini d'états possibles.* Paris: Gauthier-Villars, 1952.

15. Shannon, C., and Weaver, W. *The Mathematical Theory of Communication.* Urbana: University of Illinois Press, 1949.

16. Ashby, W. Ross *Introduction to Cybernetics*. London: Chapman and Hall, 1956.

17. Moles, A. *La Création scientifique*. Geneva: Kister, 1957.

18. Xenakis, I. "Notes sur un geste électronique," *La Revue Musicale*, Paris, 1959.

19. Xenakis, I. "Eléments de musique stochastique," *Gravesaner Blätter*, nos. 18–24. Mainz: Ars Viva Verlag, 1960. Also "La musique stochastique," *La Revue d'Esthetique*, tome 14, fasc. III, IV. Paris: J. Vrin, 1961.

20. Girault, M. *Initiation aux processus aléatoires*. Paris: Dunod, 1959.

21. Williams, J. D. *The Compleat Strategyst*. New York: McGraw-Hill, 1954.

22. Vajda, S. *Theory of Games and Linear Programming*. London: Methuen, 1956.

23. Beranek, Leo L. *Acoustics*. New York: McGraw-Hill, 1954.

24. Appelman, D. Ralph. *The Science of Vocal Pedagogy*. Bloomington: Indiana University Press, 1967.

25. Hindemith, Paul. *The Craft of Musical Composition*. 2 vols. New York: Associated Music Publishers, 1942.

26. Risset, Jean Claude. "An Introductory Catalogue of Computer Synthesized Sounds." Unpublished. Murray Hill, New Jersey: Bell Telephone Laboratories, 1969.

27. Von Foerster, Heinz, and Beauchamp, James W., eds. *Music by Computers*. New York: John Wiley and Sons, 1969.

28. Schaeffer, Pierre. *Traité des objets musicaux: Essai interdisciplines*. Paris: Editions du Seuil, 1966.

29. Mathews, Max V. *The Technology of Computer Music*. Cambridge: M.I.T. Press, 1969.

30. Feller, William. *An Introduction to Probability Theory and Its Applications*. 2 vols. New York: John Wiley and Sons, 1966.

The following may also be read to advantage:

Hiller, L. A., and Isaacson, L. M. *Experimental Music*. New York: McGraw-Hill, 1959.

Tortrat, A. *Principes de statistiques mathématiques*. Paris: Dunod, 1961.

Yaglom, A. M. and I. M. *Probabilité et information*. Paris: Dunod, 1959.

Dugué, D. *Ensembles mesurables et probabilisables*. Paris: Dunod, 1958.

Fucks, Wilhelm. "Musical Analysis by Mathematics," *Gravesaner Blätter*, nos. 23/24. Mainz: Ars Viva Verlag, 1961.

Mathews, M. V.; Pierce, J. R.; and Guttman, N "Musical Sounds From Digital Computers," *Gravesaner Blätter*, nos. 23/24. Mainz: Ars Viva Verlag, 1961.

Xenakis, I. *Musique. Architecture.* Paris: Casterman, 1971.

In particular for Chap. VI:

Blanché, R. *Introduction à la logique contemporaine.* Paris: Armand Colin, 1957.

Boole, G. *The Mathematical Analysis of Logic.* Oxford: Blackwell, 1951.

Barbut, M. *Médiane, distributivité, éloignements.* Paris: Ecole Pratique des Hautes Etudes, 6th section, 1961.

———— *Des trucs et des machins II: une illustration, la dualité des espaces vectoriels.* Paris: Ecole Pratique des Hautes Etudes, 6th section, 1961.

Bourbaki, N. *Théorie des ensembles.* fasc. des résultats. Paris: Hermann, 1958.

Guilbaud, G. Th. *Algèbres mexicaines et booléennes.* Paris: Course at the Ecole Pratique des Haute Etudes, 6th section, 1960/61.

———— *Des trucs et des machins: comment faut-il enseigner les rudiments de la théorie dite des ensembles?* Paris: Ecole Pratique des Hautes Etudes, 6th section, 1961.

Piaget, J. *Le développement de la notion de temps chez l'enfant.* Paris: Presses Universitaires, 1946.

Ville, M. J. *Eléments de l'algèbre de Boole.* Paris: Institut Henri Poincaré, 1955.

Musical works mentioned in this book:

The scores of *Metastasis* (1953–54), *Pithoprakta* (1955–56), *ST/10-1, 080262* (1956–62), *ST/48-1,24016* (1956–62), *Herma* (1960), *Morsima-Amorsima* (1956–62), *Stratégie* (1959–62), *Akrata* (1964–65), and *Nomos alpha* (1965) are published by Boosey & Hawkes, New York; *Syrmos* (1959), *Duel* (1959), *Terrêtektorh* (1966), *Nomos gamma* (1967–68), and *Hibiki-Hana-Ma* (1970) are published by Salabert, Paris; *Achorripsis* (1956–57) by Bote and Bock, Berlin; *Analogique A* (1959), *Analogique B* (1959), and *Atrées* (1956–62) by E.F.M.-O.R.T.F., Paris; and *Diamorphoses* (1957), *Concret P-H* (1957), and *Orient-Occident* (1960) by GRM-O.R.T.F., Paris. Most of these works have been recorded, by Chant du monde, Vanguard, Angel, Erato, Philips, Mainstream, EMI, Vox, Musical Heritage Society.

Notes

I. Free Stochastic Music

1. Jean Piaget, *Le développement de la notion de temps chez l'enfant* (Paris: Presses Universitaires de France, 1946).

2. I. Xenakis, *Gravesaner Blätter*, no. 1 (1955).

3. I. Xenakis, *Revue technique Philips*, vol. 20, no. 1 (1958), and Le Corbusier, *Modulor 2* (Boulogne-Seine: Architecture d'Aujourd'hui, 1955).

4. I. Xenakis, "Wahrscheinlichkeitstheorie und Musik," *Gravesaner Blätter*, no. 6 (1956).

5. Ibid.

6. Ibid.

II. Markovian Stochastic Music—Theory

1. The description of the elementary structure of the sonic symbols that is given here serves as a point of departure for the musical realization, and is consequently only a hypothesis, rather than an established scientific fact. It can, nevertheless, be considered as a first approximation to the considerations introduced in information theory by Gabor [1]. In the so-called Gabor matrix a sonic event is resolved into elementary acoustic signals of very short effective durations, whose amplitude can be divided equally into quanta in the sense of information theory. However, these elementary signals constitute sinusoidal functions having a Gaussian "bell" curve as an envelope. But one can pretty well represent these signals of Gabor's by sine waves of short duration with an approximately rectangular envelope.

2. The choice of the logarithmic scale and of the base between 2 and 3 is made in order to establish our ideas. In any case, it corresponds to the results of research in experimental music made by the author, e.g., *Diamorphoses*.

264

V. Free Stochastic Music by Computer

1. See *Gravesaner Blätter*, nos. 11/12 (Mainz: Ars Viva Verlag, 1957).

2. $(V3)e^R$ must be equal to the upper limit, e.g., to 150 sounds/sec. in the case of a large orchestra.

VI. Symbolic Music

1. A second-degree acoustic and musical experience makes it necessary to abandon the Fourier analysis, and therefore the predominance of frequency in sound construction. But this problem will be treated in Chap. IX.

VII. Towards a Metamusic

1. Cf. I. Xenakis, *Gravesaner Blätter*, no. 29 (Gravesano, Tessin, Switzerland, 1965).

2. Cf. I. Xenakis, *Gravesaner Blätter*, nos. 1, 6; the scores of *Metastasis* and *Pithoprakta* (London: Boosey and Hawkes, 1954 and 1956); and the recording by Le Chant du Monde, L.D.X. A-8368 or Vanguard.

3. I do not mention here the fact that some present-day music uses quarter-tones or sixth-tones because they really do not escape from the tonal diatonic field.

4. Cf. Chap. VI.

5. Johannis Tinctoris, *Terminorum Musicae Diffinitorum* (Paris: Richard-Masse, 1951).

6. Jacques Chailley, "Le mythe des modes grecs," *Acta Musicologica*, vol. XXVIII, fasc. IV (Basel: Bärenreiter-Verlag, 1956).

7. R. Westphal, *Aristoxenos von Tarent, Melik und Rhythmik* (Leipzig: Verlag von Ambr. Abel (Arthur Meiner), 1893), introduction in German, Greek text.

8. G. Th. Guilbaud, *Mathématiques*, Tome I (Paris: Presses Universitaires de France, 1963).

9. Aristidou Kointilianou, *Peri Mousikes Proton* (Leipzig: Teubner, 1963), at Librairie des Méridiens, Paris.

10. The Aristoxenean scale seems to be one of the experimental versions of the ancient diatonic, but does not conform to the theoretical versions of either the Pythagoreans or the Aristoxeneans, $X(9/8)(9/8) = 4/3$ and $6 + 12 + 12 = 30$ segments, respectively. Archytas' version, $X(7/8)(9/8) = 4/3$, or Euclid's are significant. On the other hand, the so-called Zarlino scale is nothing but the so-called Aristoxenean scale, which, in reality, only dates back to Ptolemy and Didymos.

11. Avraam Evthymiadis, Στοιχειώδη Μαθήματα Βυζαντινῆς Μουσικῆς (Thessaloniki: O.X.A., Apostoliki Diakonia, 1948).

12. In-Quintilian and Ptolemy the perfect fourth was divided into 60 equal tempered segments.

13. See Westphal, pp. XLVIIff. for the displacement of the tetrachord mentioned by Ptolemy: lichanos (16/15) mese (9/8) paramese (10/9) trite (Harmonics 2.1, p. 49).

14. In Ptolemy the names of the chromatic tetrachords were permuted: the soft chromatic contained the interval 6/9, the hard or syntonon the interval 7/6. Cf. Westphal, p. XXXII.

15. Selidion 1: a mixture of the syntonon chromatic (22/21, 12/11, 7/6) and toniaion diatonic (28/27, 7/8, 9/8); selidion 2: a mixture of the soft diatonic (21/20, 10/9, 8/7) and the toniaion diatonic (28/27, 8/7, 9/8), etc. Westphal, p. XLVIII.

16. Egon Wellesz, *A History of Byzantine Music and Hymnography* (Oxford: Clarendon Press, 1961), pp. 71ff. On p. 70 he again takes up the myth that the ancient scales descended.

17. The same negligence can be found among the students of ancient Hellenic culture; for example, the classic Louis Laloy in *Aristoxène de Tarente*, 1904, p. 249.

18. Alain Daniélou lived in India for many years and learned to play Indian instruments. Mantle Hood did the same with Indonesian music, and let us not forget Than Van Khé, theoretician and practicing performer and composer of traditional Vietnamese music.

19. Cf. Wellesz. Also the transcriptions by C. Höeg, another great Byzantinist who neglected the problems of structure.

20. Imagine the bewilderment of the "specialists" when they discovered that the Byzantine musical notation is used today in traditional Romanian folk music! *Rapports Complémentaires du XIIᵉ Congrès international des Etudes byzantines*, Ochrida, Yugoslavia, 1961, p. 76. These experts without doubt ignore the fact that an identical phenomenon exists in Greece.

21. Cf. my text on disc L.D.X. A-8368, issued by Le Chant du Monde. See also *Gravesaner Blätter*, no. 29, and Chap. VI of the present book.

22. Among themselves the elementary displacements are like the integers, that is, they are defined like elements of the same axiomatics.

23. Alain Daniélou, *Northern Indian Music* (Barnet, Hertfordshire: Halcyon Press, 1954), vol. II, p. 72.

24. This perhaps fulfills Edgard Varèse's wish for a spiral scale, that is, a cycle of fifths which would not lead to a perfect octave. This information, unfortunately abridged, was given me by Odile Vivier.

25. These last structures were used in *Akrata* (1964) for sixteen winds, and in *Nomos alpha* (1965) for solo cello.

VIII. Towards a Philosophy of Music

1. The "unveiling of the historical tradition" is used here in E. Husserl's sense; cf. *Husserliana*, VI: "Die Krisis der Europäischen Wissenschaften und die transzendentale Phänomenologie (Eine Einleitung in die phänomenologische Philosophie)", *Pure Geometry* (The Hague: M. Nijhoff, 1954), pp. 21–25, and Appendix III, pp. 379–80.

2. Cf. *Upanishads* and *Bhagavad Gita*, references by Ananda K. Coomaraswamy in *Hinduism and Buddhism* (New York: Philosophical Library, 1943).

3. "Perhaps the oddest thing about modern science is its return to pythagoricism." Bertrand Russell, *The Nation*, 27 September 1924.

4. In this translation I have considered the original Greek text and the translations by John Burnet in *Early Greek Philosophy* (New York: Meridian Books, 1962) and by Jean Beaufret in *Le Poème de Parménide* (Paris: P.U.F., 1955).

5. Elements are always real: (earth, water, air) = (matter, fire) = energy. Their equivalence had already been foreseen by Heraclitus.

6. Lucretius, *De la Nature*, trans. A. Ernout (Paris, 1924).

7. The term stochastic is used for the first time in this work. Today it is synonymous with probability, aleatory, chance.

8. E. Borel, *Eléments de la théorie des probabilités* (Paris: Albin Michel, 1950), p. 82.

9. Uncertainty, measured by the entropy of information theory, reaches a maximum when the probabilities p and $(1 - p)$ are equal.

10. Cf. I. Xenakis, *Gravesaner Blätter*, nos. 1, 6, 11/12 (1955–8).

11. I prepared a new interpretation of Messiaen's "modes of limited transpositions," which was to have been published in a collection in 1966, but which has not yet appeared.

12. Around 1870 A. de Bertha created his "gammes *homotones première et seconde*," scales of alternating whole and half tones, which would be written in our notation as $(3_n \vee 3_{n+2}, 3_n \vee 3_{n+1})$.

13. In 1895, Loquin, professor at the Bordeaux Conservatory, had already preconceived the equality of the twelve tones of the octave.

14. The following is a new axiomatization of the sieves, more natural than the one in Chaps. VI and VII.

Basic Assumptions. 1. The sensations create *discrete* characteristics, values, stops (pitches, instants, intensities, . . .), which can be represented as points. 2. Sensations plus comparisons of them create *differences* between the above characteristics or points, which can be described as the movement, the displacement, or the step from one discrete characteristic to another, from one point to another. 3. We are able to repeat, iterate, concatenate the above steps. 4. There are two orientations in the iterations—more iterations, fewer iterations.

Formalization. Sets. The basic assumptions above engender three fundamental sets: Ω, Δ, E, respectively. From the first assumption characteristics will belong to various specific domains Ω. From the second, displacements or steps in a specific domain Ω will belong to set Δ, which is independent of Ω. From the third, concatenations or iterations of elements of Δ form a set E. The two orientations in the fourth assumption can be represented by $+$ and $-$.

Product Sets. a. $\Omega \times \Delta \subseteq \Omega$ (a pitch-point combined with a displacement produces a pitch-point). b. $\Delta \times E \subseteq \Delta$ (a displacement combined with an iteration or a concatenation produces a displacement). We can easily identify E as the set N of natural numbers plus zero. Moreover, the fourth basic assumption leads directly to the definition of the set of integers Z from E.

We have thus bypassed the direct use of Peano axiomatics (introduced in Chaps. VI and VII) in order to generate an *Equally Tempered Chromatic Gamut* (defined as an ETCHG sieve). Indeed it is sufficient to choose any displacement ELD belonging to set Δ and form the product $\{ELD\} \times Z$. Set Δ (set of melodic intervals, e.g.), on the other hand, has a group structure.

15. Cf. Olivier Messiaen, *Technique de mon langage musical* (Paris: Durand, 1944).

16. "... therefore tones higher than needed become relaxed [lower], as they should be, by curtailment of movement; conversely those lower than needed become tensed [higher], as they should be, by adjunction of movement. This is why it is necessary to say that tones are constituted of discrete pieces, since it is by adjunction and curtailment that they become as they should be. All things composed of discrete pieces are said to be in numerical ratio to each other. Therefore we must say that tones are also in numerical ratio to each other. But among numbers, some are said to be in multiplicative ratio, others in an *epimorios* $[1 + 1/x]$, or others in an *epimeris* ratio [an integer plus a fraction having a numerator other than one]; therefore it is necessary to say that tones are also in these same ratios to each other. ..." Euclid, *Katatomé Kanonos* (12–24), in Henricus Menge, *Phaenomena et Scripta Musica* (Leipzig: B. G. Teubner, 1916). This remarkable text already attempts to establish axiomatically the correspondence between tones and numbers. This is why I bring it in in the context of this article.

17. Cf. my analysis of *Metastasis*, in Le Corbusier, *Modulor 2* (Boulogne-Seine: Architecture d'Aujourd'hui, 1955).

18. Cf. score by Boosey and Hawkes, eds., and record by Pathé-Marconi and Angel.

19. *Hibiki-Hana-Ma*, the electro-acoustic composition that I was commissioned to write for the Japanese Steel Federation Pavilion at the 1970 Osaka World Expo, used 800 loudspeakers, scattered in the air and in the ground. They were divided into approximately 150 independent groups. The sounds were designed to traverse these groups according to various kinematic diagrams. After the Philips Pavilion at the 1958 Brussels World's Fair, the Steel Pavilion was the most advanced attempt at placing sounds in space. However, only twelve independent magnetic tracks were available (two synchronized six-track tape recorders).

20. Mario Bois, *Iannis Xenakis: The Man and His Music* (New York: Boosey and Hawkes, 1967).

21. Jean Piaget, *Le développement de la notion de temps chez l'enfant*, and *La représentation de l'espace chez l'enfant* (Paris: Presses Universitaires de France, 1946 and 1948).

Index